The Art of High Performance SQL Code:

SQL Server Execution Plans

by Grant Fritchey

First published 2008 by Simple-Talk Publishing

Typeset by Andrew Clarke

CONTENTS

4

ABOUT THE AUTHOR

Grant Fritchey is currently working as a development DBA for FM Global, an industry-leading engineering and insurance company. In his previous time as a DBA, he has worked at three failed dotcoms, a major consulting company and a global bank. He has developed large scale applications in languages such as VB, C# and Java and has lived with SQL Server from the hoary days of 6.0, right through to 2008. His nickname at work is "The Scary DBA". He even has an official name plate, and he displays it proudly.

Grant volunteers for the Professional Association of SQL Server Users (PASS) and has written and published articles on various topics relating to SQL Server at Simple-Talk, SQL Server Central, the PASS web site, SQL Standard and the SQL Server Worldwide Users Group. He is one of the founding officers of the Southern New England SQL Server Users Group (SNESSUG).

Outside work, Grant kayaks, learns and teaches self-defense, brews his own beer, chops wood to heat his house, raises his kids and helps lead a pack of Cub Scouts.

ACKNOWLEDGEMENTS

I wrote this book with a lot of help. Firstly, and most importantly, thanks to Tony Davis for offering me this project and then supporting me so well throughout. I couldn't have done it without you. Next, I want to thank my wife & kids who put up with me when I was getting cranky because of troubles writing this book. You guys are troopers.

I also want to thank all the people who answer questions over at the forums at SQL Server Central. I got stuck a couple of times and you guys helped. Finally, I want to thank my co-workers who refrained from killing me when I sent them chapters and pushed for comments, questions and suggestions… repeatedly.

To everyone who helped: you guys get credit for everything that's right in the book. Anything that's wrong is all my fault.

Cheers!

Grant Fritchey

INTRODUCTION

Every day, out in the various discussion boards devoted to Microsoft SQL Server, the same types of questions come up again and again:

- Why is this query running slow?
- Is my index getting used?
- Why isn't my index getting used?
- Why does this query run faster than this query?
- And on and on.

The correct response is probably different in each case, but in order to arrive at the answer you have to ask the same return question in each case: *have you looked at the execution plan?*

Execution plans show you what's going on behind the scenes in SQL Server. They can provide you with a wealth of information on how your queries are being executed by SQL Server, including:

- Which indexes are getting used and where no indexes are being used at all.
- How the data is being retrieved, and joined, from the tables defined in your query.
- How aggregations in **GROUP BY** queries are put together.
- The anticipated load, and the estimated cost, that all these operations place upon the system.

All this information makes the execution plan a fairly important tool in the tool belt of database administrator, database developers, report writers, developers, and pretty much anyone who writes TSQL to access data in a SQL Server database.

Given the utility and importance of the tool, you'd think there'd be huge swathes of information devoted to this subject. To be sure, fantastic information is available from various sources, but there really isn't any one place you can go to for focused, practical information on how to use and interpret execution plans.

This is where my book comes in. My goal was to gather as much useful information on execution plans as possible into a single location, and to organize it in such as way that it provided a clear route through the subject, right from the basics of capturing plans, through their interpretation, and then on to how to use them to understand how you might optimize your SQL queries, improve your indexing strategy, and so on.

Specifically, I cover:

- How to capture execution plans in graphical, as well as text and XML formats
- A documented method for interpreting execution plans, so that you can create these plans from your own code and make sense of them in your own environment
- How SQL Server represents and interprets the common SQL Server objects – indexes, views, derived tables etc – in execution plans
- How to spot some common performance issues such as bookmark lookups or unused/missing indexes
- How to control execution plans with hints, plans guides and so on, and why this is a double-edged sword
- How XML code appears in execution plans
- Advanced topics such as parallelism, forced parameterization and plan forcing.

Along the way, I tackle such topics as SQL Server internals, performance tuning, index optimization and so on. However, my focus is always on the details of the execution plan, and how these issues are manifest in these plans. If you are specifically looking for information on how to optimize SQL, or build efficient indexes, then you need a book dedicated to these topics. However, if you want to understand how these issues are interpreted within an execution plan, then this is the place for you.

FOREWORD

I have attended many SQL Server conferences since 2000, and I have spoken with hundreds of people attending them. One of the most significant trends I have noticed over the past eight years is the huge number of people who have made the transition from IT Professional or Developer, to SQL Server Database Administrator. In some cases, the transition has been planned and well thought-out. In other cases, it was an accidental transition, when an organization desperately needed a DBA, and the closest warm body was chosen for the job.

No matter the route you took to get there, all DBAs have one thing in common: we have had to learn how to become DBAs through self-training, hard work, and trial and error. In other words, there is no school you can attend to become a DBA, it is something you have to learn on your own. Some of us are fortunate to attend a class or two, or to have a great mentor to help us along. However, in most cases, DBAs become DBAs the hard way: we are thrown into the water and we either sink or swim.

One of the biggest components of a DBA's self-learning process is reading. Fortunately, there are many good books on the basics of being a DBA that make a good starting point for your learning process. Once you have read the basic books and have gotten some experience under your belt, you will soon want to know more of the details of how SQL Server works. While there are a few good books on the advanced use of SQL Server, there are still many areas that aren't well covered. One of those areas of missing knowledge is a dedicated book on SQL Server execution plans.

That's where *Dissecting SQL Server Execution Plans* comes into play. It is the first book available anywhere that focuses entirely on what SQL Server execution plans are, how to read them, and how to apply the information you learn from them in order to boost the performance of your SQL Servers.

This was not an easy book to write because SQL Server execution plans are not well documented anywhere. Grant Fritchey spent a huge amount of time researching SQL Server execution plans, and conducting original research as necessary, in order to write the material in this book. Once you understand the fundamentals of SQL Server, this book should be on top of your reading list, because understanding SQL

Server execution plans is a critical part of becoming an Exceptional DBA.

As you read the book, take what you have learned and apply it to your own unique set of circumstances. Only by applying what you have read will you be able to fully understand and grasp the power of what execution plans have to offer.

Brad McGehee

Director of DBA Education, Red-Gate Software Cambridge

Cambridge 2008

CHAPTER 1: EXECUTION PLAN BASICS

An execution plan, simply put, is the result of the query optimizer's attempt to calculate the most efficient way to implement the request represented by the T-SQL query you submitted.

Execution plans can tell you how a query will be executed, or how a query was executed. They are, therefore, the DBA's primary means of troubleshooting a poorly performing query. Rather than guess at why a given query is performing thousands of scans, putting your I/O through the roof, you can use the execution plan to identify the exact piece of SQL code that is causing the problem. For example, it may be scanning an entire table-worth of data when, with the proper index, it could simply backpack out only the rows you need. All this and more is displayed in the execution plan.

The aim of this chapter is to enable you to capture actual and estimated execution plans, in either graphical, text or XML format, and to understand the basics of how to interpret them. In order to do this, we'll cover the following topics:

- **A brief backgrounder on the query optimizer** – execution plans are a result of the optimizer's calculations so it's useful to know at least a little bit about what the optimizer does, and how it works
- Actual and Estimated execution plans – what they are and how they differ
- **Capturing and interpreting the different visual execution plan formats** – we'll investigate graphical, text and XML execution plans for a very basic SELECT query
- **Automating execution plan capture** – using the SQL Server Profiler tool

What Happens When a Query is Submitted?

When you submit a query to a SQL Server database, a number of processes on the server go to work on that query. The purpose of all these processes is to manage the system such that it will provide your data back to you, or store it, in as timely a manner as possible, whilst maintaining the integrity of the data.

These processes are run for each and every query submitted to the system. While there are lots of different actions occurring simultaneously within SQL Server, we're going to focus on the processes around T-SQL. They break down roughly into two stages:

1. Processes that occur in the relational engine
2. Processes that occur in the storage engine.

In the relational engine the query is parsed and then processed by the Query Optimizer, which generates an execution plan. The plan is sent (in a binary format) to the storage engine, which it then uses to retrieve or update the underlying data. The storage engine is where processes such as locking, index maintenance and transactions occur. Since **execution plans** are created in the relational engine, that's where we'll be focusing our attention.

Query Parsing

When you pass a T-SQL query to the SQL Server system, the first place it goes to is the relational engine.[1]

As the T-SQL arrives, it passes through a process that checks that the T-SQL is written correctly, that it's well formed. This process is known as query *parsing*. The output of the **Parser** process is a parse tree, or query tree (or even sequence tree). The parse tree represents the logical steps necessary to execute the query that has been requested.

If the T-SQL string is not a data manipulation language (DML) statement, it will be not be optimized because, for example, there is only one "right way" for the SQL Server system to create a table; therefore, there are no opportunities for improving the performance of that type of statement. If the T-SQL string is a DML statement, the parse tree is passed to a process called the **algebrizer**. The algebrizer resolves all the names of the various objects, tables and columns, referred to within the query string. The algebrizer identifies, at the individual column level, all the types (**varchar(50)** versus **nvarchar(25)** and so on) of the objects being accessed. It also determines the location of aggregates (such as **GROUP BY**, and **MAX**) within the query, a process called *aggregate*

---

[1] A T-SQL Query can be an ad hoc query from a command line or a call to request data from a stored procedure, any T-SQL within a single batch or a stored procedure, or between "GO" statements.

binding. This algebrizer process is important because the query may have aliases or synonyms, names that don't exist in the database, that need to be resolved, or the query may refer to objects not in the database.

The algebrizer outputs a binary called the **query processor tree**, which is then passed on to the **query optimizer**.

The Query Optimizer

The query optimizer is essentially a piece of software that "models" the way in which the database relational engine works. Using the query processor tree and the **statistics** it has about the data, and applying the model, it works out what it thinks will be the optimal way to execute the query – that is, it generates an execution plan.

In other words, the optimizer figures out how best to implement the request represented by the T-SQL query you submitted. It decides if the data can be accessed through indexes, what types of joins to use and much more. The decisions made by the optimizer are based on what it calculates to be the cost of a given execution plan, in terms of the required CPU processing and I/O, and how fast it will execute. Hence, this is known as a **cost-based** plan.

The optimizer will generate and evaluate many plans (unless there is already a cached plan) and, generally speaking, will choose the lowest-cost plan i.e. the plan it thinks will execute the query as fast as possible and use the least amount of resources, CPU and I/O. The calculation of the execution speed is the most important calculation and the optimizer will use a process that is more CPU-intensive if it will return results that much faster. Sometimes, the optimizer will select a less efficient plan if it thinks it will take more time to evaluate many plans than to run a less efficient plan.

If you submit a very simple query – for example, a single table with no indexes and with no aggregates or calculations within the query – then rather than spend time trying to calculate the absolute optimal plan, the optimizer will simply apply a single, **trivial plan** to these types of queries.

If the query is non-trivial, the optimizer will perform a cost-based calculation to select a plan. In order to do this, it relies on **statistics** that are maintained by SQL Server.

Statistics are collected on columns and indexes within the database, and describe the data distribution and the uniqueness, or selectivity, of the data. The information that makes up statistics is represented by a **histogram**, a tabulation of counts of the occurrence of a particular value, taken from 200 data points evenly distributed across the data. It's this "data about the data" that provides the information necessary for the optimizer to make its calculations.

If statistics exist for a relevant column or index, then the optimizer will use them in its calculations. Statistics, by default, are created and updated automatically within the system for all indexes or for any column used as a predicate, as part of a **WHERE** clause or **JOIN ON** clause. Table variables do not ever have statistics generated on them, so they are always assumed by the optimizer to have a single row, regardless of their actual size. Temporary tables do have statistics generated on them and are stored in the same histogram as permanent tables, for use within the optimizer.

The optimizer takes these statistics, along with the query processor tree, and heuristically determines the best plan. This means that it works through a series of plans, testing different types of join, rearranging the join order, trying different indexes, and so on, until it arrives at what it thinks will be the fastest plan. During these calculations, a number is assigned to each of the steps within the plan, representing the optimizer's estimation of the amount of time it thinks that step will take. This shows what is called the **estimated cost** for that step. The accumulation of costs for each step is the cost for the execution plan itself.

It's important to note that the estimated cost is just that – an estimate. Given an infinite amount of time and complete, up-to-date statistics, the optimizer would find the perfect plan for executing the query. However, it attempts to calculate the best plan it can in the least amount of time possible, and is obviously limited by the quality of the statistics it has available. Therefore these cost estimations are very useful as measures, but may not precisely reflect reality.

Once the optimizer arrives at an execution plan, the actual plan is created and stored in a memory space known as the **plan cache** – unless an identical plan already exists in the cache (more on this shortly, in the section on *Execution Plan Reuse*). As the optimizer generates potential plans, it compares them to previously generated plans in the cache. If it finds a match, it will use that plan.

Query Execution

Once the execution plan is generated, the action switches to the storage engine, where the query is actually executed, according to the plan.

We will not go into detail here, except to note that the carefully generated execution may be subject to *change* during the actual execution process. For example, this might happen if:

- A determination is made that the plan exceeds the threshold for a parallel execution (an execution that takes advantage of multiple processors on the machine – more on parallel execution in Chapter 3).
- The statistics used to generate the plan were out of date, or have changed since the original execution plan was created by the optimizer.

The results of the query are returned to you after the relational engine changes the format to match that requested in your T-SQL statement, assuming it was a **SELECT**.

Estimated and Actual Execution Plans

As discussed previously, there are two distinct types of execution plan. First, there is the plan that represents the output from the optimizer. This is known as an **Estimated execution plan**. The operators, or steps, within the plan will be labeled as logical, because they're representative of the optimizer's view of the plan.

Next is the plan that represents the output from the actual query execution. This type of plan is known, funnily enough, as the **Actual execution plan**. It shows what actually happened when the query executed.

Execution Plan Reuse

It is expensive for the Server to generate execution plans so SQL Server will keep and reuse plans wherever possible. As they are created, plans are stored in a section of memory called the **plan cache** (previously called the **procedure cache**).

When a query is submitted to the server, an *estimated* execution plan is created by the optimizer. Once that plan is created, and before it gets passed to the storage engine, the optimizer compares this estimated plan to *actual* execution plans that already exist in the plan cache. If an actual plan is found that matches the estimated one, then the optimizer will reuse the existing plan, since it's already been used before by the query engine. This reuse avoids the overhead of creating actual execution plans for large and complex queries or even simple plans for small queries called thousands of times in a minute.

Each plan is stored once, unless the cost of the plan lets the optimizer know that a parallel execution might result in better performance (more on parallelism in Chapter 8). If the optimizer sees parallelism as an option, then a second plan is created and stored with a different set of operations to support parallelism. In this instance, one query gets two plans.

Execution plans are not kept in memory forever. They are slowly aged out of the system using an "age" formula that multiplies the estimated cost of the plan by the number of times it has been used (e.g. a plan with a cost of 10 that has been referenced 5 times has an "age" value f of 50). The lazywriter process, an internal process that works to free all types of cache (including plan cache), periodically scans the objects in the cache and decreases this value by one each time.

If the following criteria are met, the plan is removed from memory:

- More memory is required by the system
- The "age" of the plan has reached zero
- The plan isn't currently being referenced by an existing connection

Execution plans are not sacrosanct. Certain events and actions can cause a plan to be recompiled. It is important to remember this because recompiling execution plans can be a very expensive operation. The following actions can lead to recompilation of an execution plan:

- Changing the structure or schema of a table referenced by the query
- Changing an index used by the query
- Dropping an index used by the query
- Updating the statistics used by the query
- Calling the function, **sp_recompile**
- Subjecting the keys in tables referenced by the query to a large number of inserts or deletes
- For tables with triggers, significant growth of the **inserted** or **deleted** tables
- Mixing DDL and DML within a single query, often called a deferred compile
- Changing the **SET** options within the execution of the query
- Changing the structure or schema of temporary tables used by the query
- Changes to dynamic views used by the query
- Changes to cursor options within the query

- Changes to a remote rowset, like in a distributed partitioned view
- When using client side cursors, if the **FOR BROWSE** options are changed

Since the cache plays such an important role in how execution plans operate, you need a few tools for querying and working with the plan cache. First off, while testing, you may want to see how long a plan takes to compile, or to investigate how minor adjustments might create slightly different plans. To completely clear the cache, run this:

```
DBCC FREEPROCCACHE
```

You're going to want to see the objects within the cache in order to see how the optimizer and storage engine created your plan. With dynamic management views and dynamic management functions, we can easily put together a query to get a very complete set of information about the execution plans on our system:

```
SELECT   [cp].[refcounts]
        ,[cp].[usecounts]
        ,[cp].[objtype]
        ,[st].[dbid]
        ,[st].[objectid]
        ,[st].[text]
        ,[qp].[query_plan]
FROM     sys.dm_exec_cached_plans cp
         CROSS APPLY sys.dm_exec_sql_text(cp.plan_handle) st
         CROSS APPLY sys.dm_exec_query_plan(cp.plan_handle)
qp ;
```

With this query we can see the SQL called and the XML plan generated by the execution of that SQL. You can use the XML directly or open it as a graphical execution plan.

Why the Actual and Estimated Execution Plans Might Differ

Generally, you probably won't see any differences between your estimated and actual execution plans. However, circumstances can arise that can cause differences between the estimated and actual execution plans.

When Statistics are Stale

The main cause of a difference between the plans is differences between the statistics and the actual data. This generally occurs over time as data is added and deleted. This causes the key values that define the index to change, or their distribution (how many of what type) to change. The automatic update of statistics that occurs, assuming it's turned on, only samples a subset of the data in order to reduce the cost of the operation. This means that, over time, the statistics become a less-and-less accurate reflection of the actual data. Not only can this cause differences between the plans, but you can get bad execution plans because the statistical data is not up to date.2

When the Estimated Plan is Invalid

In some instances, the estimated plan won't work at all. For example, try generating an estimated plan for this simple bit of code:

```
CREATE TABLE TempTable
    (
     Id INT IDENTITY(1, 1)
    ,Dsc NVARCHAR(50)
    );

INSERT INTO TempTable ( Dsc )
        SELECT  [Name]
        FROM    [Sales].[Store];

SELECT  *
FROM    TempTable;

DROP TABLE TempTable;
```

You will get this error:

```
Msg 208, Level 16, State 1, Line 7
Invalid object name 'TempTable'.
```

---

2 An example demonstrating how a drastic change in the data can affect the execution plan is given in the Statistics and Indexes section of Chapter 4.

The optimizer, which is what is used to generate Estimated Execution plans, doesn't execute T-SQL. It does run the statements through the algebrizer, the process outlined earlier that is responsible for verifying the names of database objects. Since the query has not yet been executed, the temporary table does not yet exist. This is the cause of the error. Running this same bit of code through the Actual execution plan will work perfectly fine.

When Parallelism is Requested

When a plan meets the threshold for parallelism (more about this in Chapter 8) two plans are created. Which plan is actually executed is up to the query engine. So you might see a plan with, or without, parallel operators in the estimated execution plan. When the query actually executes, you may see a completely different plan if the query engine determines that it either can't support a parallel query at that time or that a parallel query is called for.

Execution Plan Formats

SQL Server offers only one type of execution plan (be it estimated or actual), but three different formats in which to view that execution plan.

- Graphical Plans
- Text Plans
- XML Plans

The one you choose will depend on the level of detail you want to see, and on the individual DBA's preferences and methods.

Graphical Plans

These are quick and easy to read but the detailed data for the plan is masked. Both Estimated and Actual execution plans can be viewed in graphical format.

Text Plans

These are a bit harder to read, but more information is immediately available. There are three text plan formats:

- **SHOWPLAN_ALL**: a reasonably complete set of data showing the Estimated execution plan for the query
- **SHOWPLAN_TEXT**: provides a very limited set of data for use with tools like **osql.exe**. It too only shows the Estimated execution plan

- **STATISTICS PROFILE:** similar to **SHOWPLAN_ALL** except it represents the data for the Actual execution plan

XML Plans

XML plans present the most complete set of data available on a plan, all on display in the structured XML format. There are two varieties of XML plan:

- **SHOWPLAN_XML:** The plan generated by the optimizer prior to execution.
- **STATISTICS_XML:** The XML format of the Actual execution plan.

Getting Started

Execution plans are there to assist you in writing efficient T-SQL code, troubleshooting existing T-SQL behavior or monitoring and reporting on your systems. How you use them and view them is up to you, but first you need to understand the information contained within the plans and how to interpret it. One of the best ways to learn about execution plans is to see them in action, so let's get started.

Please note that occasionally, especially when we move on to more complex plans, the plan that you see may differ slightly from the one presented in the book. This might be because we are using different versions of SQL Server (different SP levels and hot fixes), that we are using slightly different versions of the AdventureWorks database, or because of how the AdventureWorks database has been altered over time as each of us has played around in it. So while most of the plans you get should be very similar to what we display here, don't be too surprised if you try the code and see something different

Sample Code

Throughout the following text, I'll be supplying T-SQL code that you're encouraged to run for yourself. All of the source code is freely downloadable from the **Simple Talk Publishing** website (http://www.simple-talk.com/).

The examples are written for SQL 2005 sample database, **Adventureworks**. You can get hold of get a copy of **Adventureworks** from here:

http://www.codeplex.com/MSFTDBProdSamples

If you are working with procedures and scripts other than those supplied, please remember that encrypted procedures will not display an execution plan.

The plans you see may not precisely reflect the plans generated for the book. Depending on how old a given copy of AdventureWorks may be, the statistics could be different, the indexes may be different, the structure and data may be different. So please be aware that you won't always see the same thing if you run the examples.

The initial execution plans will be simple and easy to read from the samples presented in the text. As the queries and plans become more complicated, the book will describe the situation but, in order to easily see the graphical execution plans or the complete set of XML, it will be necessary to generate the plans. So, please, read next to your machine, so that you can try running each query yourself!

Permissions Required to View Execution Plans

In order to see the execution plans for the following queries you must have the correct permissions within the database. Once that's set, assuming you're not **sysadmin, dbcreator** or **db_owner**, you'll need to be granted the **ShowPlan** permission within the database being tested. Further, you'll need this permission on each database referenced by the queries for which you hope to generate a plan. Run the statement:

```
GRANT SHOWPLAN TO [username]
```

Substituting the user name will enable execution plans for that user on that database.

Working with Graphical Execution Plans

In order to focus on the basics of capturing Estimated and Actual execution plans, the first query will be one of the simplest possible queries, and we'll build from there. Open up Management Studio, and type the following into the query window:

```
SELECT *
  FROM [dbo].[DatabaseLog];
```

Getting the Estimated Plan

We'll start by viewing the graphical **estimated execution plan** that is generated by the query optimizer, so there's no need to actually run the query yet.

We can find out what the optimizer estimates to be the least costly plan in one of following ways:

- Click on the "Display Estimated Execution Plan" icon on the tool bar.
- Right-click the query window and select the same option from the menu.
- Click on the Query option in the menu bar and select the same choice.
- Simply hit CTRL-L on the keyboard.

I tend to click the icon more often than not but, either way, we see our very first **Estimated execution plan,** as in Figure 1.

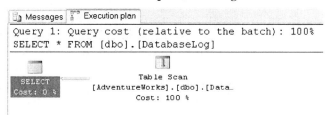

Figure 1

We'll explain what this plan means shortly, but first, let's capture the Actual execution plan.

Getting the Actual Plan

Actual execution plans, unlike Estimated execution plans, do not represent the calculations of the optimizer. Instead this execution plan shows what happened when the query was executed. The two will often be identical but will sometimes differ, due to changes to the execution plan made by the storage engine.

Again, there are several ways to generate our first graphical Actual Execution Plan:

- Click on the icon on the tool bar called "Include Actual Execution Plan."
- Right-click within the query window and choose the "Include Actual Execution Plan" menu item.

- Choose the same option in the Query menu choice.
- Type Control-M.

Each of these methods functions as an "on" switch and an execution plan will be created for all queries run from that query window until you turn it off again.

So, activate execution plans by your preferred method and execute the query. You should see an execution plan like the one in Figure 2.

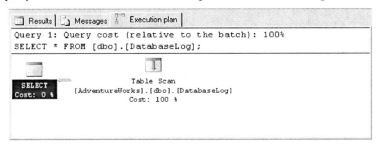

Figure 2

In this simple case the Actual plan is identical to the Estimated plan.

Interpreting Graphical Execution Plans

The icons you see in Figures 1 and 2 are the first two of approximately 78 operators that represent various actions and decisions that potentially make up an execution plan. On the left is the SELECT icon, an icon that you'll see quite a lot of and that you can usually completely ignore. It's the final result and formatting from the relational engine. The icon on the right represents a **table scan**[3]. This is the first, and one of the

---

[3] A **table scan** occurs when the storage engine is forced to walk through the table, row by row, either returning everything, as in our case, because we're not using a **WHERE** clause and we're not hitting a covering index (an index that includes all the columns referred to in the query for a given table), or searching everything to identify the appropriate rows to return to the user. As you might imagine, as the number of rows in the table grows, this operation gets more and more expensive.

easiest, icons to look for when trying to track down performance problems.

Usually, you read a graphical execution plan from right to left and top to bottom. You'll also note that there is an arrow pointing between the two icons. This arrow represents the data being passed between the operators, as represented by the icons. So, in this case, we simply have a table scan operator producing the result set (represented by the Select operator). The thickness of the arrow reflects the amount of data being passed, thicker meaning more rows. This is another visual clue as to where performance issues may lie. You can hover with the mouse pointer over these arrows and it will show the number of rows that it represents. For example, if your query returns two rows, but the execution plan shows a big thick arrow indicating many rows being processed, then that's something to possibly investigate.

Below each icon is displayed a number as a percentage. This number represents the relative cost to the query for that operator. That cost, returned from the optimizer, is the estimated execution time for that operation. In our case, all the cost is associated with the table scan. While a cost may be represented as 0% or 100%, remember that, as these are ratios, not actual numbers, even a 0% operator will have a small cost associated with it.

Above the icons is displayed as much of the query string as will fit and a "cost (relative to batch)" of 100%. Just as each query can have multiple steps, and each of those steps will have a cost relative to the query, you can also run multiple queries within a batch and get execution plans for them. They will then show up as different costs as a part of the whole.

ToolTips

Each of the icons and the arrows has, associated with it, a pop-up window called a **ToolTip**, which you can access by hovering your mouse pointer over the icon.

Pull up the Estimated execution plan, hover over the **SELECT** operator, and you should see the ToolTip window shown in Figure 3.

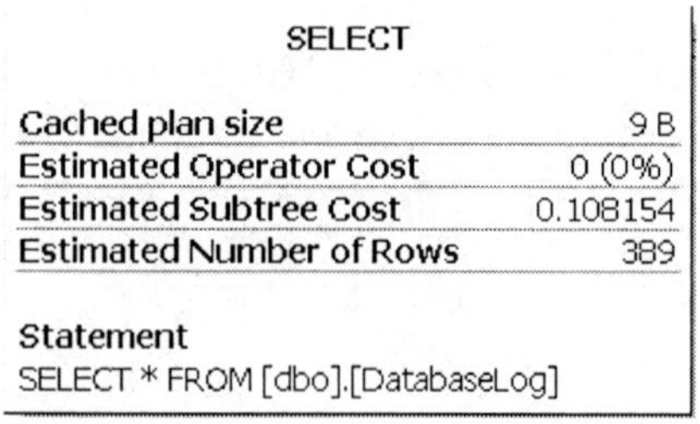

SELECT	
Cached plan size	9 B
Estimated Operator Cost	0 (0%)
Estimated Subtree Cost	0.108154
Estimated Number of Rows	389

Statement
SELECT * FROM [dbo].[DatabaseLog]

Figure 3

Here we get the numbers generated by the optimizer on the following:

- **Cached plan size** – how much memory the plan generated by this query will take up in stored procedure cache. This is a useful number when investigating cache performance issues because you'll be able to see which plans are taking up more memory.
- **Estimated Operator Cost** – we've already seen this as the percentage cost in Figure 1.
- **Estimated Subtree Cost** – tells us the accumulated optimizer cost assigned to this step and all previous steps, but remember to read from right to left. This number is meaningless in the real world, but is a mathematical evaluation used by the query optimizer to determine the cost of the operator in question; it represents the amount of time that the optimizer thinks this operator will take.
- **Estimated number of rows** – calculated based on the statistics available to the optimizer for the table or index in question.

Below this information, we see the statement that represents the entire query that we're processing. If we look at the ToolTip information for the Table Scan we see the information in Figure 4.

Table Scan	
Scan rows from a table.	
Physical Operation	Table Scan
Logical Operation	Table Scan
Estimated I/O Cost	0.107569
Estimated CPU Cost	0.0005849
Estimated Operator Cost	0.108154 (100%)
Estimated Subtree Cost	0.108154
Estimated Number of Rows	389
Estimated Row Size	8569 B
Ordered	False
Node ID	0

Object
[AdventureWorks].[dbo].[DatabaseLog]
Output List
[AdventureWorks].[dbo].
[DatabaseLog].DatabaseLogID, [AdventureWorks].
[dbo].[DatabaseLog].PostTime, [AdventureWorks].
[dbo].[DatabaseLog].DatabaseUser,
[AdventureWorks].[dbo].[DatabaseLog].Event,
[AdventureWorks].[dbo].[DatabaseLog].Schema,
[AdventureWorks].[dbo].[DatabaseLog].Object,
[AdventureWorks].[dbo].[DatabaseLog].TSQL,
[AdventureWorks].[dbo].[DatabaseLog].XmlEvent

Figure 4

Each of the different operators will have a distinct set of data. The operator in Figure 4 is performing work of a different nature than that in Figure 3, and so we get a different set of details. First, the Physical and Logical Operations are listed. The logical operators are the results of the optimizer's calculations for what should happen when the query executes. The physical operators represent what actually occurred. The logical and physical operators are usually the same, but not always – more on that in Chapter 2.

After that, we see the estimated costs for I/O, CPU, Operator and Subtree. The Subtree is simply the section of the execution tree that we have looked at so far, working right to left again, and top to bottom. All estimations are based on the statistics available on the columns and indexes in any table.

The I/O Cost and CPU cost are not actual operators, but rather the cost numbers assigned by the Query Optimizer during its calculations. These numbers are useful when determining whether most of the cost is I/O-based (as in this case), or if we're putting a load on the CPU. A bigger number means more processing in this area. Again, these are not hard and absolute numbers, but rather pointers that help to suggest where the actual cost in a given operation may lie.

You'll note that, in this case, the operator cost and the subtree cost are the same, since the table scan is the only operator. For more complex trees, with more operators, you'll see that the cost accumulates as the individual cost for each operator is added to the total. You get the full cost of the plan from the final operation in the query plan, in this case the **Select** operator.

Again we see the estimated number of rows. This is displayed for each operation because each operation is dealing with different sets of data. When we get to more complicated execution plans, you'll see the number of rows change as various operators perform their work on the data as it passes between each operator. Knowing how the rows are added or filtered out by each operator helps you understand how the query is being performed within the execution process.

Another important piece of information, when attempting to troubleshoot performance issues, is the Boolean value displayed for **Ordered**. This tells you whether or not the data that this operator is working with is in an ordered state. Certain operations, for example, an **ORDER BY** clause in a **SELECT** statement, may require data to be placed in a particular order, sorted by a particular value or set of values. Knowing whether or not the data is in an **Ordered** state helps show where extra processing may be occurring to get the data into that state.

Finally, **Node ID** is the ordinal, which simply means numbered in order, of the node itself, interestingly enough numbered left to right, despite the fact that the operations are best read right to left.

All these details are available to help you understand what's happening within the query in question. You'll be able to walk through the various operators, observing how the subtree cost accumulates, how the number of rows changes, and so on. With these details you'll be able to identify processes that are using excessive amounts of CPU or tables that need more indexes, or indexes that are not used, and so on.

Operator Properties

More information is available than that presented in the ToolTips. Right-click any icon within a graphical execution plan and select the "Properties" menu item to get a detailed list of information about that operation. Figure 5 shows the details from the original table scan.

Figure 5

Most of this information should be familiar, but some of it is new. Starting from the top, **Defined Values** displays the information that this operation adds to the process. These can be a part of the basic query, in this case the columns being selected, or they can be internally created values as part of the query processing, such as a flag used to determine referential integrity, or a placeholder for counts for aggregate functions.

Under the **Defined Values** property, we get a description of the operation and then some familiar **Estimated Cost** data. After that we see:

- **Estimated Rebinds** and **Rewinds**, values which describe the number of times an **Init()** operator is called in the plan.
- The **Forced Index** value would be **True** when a query hint is used to put a specific index to use within a query. SQL Server supplies the functionality in query hints as a way to give you some control over how a query is executed. Query hints are covered in detail in Chapter 4.
- **NoExpandHint** this is roughly the same concept as Forced Index, but applied to indexed views.

By expanding the **Object** property, you can see details on the object in question. The **Output List** property provides details of each of the output columns. You'll also find out whether or not this operator is taking part in a parallel operation, (when multiple CPUs are used by one operator).

Working with Text Execution Plans

The graphical execution plans are very useful because they're so easy to read. However, a lot of the data about the operators is not immediately visible to you. Some can be seen in a limited form in the ToolTip windows, and the complete set is available in the Properties window. Wouldn't it be great if there was a way to see all that information at once?

In the case of really large queries with incredibly complex plans or large number of batch statements, wouldn't it be handy to be able to search through for particular bits of information, table scans or the highest operator cost or something? Well, you can. Two methods exist: Text Execution Plans and XML Execution Plans.

Microsoft is planning on deprecating Text Execution Plans, so we'll cover them in relatively little detail.

Getting the Estimated Text Plan

To activate the text version of the Estimated text execution plan, simply issue the following command at the start of the query:

```
SET SHOWPLAN_ALL ON;
```

It's important to remember that, with SHOWPLAN_ALL set to ON, execution information is collected for all subsequent T-SQL statements, but those statements are not actually executed. Hence, we get the estimated plan. It's very important to remember to turn **SHOWPLAN_ALL OFF** after you have captured the information you require. If you forget, and submit a **CREATE**, **UPDATE** or **DELETE** statement with **SHOWPLAN_ALL** turned on, then those statements *won't* be executed, and a table you might expect to exist, for example, will not.

To turn **SHOWPLAN_ALL** off, simply issue:

```
SET SHOWPLAN_ALL OFF;
```

We can also use the equivalent commands for **SHOWPLAN_TEXT**. The text-only show plan is meant for use with tools like **osql.exe**, where the result sets can be readily parsed and stored by a tool dealing with text values, as opposed to actual result sets, as the **SHOWPLAN_ALL** function does.

We focus only on **SHOWPLAN_ALL** here.

Getting the Actual Text Plan

In order to activate and deactivate the text version of the Actual execution plan, use:

```
SET STATISTICS PROFILE ON
```

And:

```
SET STATISTICS PROFILE OFF
```

Interpreting Text Plans

We'll stick with the same basic query we used when discussing graphical plans, so execute the following:

```
GO
SELECT *
    FROM [dbo].[DatabaseLog];
GO
SET SHOWPLAN_ALL OFF;
GO
```

When you execute this query, the estimated plan is shown in the results pane. Here is the first column of the results:

	StmtText	StmtId	NodeId	Parent	PhysicalOp	LogicalOp	Argument
1	SELECT * FROM [dbo].[DatabaseLog];	1	1	0	NULL	NULL	1
2	I-Table Scan(OBJECT:([AdventureWorks].[d...	1	2	1	Table Scan	Table Scan	OBJECT:([AdventureWorks].[dbo].[Databas...

Figure 6

This screen shot was trimmed to keep the text as readable as possible. The text plan generated roughly parallels the graphical plan. The first row is the **SELECT** statement that was submitted. The rows following are the physical operations occurring within the query plan. In or case that means one row i.e. the table scan.

As we progress and view more complex text plans, in later chapters, you'll quickly realize that they are not as readily readable as the graphical plan. There's also no easy route through the query, such as we have with the "read it right to left" approach in the graphical plans. You start in the middle and move outwards, helped by the indentation of the data and the use of pipe (|) to connect the statements parent to child.

In addition to the first column, the details that were hidden in the ToolTip or in the Properties window are displayed in a series of columns. Most of the information that you're used to seeing is here, plus a little more. So, while the **NodeId** was available in the graphical plan, because of the nature of the graphical plan, nothing was required to identify the parent of a given node. In the **SHOWPLAN_ALL** we get a column showing the **Parent** NodeId. As you scan right you'll see many other familiar columns, such as the **TotalSubTreeCost**, **EstimateRows** and so on. Some of the columns are hard to read, such as the Defined List (the values or columns introduced by this operation to the data stream), which is displayed as just a comma-separated list.

Working with XML Execution Plans

XML Plans are the new and recommended way of displaying the execution plans in SQL Server 2005. They offer functionality not previously available.

Getting the Actual and Estimated XML Plans

In order to activate and deactivate the XML version of the Estimated execution plan, use:

```
SET SHOWPLAN_XML ON
...
SET SHOWPLAN_XML OFF
```

As for **SHOWPLAN_ALL**, the **SHOWPLAN_XML** command is essentially an instruction not to execute any T-SQL statements that follow, but instead to collect execution plan information for those statements, in the form of an XML document. Again, it's important to turn SHOWPLAN_XML off as soon as you have finished collecting plan information, so that subsequent T-SQL execute as intended.

For the XML version of the Actual plan, use:

```
SET STATISTICS XML ON
...
SET STATISTICS XML OFF
```

Interpreting XML Plans

Once again, let's look at the same execution plan as we evaluated with the text plan.

```
GO
SET SHOWPLAN_XML ON;
GO
SELECT *
  FROM [dbo].[DatabaseLog];
SET SHOWPLAN_XML OFF;
GO
```

The result, in the default grid mode, is shown in figure 7:

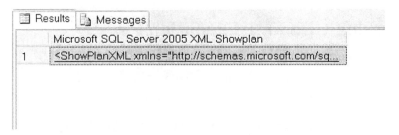

Figure 7

The link is a pointer to an XML file located here:

```
\Microsoft SQL Server\90\Tools\Binn\schemas\sqlserver\2003\0
3\showplan\showplanxml.xsd
```

Clicking on this link opens the execution plan in XML format in a browser window within the SQL Server Management Studio (SSMS). You can view the output in text, grid or file (default is grid). You can change the output format from the **Query** | **Results To** menu option.

A lot of information is put at your fingertips with XML plans – much of which we won't encounter here with our simple example, but will get to in later, more complex plans. Nevertheless, even this simple plan will give you a good feel for the XML format.

The results, even for our simple query, are too large to output here. I'll go over them by reviewing various elements and attributes. The full schema is available here:

```
http://schemas.microsoft.com/sqlserver/2004/07/showplan/
```

Listed first are the **BatchSequence**, **Batch** and **Statements** elements. In this example, we're only looking at a single Batch and a single Statement, so nothing else is displayed. Next, like all the other execution plans we've reviewed so far, we see the query in question as part of the **StmtSimple** element. Within that, we receive a list of attributes of the statement itself, and some physical attributes of the **QueryPlan**:

```
<StmtSimple StatementText="SELECT * &#xD;&#xA; FROM
[dbo].[DatabaseLog];&#xD;&#xA;" StatementId="1"
StatementCompId="1" StatementType="SELECT"
StatementSubTreeCost="0.108154" StatementEstRows="389"
StatementOptmLevel="TRIVIAL">
        <StatementSetOptions QUOTED_IDENTIFIER="false"
ARITHABORT="true" CONCAT_NULL_YIELDS_NULL="false"
```

```
ANSI_NULLS="false" ANSI_PADDING="false"
ANSI_WARNINGS="false" NUMERIC_ROUNDABORT="false" />
        <QueryPlan CachedPlanSize="9">
```

Clearly a lot more information is on immediate display than was provided for **SHOWPLAN_ALL**. Notice that the optimizer has chosen a trivial execution plan, as we might expect. Information such as the **CachedPlanSize** will help you to determine if, for example, your query exceeds one page in length, and gets sent into the **LeaveBehind** memory space.

After that, we have the **RelOp** element, which provides the information we're familiar with, regarding a particular operation, in this case the table scan.

```
            <RelOp NodeId="0" PhysicalOp="Table Scan"
LogicalOp="Table Scan" EstimateRows="389"
EstimateIO="0.107569" EstimateCPU="0.0005849"
AvgRowSize="8569" EstimatedTotalSubtreeCost="0.108154"
Parallel="0" EstimateRebinds="0" EstimateRewinds="0">
```

Not only is there more information than in the text plans, but it's also much more readily available and easier to read than in either the text plans or the graphical plans (although the flow through the graphical plans is much easier to read). For example, a problematic column, like the Defined List mentioned earlier, that is difficult to read, becomes the **OutputList** element with a list of **ColumnReference** elements, each containing a set of attributes to describe that column:

```
        <OutputList>
            <ColumnReference Database="[AdventureWorks]"
Schema="[dbo]" Table="[DatabaseLog]"
            Column="DatabaseLogID" />
            <ColumnReference Database="[AdventureWorks]"
Schema="[dbo]" Table="[DatabaseLog]" Column="PostTime" />
            <ColumnReference Database="[AdventureWorks]"
Schema="[dbo]" Table="[DatabaseLog]"
            Column="DatabaseUser" />
            <ColumnReference Database="[AdventureWorks]"
Schema="[dbo]" Table="[DatabaseLog]" Column="Event" />
            <ColumnReference Database="[AdventureWorks]"
Schema="[dbo]" Table="[DatabaseLog]" Column="Schema" />
            <ColumnReference Database="[AdventureWorks]"
Schema="[dbo]" Table="[DatabaseLog]" Column="Object" />
            <ColumnReference Database="[AdventureWorks]"
Schema="[dbo]" Table="[DatabaseLog]" Column="TSQL" />
```

```
                        <ColumnReference Database="[AdventureWorks]"
Schema="[dbo]" Table="[DatabaseLog]" Column="XmlEvent" />

                  </OutputList>
```

This makes XML not only easier to read, but much more readily translated directly back to the original query.

Back to the plan, after **RelOp** element referenced above we have the table scan element:

```
<TableScan Ordered="0" ForcedIndex="0" NoExpandHint="0">
```

Followed by a list of defined values that lays out the columns referenced by the operation:

```
                  <DefinedValues>
                    <DefinedValue>
                      <ColumnReference
Database="[AdventureWorks]" Schema="[dbo]"
Table="[DatabaseLog]" Column="DatabaseLogID" />
                    </DefinedValue>
                    <DefinedValue>
                  ...<output cropped>........
```

Saving XML Plans as Graphical Plans

You can save the execution plan without opening it by right-clicking within the results and selecting "Save As." You then have to change the filter to "*.*" and when you type the name of the file you want to save add the extension ".sqlplan." This is how the Books Online recommends saving an XML execution plan. In fact, what you get when you save it this way is actually a **graphical execution plan** file. This can actually be a very useful feature. For example, you might collect multiple plans in XML format, save them to file and then open them in easy-to-view (and compare) graphical format.

One of the benefits of extracting an XML plan and saving it as a separate file is that you can share it with others. For example, you can send the XML plan of a slow-running query to a DBA friend and ask them their opinion on how to rewrite the query. Once the friend receives the XML plan, they can open it up in Management Studio and review it as a graphical execution plan.

In order to actually save an XML plan as XML, you need to first open the results into the XML window. If you attempt to save to XML directly from the result window you only get what is on display in the result window. Another option is to go to the place where the plan is stored, as defined above, and copy it.

Automating Plan Capture Using SQL Server Profiler

During development you will capture execution plans for targeted T-SQL statements, using one of the techniques described in this chapter. You will activate execution plan capture, run the query in question, and then disable it again.

However, if you are troubleshooting on a test or live production server, the situation is different. A production system may be subject to tens or hundreds of sessions executing tens or hundreds or queries, each with varying parameter sets and varying plans. In this situation we need a way to automate plan capture so that we can collect a large number of plans simultaneously. In SQL Server 2005 you can use Profiler to capture XML execution plans, as the queries are executing. You can then examine the collected plans, looking for the queries with the highest costs, or simply searching the plans to find, for example, Table Scan operations that you'd like to eliminate.

SQL Server 2005 Profiler is a powerful tool that allows you to capture data about events, such as the execution of T-SQL or a stored procedure, occurring within SQL Server. Profiler events can be tracked manually, through a GUI interface, or traces can be defined through T-SQL (or the GUI) and automated to run at certain times and for certain periods.

These traces can be viewed on the screen or sent to or to a file or a table in a database.[4]

---

[4] Detailed coverage of Profiler is out of scope for this book, but more information can be found in Books Online (http://msdn2.microsoft.com/en-us/library/ms173757.aspx).

Execution Plan events

The various trace events that will generate an execution plan are as follow:

- **Showplan Text**: This event fires with each execution of a query and will generate the same type of estimated plan as the **SHOWPLAN_TEXT** T-SQL statement. Showplan Text will work on SQL 2005 databases, but it only shows a subset of the information available to ShowPlan XML. We've already discussed the shortcomings of the text execution plans, and this is on the list for deprecation in the future.
- **Showplan Text (unencoded)**: Same as above, but it shows the information as a string instead of binary. This is also on the list for deprecation in the future.
- **Showplan All**: This event fires as each query executes and will generate the same type of estimated execution plan as the **SHOWPLAN_ALL** TSQL statement. This has the same shortcomings as Showplan Text, and is on the list for future deprecation.
- **Showplan All for Query Compile**: This event generates the same data as the Showplan All event, but it only fires when a query compile event occurs. This is also on the list for deprecation in the future.
- **Showplan Statistics Profile**: This event generates the actual execution plan in the same way as the TSQL command **STATISTICS PROFILE**. It still has all the shortcomings of the text output, including only supplying a subset of the data available to **STATISTICS XML** in TSQL or the **Showplan XML Statistics Profile** event in SQL Server Profiler. The **Showplan Statistics Profile** event is on the list for deprecation.
- **Showplan XML**: The event fires with each execution of a query and generates an estimated execution plan in the same way as **SHOWPLAN_XML**.
- **Showplan XML For Query Compile**: Like Showplan XML above, but it only fires on a compile of a given query.
- **Performance Statistics**: Similar to the Showplan XML For Query Compile event, except this event captures performance metrics for the query as well as the plan. This only captures XML output for certain event subclasses, defined with the event. It fires the first time a plan is cached, compiled, recompiled or removed from cache.

- **Showplan XML Statistics Profile**: This event will generate the actual execution plan for each query, as it runs.

Capturing all of the execution plans, using Showplan XML or Showplan XML Statistics Profile, inherently places a sizeable load on the server. These are not lightweight event capture scenarios. Even the use of the less frequent Showplan XML for Query Compile will cause a small performance hit. Use due diligence when running traces of this type against any production machine.

Capturing a Showplan XML Trace

The SQL Server 2005 Profiler Showplan XML event captures the XML execution plan used by the query optimizer to execute a query. To capture a basic Profiler trace, showing estimated execution plans, start up Profiler, create a new trace and connect to a server[5].

Switch to the "Events Selection" tab and click on the "Show all events" check box. The Showplan XML event is located within the Performance section, so click on the plus (+) sign to expand that selection. Click on the Showplan XML event.

While you can capture the Showplan XML event by itself in Profiler, it is generally more useful if you capture it along with some other basic events, such as:

- RPC: Completed
- SQL:BatchStarting
- SQL:BatchCompleted

---

[5] By default, only an SA, or a member of the SYSADMIN group can create and run a Profiler trace – or a use who has been granted the ALTER TRACE permission.

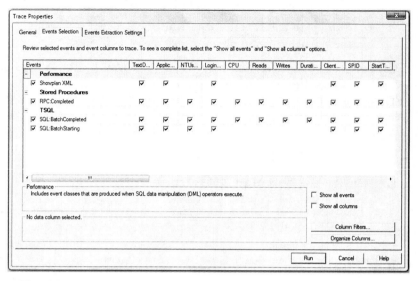

Figure 8

These extra events provide additional information to help put the XML plan into context. For example, you can see what occurred just before and after the event you are interested in.

Once Showplan XML is selected, or any of the other XML events, a third tab appears called **Events Extraction Settings**. On this tab, you can choose to output the XML as it's generated to a separate file, for later use. Not only can you define the file, but also determine whether or not all the XML will go into a single file or a series of files, unique to each execution plan.

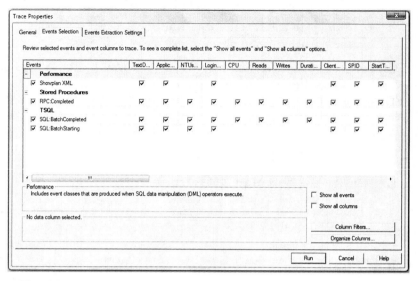

Figure 9

Click on the "Run" button in order to start the trace. When you capture the above events, you get a trace like the one shown in Figure 10.

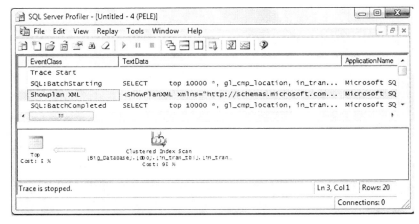

Figure 10

Notice that I have clicked on the Showplan XML event. Under the **TextData** column, you see the actual XML plan code. While you can't see all of it in the screen shot above, it is all there and can be saved to an individual file. In the second window, you can see the graphical execution plan, which is how most people prefer to read and analyze execution plans. So, in effect, the Showplan XML event available in Profiler not only shows you the XML plan code, but also the graphical execution plan.

At this stage, you can also save the code for this particular Showplan XML event to a separate file. Simply right-click on the Showplan XML event you want to save, then select "Extract Event Data."

Figure 11

This brings up a dialog box where you can enter the path and filename of the XML code you want to store. Instead of storing the XML code with the typical XML extension, the extension used is .SQLPlan. By using this extension, when you double-click on the file from within Windows Explorer, the XML code will open up in Management Studio in the form of a graphical execution plan.

Whether capturing Estimated execution plans or Actual execution plans, the Trace events operate in the same manner as when you run the T-SQL statements through the query window within Management Studio. The main difference is that this is automated across a large number of queries, from ad-hoc to stored procedures, running against the server.

Summary

In this chapter we've approached how the optimizer and the storage engine work together to bring data back to your query. These operations are expressed in the estimated execution plan and the actual execution plan. You were given a number of options for obtaining either of these plans, graphically, output as text, or as XML. Either the graphical plans or the XML plans will give you all the data you need, but it's going to be up to you to decide which to use and when based on the needs you're addressing and how you hope to address them.

Chapter 2: Reading Graphical Execution Plans for Basic Queries

The aim of this chapter is to enable you to interpret *basic* graphical execution plans, in other words, execution plans for simple **SELECT**, **UPDATE**, **INSERT** or **DELETE** queries, with only a few joins and no advanced functions or hints. In order to do this, we'll cover the following graphical execution plan topics:

- **Operators** – introduced in the last chapter, now you'll see more
- **Joins** – what's a relational system without the joins between tables
- **WHERE** clause – you need to filter your data and it does affect the execution plans
- **Aggregate**s – how grouping data changes execution plans
- **Insert**, **Update** and **Delete** execution plans

The Language of Graphical Execution Plans

In some ways, learning how to read graphical execution plans is similar to learning a new language, except that the language is icon-based, and the number of words (icons) we have to learn is minimal. Each icon represents a specific operator within the execution plan. We will be using the terms 'icon' and 'operator' interchangeably in this chapter.

In the previous chapter, we only saw two operators (**Select** and **Table Scan**). However, there are a total of 79 operators available. Fortunately for us, we don't have to memorize all 79 of them before we can read a graphical execution plan. Most queries use only a small subset of the icons, and those are the ones we are going to focus on in this chapter. If you run across an icon not covered here, you can find out more information about it on Books Online:

```
http://msdn2.microsoft.com/en-us/library/ms175913.aspx
```

Four distinct types of operator are displayed in a graphical execution plan:

- **Logical and physical operators**, also called iterators, are displayed as blue icons and represent query execution or Data Manipulation Language (DML) statements.
- **Parallelism physical operators** are also blue icons and are used to represent parallelism operations. In a sense, they are a subset of logical and physical operators, but are considered separate because they entail an entirely different level of execution plan analysis.
- **Cursor operators** have yellow icons and represent Transact-SQL cursor operations
- **Language elements** are green icons and represent Transact-SQL language elements, such as Assign, Declare, If, Select (Result), While, and so on.

In this chapter we'll focus mostly on logical and physical operators, including the parallelism physical operators. Books Online lists them in alphabetical order, but this is not the easiest way to learn them, so we will forgo being "alphabetically correct" here. Instead, we will focus on the most-used icons. Of course, what is considered most-used and least-used will vary from DBA to DBA, but the following are what I would consider the more common operators, listed from left-to-right and top-to-bottom, roughly in the order of most common to least common:

Select (Result)	Sort	**Clustered Index Seek**	Clustered Index Scan and	Non-clustered Index Scan
Non-clustered Index Seek	Table Scan	RID Lookup	Key Lookup	Hash Match
Nested Loops	Merge Join	Top	Compute Scalar	Constant Scan
Filter	Lazy Spool	Spool	Eager Spool	Stream Aggregate
Distribute Streams	Repartition Streams	Gather Streams	Bitmap	Split

Those picked out in bold are covered in this chapter. The rest will be covered when we move onto more complex queries in later chapters.

Operators have behavior that is worth understanding. Some operators – primarily **sort, hash match (aggregate)** and **hash join** – require a variable amount of memory in order to execute. Because of this, a query with one of these operators may have to wait for available memory prior to execution, possibly adversely affecting performance. Most operators behave in one of two ways, non-blocking or blocking. A non-blocking operator creates output data at the same time as it receives the input. A blocking operator has to get all the data prior to producing its output. A blocking operator might contribute to concurrency problems, hurting performance.

Some Single table Queries

Let's start by looking at some very simple plans, based on single table queries.

Clustered Index Scan

Consider the following simple (but inefficient!) query against the **Person.Contact** table in the AdventureWorks database:

```
SELECT *
FROM    Person.Contact
```

Following is the actual execution plan:

```
Query 1: Query cost (relative to the batch): 100%
SELECT * FROM Person.Contact
```

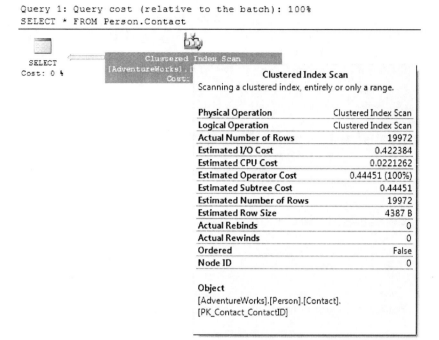

Figure 1

We can see that a clustered index scan operation is performed to retrieve the required data. If you place the mouse pointer over the Clustered Index Scan icon, to bring up the ToolTip window, you will see that the clustered index used was **PK_Contact_ContactID** and that the estimated number of rows involved in the operation was 19972.

Indexes in SQL Server are stored in a B-tree (a series of nodes that point to a parent). A clustered index not only stores the key structure, like a regular index, but also sorts and stores the data, which is the main reason why there can be only one clustered index per table.

As such, a clustered index **scan** is almost the same in concept as a table scan. The entire index, or a large percentage of it, is being traversed, row-by-row, in order to identify the data needed by the query.

An index scan often occurs, as in this case, when an index exists but the optimizer determines that so many rows need to be returned that it is quicker to simply scan all the values in the index rather than use the keys provided by that index.

An obvious question to ask if you see an index scan in your execution plan is whether you are returning more rows than is necessary. If the number of rows returned is higher than you expect, that's a strong indication that you need to fine-tune the **WHERE** clause of your query so that only those rows that are actually needed are returned. Returning unnecessary rows wastes SQL Server resources and hurts overall performance.

Clustered Index Seek

We can easily make the previous query more efficient by adding a **WHERE** clause:

```
SELECT *
FROM     Person.Contact
```

The plan now looks as shown in figure 2:

```
Query 1: Query cost (relative to the batch): 100%
SELECT * FROM [Person].[Contact] WHERE [ContactID]=@1
```

Clustered Index Seek	
Scanning a particular range of rows from a clustered index.	
Physical Operation	Clustered Index Seek
Logical Operation	Clustered Index Seek
Actual Number of Rows	1
Estimated I/O Cost	0.003125
Estimated CPU Cost	0.0001581
Estimated Operator Cost	0.0032831 (100%)
Estimated Subtree Cost	0.0032831
Estimated Number of Rows	1
Estimated Row Size	4387 B
Actual Rebinds	0
Actual Rewinds	0
Ordered	True
Node ID	0

Object
[AdventureWorks].[Person].[Contact].
[PK_Contact_ContactID]
Seek Predicates
Prefix: [AdventureWorks].[Person].[Contact].ContactID
= Scalar Operator(CONVERT_IMPLICIT(int,[@1],0))

Figure 2

Index seeks are completely different from scans, where the engine walks through the rows to find what it needs. An index seek, clustered or not, occurs when the optimizer is able to locate an index that it can use to retrieve the required records. Therefore, it tells the storage engine to look up the values based on the keys of the given index. Indexes in SQL Server are stored in a B-tree (a series of nodes that point to a parent). A **clustered index** stores not just the key structure, like a regular index, but also sorts and stores the data, which is the main reason why there can be only one clustered index per table.

When an index is used in a seek operation, the key values are used to quickly identify the row, or rows, of data needed. This is similar to looking up a word in the index of a book to get the correct page number. The added value of the clustered index seek is that, not only is the index seek an inexpensive operation as compared to an index scan, but no extra steps are required to get the data because it is stored in the index.

In the above example, we have a **Clustered Index Seek** operation carried out against the **Person.Contact** table, specifically on the **PK_Contact_ContactId**, which is happens to be both the primary key and the clustered index for this table.

Note on the ToolTips window for the Clustered Index Seek that the **Ordered** property is now true, indicating that the data was ordered by the optimizer.

Non-clustered Index Seek

Let's run a slightly different query against the **Person.Contact** table; one that uses a non-clustered index:

```
SELECT   ContactID
FROM     Person.Contact
WHERE    EmailAddress LIKE 'sab%'
```

We get a non-clustered index seek. Notice in the ToolTip shown in figure 3 that the non-clustered index, **IX_Contact_EmailAddress** has been used.

NOTE: The non-clustered Index Seek icon is misnamed and called an Index Seek in the execution plan below. Apparently, this was a mistake by Microsoft and hopefully will be fixed at some point. No big deal, but something for you to be aware of.

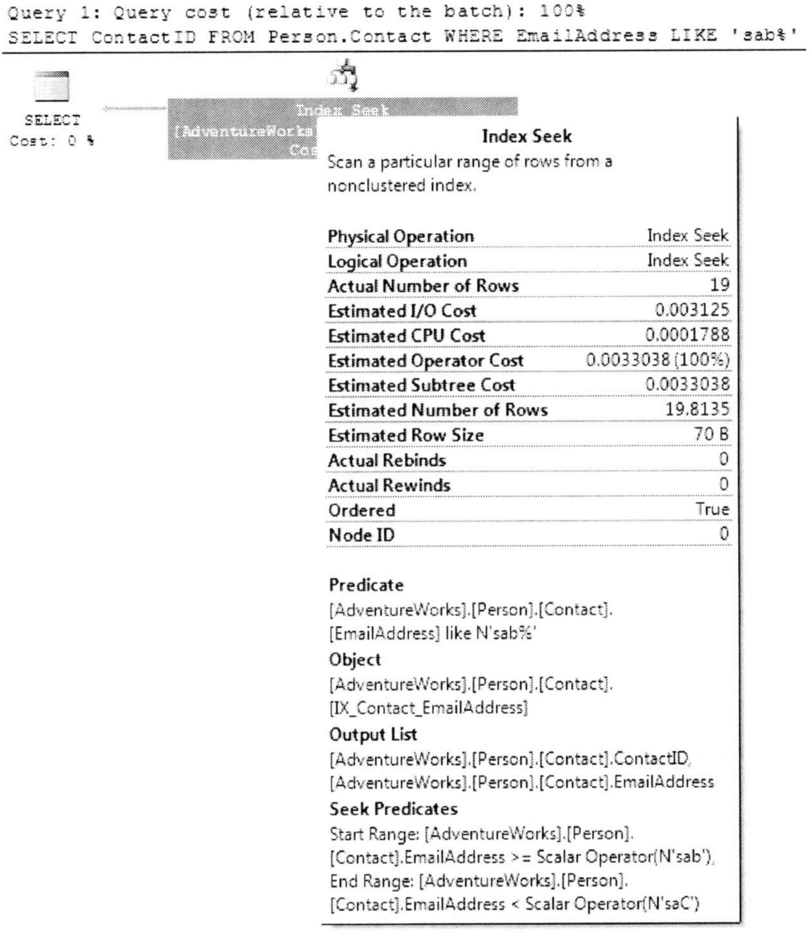

```
Query 1: Query cost (relative to the batch): 100%
SELECT ContactID FROM Person.Contact WHERE EmailAddress LIKE 'sab%'
```

Index Seek	
Scan a particular range of rows from a nonclustered index.	
Physical Operation	Index Seek
Logical Operation	Index Seek
Actual Number of Rows	19
Estimated I/O Cost	0.003125
Estimated CPU Cost	0.0001788
Estimated Operator Cost	0.0033038 (100%)
Estimated Subtree Cost	0.0033038
Estimated Number of Rows	19.8135
Estimated Row Size	70 B
Actual Rebinds	0
Actual Rewinds	0
Ordered	True
Node ID	0

Predicate
[AdventureWorks].[Person].[Contact].
[EmailAddress] like N'sab%'
Object
[AdventureWorks].[Person].[Contact].
[IX_Contact_EmailAddress]
Output List
[AdventureWorks].[Person].[Contact].ContactID,
[AdventureWorks].[Person].[Contact].EmailAddress
Seek Predicates
Start Range: [AdventureWorks].[Person].
[Contact].EmailAddress >= Scalar Operator(N'sab'),
End Range: [AdventureWorks].[Person].
[Contact].EmailAddress < Scalar Operator(N'saC')

Figure 3

Like a clustered index seek, a non-clustered index seek uses an index to look up the rows to be returned directly. Unlike a clustered index seek, a non-clustered index seek has to use a non-clustered index to perform the operation. Depending on the query and index, the query optimizer might be able to find all the data in the non-clustered index, or it might have to look up the data in the clustered index, slightly hurting performance due to the additional I/O required to perform the extra lookups – more on this in the next section.

Key LookUp

Let's take our query from the previous sections and alter it so that it returns just a few more columns:

```
SELECT   ContactID,
         LastName,
         Phone
FROM     Person.Contact
WHERE    EmailAddress LIKE 'sab%'
```

You should see a plan like that shown in figure 4:

Figure 4

Finally, we get to see a plan that involves more than a single operation! Reading the plan from right-to-left and top-to-bottom, the first operation we see is an Index Seek against the **IX_Contact_EmailAddress** index. This is a non-unique, non-clustered index and, in the case of this query, it is *non-covering*. A non-covering index is an index that does not contain all of the columns that need to be returned by a query, forcing the query optimizer to not only read the index, but to also read the clustered index to gather all the data it needs so it can be returned.

We can see this in the ToolTips window from the *Output List* for the Index Seek, in figure 5, which shows the **EmailAddress** and **ContactID** columns.

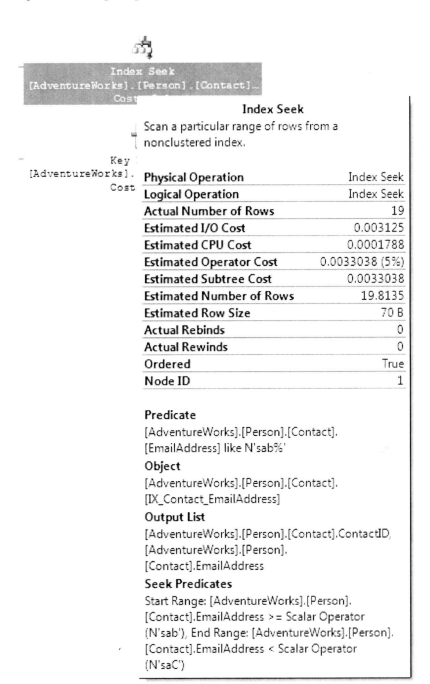

Index Seek	
Scan a particular range of rows from a nonclustered index.	
Physical Operation	Index Seek
Logical Operation	Index Seek
Actual Number of Rows	19
Estimated I/O Cost	0.003125
Estimated CPU Cost	0.0001788
Estimated Operator Cost	0.0033038 (5%)
Estimated Subtree Cost	0.0033038
Estimated Number of Rows	19.8135
Estimated Row Size	70 B
Actual Rebinds	0
Actual Rewinds	0
Ordered	True
Node ID	1

Predicate
[AdventureWorks].[Person].[Contact].
[EmailAddress] like N'sab%'
Object
[AdventureWorks].[Person].[Contact].
[IX_Contact_EmailAddress]
Output List
[AdventureWorks].[Person].[Contact].ContactID,
[AdventureWorks].[Person].
[Contact].EmailAddress
Seek Predicates
Start Range: [AdventureWorks].[Person].
[Contact].EmailAddress >= Scalar Operator
(N'sab'), End Range: [AdventureWorks].[Person].
[Contact].EmailAddress < Scalar Operator
(N'saC')

Figure 5

The key values are then used in a **Key Lookup** on the **PK_Contact_ ContactID** clustered index to find the corresponding rows, with the output list being the **LastName** and **Phone** columns, as shown in figure 6.

Key Lookup

Uses a supplied clustering key to lookup on a table that has a clustered index.

Physical Operation	Key Lookup
Logical Operation	Key Lookup
Actual Number of Rows	19
Estimated I/O Cost	0.003125
Estimated CPU Cost	0.0001581
Estimated Operator Cost	0.0610102 (95%)
Estimated Subtree Cost	0.0610102
Estimated Number of Rows	1
Estimated Row Size	88 B
Actual Rebinds	0
Actual Rewinds	0
Ordered	True
Node ID	3

Object
[AdventureWorks].[Person].[Contact].
[PK_Contact_ContactID]
Output List
[AdventureWorks].[Person].[Contact].LastName,
[AdventureWorks].[Person].[Contact].Phone
Seek Predicates
Prefix: [AdventureWorks].[Person].
[Contact].ContactID = Scalar Operator
([AdventureWorks].[Person].[Contact].[ContactID])

Figure 6

A Key Lookup[6] is a bookmark lookup on a table with a clustered index.

A Key Lookup essentially means that the optimizer cannot retrieve the rows in a single operation, and has to use a clustered key (or a row ID) to return the corresponding rows from a clustered index (or from the table itself).

The presence of a Key Lookup is an indication that query performance might benefit from the presence of a covering or included index. Both a covering or included index include all of the columns that need to be returned by a query, so all the columns of each row are found in the index, and a Key Lookup does not have to occur in order to get all the columns that need to be returned.

A Key LookUp is always accompanied by the Nested Loop join operation that combines the results of the two operations.

---

[6] Pre-SP2, this operation would have been represented with a Clustered Index scan, with a LookUp value of True.

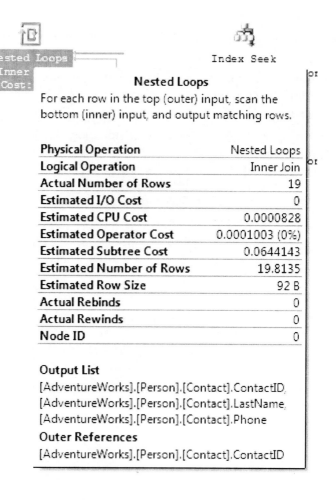

Figure 7

Typically, a Nested Loops join is a standard type of join and by itself does not indicate any performance issues. In this case, because a Key Lookup operation is required, the Nested Loops join is needed to combine the rows of the Index Seek and Key Lookup. If the Key Lookup was not needed (because a covering index was available), then the Nested Loops operator would not be needed and would not appear in the graphical execution plan.

Table Scan

This operator is fairly self-explanatory and is one we previously encountered in Chapter 1. It indicates that the required rows were returned by scanning the table, one row after another. You can see a table scan operation by executing the following query:

```
SELECT    *
FROM      [dbo].[DatabaseLog]
```

Query 1: Query cost (relative to the batch): 100%
SELECT * FROM [dbo].[DatabaseLog]

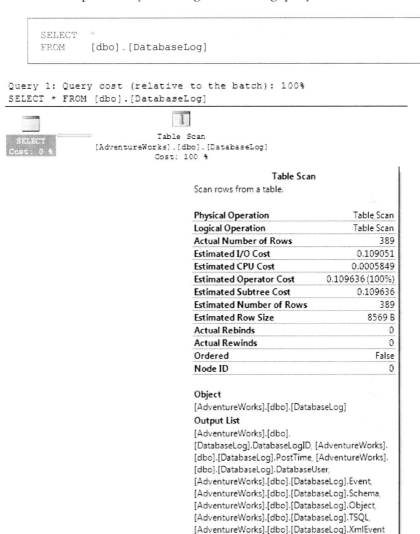

Figure 8

A table scan can occur for several reasons, but it's often because there are no useful indexes on the table, and the query optimizer has to search through every row in order to identify the rows to return. Another common reason why a table scan may occur is when all the rows of a table are returned, as is the case in this example. When all (or the majority) of the rows of a table are returned then, whether an index exists or not, it is often faster for the query optimizer to scan through each row and return them than look up each row in an index. And last, sometimes the query optimizer determines that it is faster to scan each row than it is to use an index to return the rows. This commonly occurs in tables with few rows.

Assuming that the number of rows in a table is relatively small, table scans are generally not a problem. On the other hand, if the table is large and many rows are returned, then you might want to investigate ways to rewrite the query to return fewer rows, or add an appropriate index to speed performance.

RID LookUp

If we specifically filter the results of our previous **DatabaseLog** query using the primary key column, we see a different plan that uses a combination of an Index Seek and a **RID LookUp**.

```
SELECT   *
FROM     [dbo].[DatabaseLog]
WHERE    DatabaseLogID = 1
```

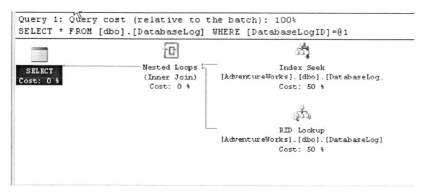

Figure 9

To return the results for this query, the query optimizer first performs an Index Seek on the primary key. While this index is useful in identifying the rows that meet the **WHERE** clause criteria, all the required data columns are not present in the index. How do we know this?

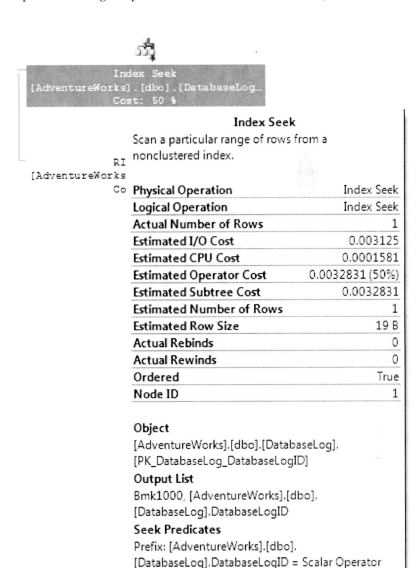

Index Seek

Scan a particular range of rows from a nonclustered index.

Physical Operation	Index Seek
Logical Operation	Index Seek
Actual Number of Rows	1
Estimated I/O Cost	0.003125
Estimated CPU Cost	0.0001581
Estimated Operator Cost	0.0032831 (50%)
Estimated Subtree Cost	0.0032831
Estimated Number of Rows	1
Estimated Row Size	19 B
Actual Rebinds	0
Actual Rewinds	0
Ordered	True
Node ID	1

Object
[AdventureWorks].[dbo].[DatabaseLog].
[PK_DatabaseLog_DatabaseLogID]
Output List
Bmk1000, [AdventureWorks].[dbo].
[DatabaseLog].DatabaseLogID
Seek Predicates
Prefix: [AdventureWorks].[dbo].
[DatabaseLog].DatabaseLogID = Scalar Operator
(CONVERT_IMPLICIT(int,[@1],0))

Figure 10

If you look at the ToolTip above for the Index Seek, we see "Bmk1000" is in the Output list. This"Bmk1000" is telling us that this Index Seek is actually part of a query plan that has a bookmark lookup.

Next, the query optimizer performs a RID LookUp, which is a type of bookmark lookup that occurs on a heap table (a table that doesn't have a clustered index), and uses a row identifier to find the rows to return.

In other words, since the table doesn't have a clustered index (that includes all the rows), it must use a row identifier that links the index to the heap. This adds additional disk I/O because two different operations have to be performed instead of a single operation, which are then combined with a Nested Loops operation.

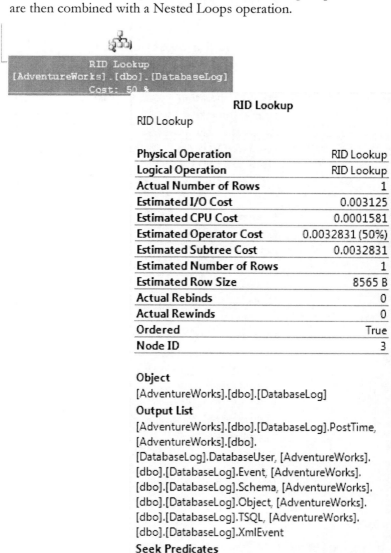

RID Lookup

RID Lookup

Physical Operation	RID Lookup
Logical Operation	RID Lookup
Actual Number of Rows	1
Estimated I/O Cost	0.003125
Estimated CPU Cost	0.0001581
Estimated Operator Cost	0.0032831 (50%)
Estimated Subtree Cost	0.0032831
Estimated Number of Rows	1
Estimated Row Size	8565 B
Actual Rebinds	0
Actual Rewinds	0
Ordered	True
Node ID	3

Object
[AdventureWorks].[dbo].[DatabaseLog]
Output List
[AdventureWorks].[dbo].[DatabaseLog].PostTime,
[AdventureWorks].[dbo].
[DatabaseLog].DatabaseUser, [AdventureWorks].
[dbo].[DatabaseLog].Event, [AdventureWorks].
[dbo].[DatabaseLog].Schema, [AdventureWorks].
[dbo].[DatabaseLog].Object, [AdventureWorks].
[dbo].[DatabaseLog].TSQL, [AdventureWorks].
[dbo].[DatabaseLog].XmlEvent
Seek Predicates
Prefix: Bmk1000 = Scalar Operator([Bmk1000])

Figure 11

In the above ToolTip for the RID Lookup, notice that "Bmk1000" is used again, but this time in the Seek Predicates section. This is telling us that a bookmark lookup (specifically a RID Lookup in our case) was used as part of the query plan. In this particular case, only one row had to be looked up, which isn't a big deal from a performance perspective. But if a RID Lookup returns many rows, you should consider taking a close look at the query to see how you can make it perform better by using less disk I/O – perhaps by rewriting the query, by adding a clustered index, or by using a covering or included index.

Table Joins

Up to now, we have worked with single tables. Let's spice things up a bit and introduce joins into our query. The following query retrieves employee information, concatenating the **FirstName** and **LastName** columns in order to return the information in a more pleasing manner.

```
SELECT   e.[Title],
         a.[City],
         c.[LastName] + ', ' + c.[FirstName] AS EmployeeName
FROM     [HumanResources].[Employee] e
JOIN [HumanResources].[EmployeeAddress] ed ON e.[EmployeeID]
= ed.[EmployeeID]
JOIN [Person].[Address] a ON [ed].[AddressID] =
[a].[AddressID]
         JOIN [Person].[Contact] c ON e.[ContactID] =
c.[ContactID];
```

The execution plan for this query is shown in figure 12.

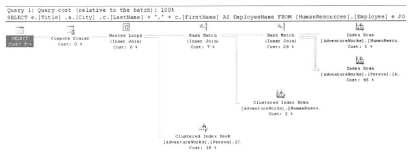

Figure 12

With this query there are multiple processing steps occurring, with varying costs to the processor. The cost accumulates as you move thorough the execution tree from right to left.

From the relative cost displayed below each operator icon, we can identify the three most costly operations in the plan, in descending order:

1. The Index Scan against the **Person.Address** table (45%)

2. The Hash Match join operation between the **HumanResources.EmployeeAddress** and **Person.Address** (28%)

3. The Clustered Index Seek on the **Person.Contact** table (18%)

Let's consider each of the operators we see in this plan.

Starting on the right of Figure 12 above, the first thing we see is an Index Scan against the **HumanResources.EmployeeAddress** table, and directly below this is another index scan against the **Person.Address** table. The latter was the most expensive operation in the plan, so let's investigate further. By bringing up the ToolTip, shown in Figure 13, we can see that the scan was against the index **IX_Address_AddressLine_AddressLine2_City_StateProvinceId_-PostalCode** and that the storage engine had to walk through 19,614 rows to arrive at the data that we needed.

Index Scan

Scan a nonclustered index, entirely or only a range.

Physical Operation	Index Scan
Logical Operation	Index Scan
Actual Number of Rows	19614
Estimated I/O Cost	0.158681
Estimated CPU Cost	0.0217324
Estimated Operator Cost	0.180413 (45%)
Estimated Subtree Cost	0.180413
Estimated Number of Rows	19614
Estimated Row Size	45 B
Actual Rebinds	0
Actual Rewinds	0
Ordered	False
Node ID	6

Object
[AdventureWorks].[Person].[Address].
[IX_Address_AddressLine1_AddressLine2_City_Sta
teProvinceID_PostalCode] [a]
Output List
[AdventureWorks].[Person].[Address].AddressID,
[AdventureWorks].[Person].[Address].City

Figure 13

The query optimizer needed to get at the **AddressId** and the **City** columns, as shown by the output list. The optimizer calculated, based on the selectivity of the indexes and columns in the table, that the best way to arrive at that data was to walk though the index. Walking through those 19,614 rows took 45% of the total query cost or an estimated operator cost of 0.180413. The estimated operator cost is the cost to the query optimizer for executing this specific operation, which is an internally calculated number used by the query optimizer to evaluate the relative costs of specific operations. The lower this number, the more efficient the operation.

Hash Match (Join)

Continuing with the above example, the output of the two index scans is combined through a **Hash Match join**, the second most expensive operation of this execution plan. The ToolTip for this operator is shown in Figure 14:

Hash Match	
Use each row from the top input to build a hash table, and each row from the bottom input to probe into the hash table, outputting all matching rows.	
Physical Operation	Hash Match
Logical Operation	Inner Join
Actual Number of Rows	290
Estimated I/O Cost	0
Estimated CPU Cost	0.111073
Estimated Operator Cost	0.111076 (28%)
Estimated Subtree Cost	0.29509
Estimated Number of Rows	282.216
Estimated Row Size	45 B
Actual Rebinds	0
Actual Rewinds	0
Node ID	4

Output List
[AdventureWorks].[HumanResources].
[EmployeeAddress].EmployeeID,
[AdventureWorks].[Person].[Address].City
Hash Keys Probe
[AdventureWorks].[Person].[Address].AddressID

Figure 14

Before we can talk about what a Hash Match join is, we need to understand two new concepts: **hashing** and **hash table**. Hashing is a programmatic technique where data is converted into a symbolic form that makes it easier to be searched for quickly. For example, a row of data in a table can be programmatically converted into a unique value that represents the contents of the row. In many ways it is like taking a row of data and encrypting it. Like encryption, a hashed value can be converted back to the original data. Hashing is often used within SQL Server to convert data into a form that is more efficient to work with, or in this case, to make searching more efficient.

A hash table, on the other hand, is a data structure that divides all of the elements into equal-sized categories, or buckets, to allow quick access to the elements. The hashing function determines which bucket an element goes into. For example, you can take a row from a table, hash it into a hash value, then store the hash value into a hash table.

Now that we understand these terms, a **Hash Match** join occurs when SQL Server joins two tables by hashing the rows from the smaller of the two tables to be joined, and then inserting them into a hash table, then processing the larger table one row at a time against the smaller hashed table, looking for matches where rows need to be joined. Because the smaller of the tables provides the values in the hash table, the table size is kept at a minimum, and because hashed values instead of real values are used, comparisons can be made very quickly. As long as the table that is hashed is relatively small, this can be a quick process. On the other hand, if both tables are very large, a Hash Match join can be very inefficient as compared to other types of joins.

In this example, the data from **HumanResources.EmployeeAddress .AddressId** is matched with **Person.Address** table.

Hash Match joins are often very efficient with large data sets, especially if one of the tables is substantially smaller than the other. Hash Match joins also work well for tables that are not sorted on join columns, and they can be efficient in cases where there are no useable indexes. On the other hand, a Hash Match join might indicate that a more efficient join method (Nested Loops or Merge) could be used. For example, seeing a Hash Match join in an execution plan sometimes indicates:

- a missing or incorrect index
- a missing **WHERE** clause
- a **WHERE** clause with a calculation or conversion that makes it non-sargeable (a commonly used term meaning that the search argument, "sarg" can't be used). This means it won't use an existing index.

While a Hash Match join may be the most efficient way for the query optimizer to join two tables, it does not mean there are not more efficient ways to join two tables, such as adding appropriate indexes to the joined tables, reducing the amount of data returned by adding a more restrictive WHERE clause, or by making the WHERE clause sargeble. In other words, a seeing a Hash Match join should be a cue for you to investigate if the join operation can be improved or not. If it can be improved, then great. If not, then there is nothing else to do, as the Hash Match join might be the best overall way to perform the join.

Worth noting in this example is the slight discrepancy between the estimated number of rows returned, 282.216 (proving this is a calculation since you can't possibly return .216 rows), and the actual number of rows, 290. A difference this small is not worth worrying about, but a larger discrepancy indicates that your statistics are out of date and need to be updated. A large difference can lead to differences in the Estimated and Actual plans.

The query proceeds from here with another index scan against the **HumanResources.Employee** table and another Hash Match between the results of the first Hash Match and the index scan.

Clustered Index Seek

After the Hash Match Join, we see a **Clustered Index Seek** operation carried out against the **Person.Contact** table, specifically on the **PK_Contact_ContactId**, which is both the primary key and clustered index for this table. This is the third most-expensive operation in the plan. The ToolTip is shown in Figure 15.

Clustered Index Seek

Scanning a particular range of rows from a clustered index.

Physical Operation	Clustered Index Seek
Logical Operation	Clustered Index Seek
Actual Number of Rows	290
Estimated I/O Cost	0.003125
Estimated CPU Cost	0.0001581
Estimated Operator Cost	0.0702501 (18%)
Estimated Subtree Cost	0.0702501
Estimated Number of Rows	1
Estimated Row Size	113 B
Actual Rebinds	0
Actual Rewinds	0
Ordered	True
Node ID	10

Object
[AdventureWorks].[Person].[Contact].
[PK_Contact_ContactID] [c]
Output List
[AdventureWorks].[Person].[Contact].FirstName,
[AdventureWorks].[Person].[Contact].LastName
Seek Predicates
Prefix: [AdventureWorks].[Person].[Contact].ContactID
= Scalar Operator([AdventureWorks].
[HumanResources].[Employee].[ContactID] as [e].
[ContactID])

Figure15

Note from the **Seek Predicates** section in figure 15 above, that the operation was joining directly between the **ContactId** column in the **HumanResources.Employee** table and the **Person.Contact** table.

Nested Loops Join

Following the clustered index seek, the data accumulated by the other operations are joined with the data collected from the seek, through a **Nested Loops Join,** as shown in Figure 16.

Nested Loops

For each row in the top (outer) input, scan the bottom (inner) input, and output matching rows.

Physical Operation	Nested Loops
Logical Operation	Inner Join
Actual Number of Rows	290
Estimated I/O Cost	0
Estimated CPU Cost	0.0011797
Estimated Operator Cost	0.0011799 (0%)
Estimated Subtree Cost	0.400857
Estimated Number of Rows	282.216
Estimated Row Size	197 B
Actual Rebinds	0
Actual Rewinds	0
Node ID	1

Output List
[AdventureWorks].[HumanResources].
[Employee].Title, [AdventureWorks].[Person].
[Address].City, [AdventureWorks].[Person].
[Contact].FirstName, [AdventureWorks].[Person].
[Contact].LastName
Outer References
[AdventureWorks].[HumanResources].
[Employee].ContactID, Expr 1009

Figure 16

The **nested loops join** is also called a nested iteration. This operation takes the input from two sets of data and joins them by scanning the outer data set (the bottom operator in a graphical execution plan) once for each row in the inner set. The number of rows in each of the two data sets was small, making this a very efficient operation. As long as the inner data set is small and the outer data set, small or not, is indexed, this becomes an extremely efficient join mechanism. Unless you have very large data sets, this is the type of join that you most want to see in an execution plan.

Compute Scalar

Finally, in the execution plan shown in figure 12, right before the Select operation, we have a Compute Scalar operation. The Tooltip for this operator is shown in Figure 19.

Compute Scalar	
Compute new values from existing values in a row.	

Physical Operation	Compute Scalar
Logical Operation	Compute Scalar
Estimated I/O Cost	0
Estimated CPU Cost	0.0000282
Estimated Operator Cost	0.000028 (0%)
Estimated Subtree Cost	0.400885
Estimated Number of Rows	282.216
Estimated Row Size	196 B
Node ID	0

Output List
[AdventureWorks].[HumanResources].
[Employee].Title, [AdventureWorks].[Person].
[Address].City, Expr1008

Figure 19

This is simply a representation of an operation to produce a scalar, a single defined value, usually from a calculation – in this case, the alias **EmployeeName** which combines the columns **Contact.LastName** and **Contact.FirstName** with a comma in between them. While this was not a zero-cost operation, 0.0000282, it's so trivial in the context of the query as to be essentially free of cost.

Merge Join

Besides the Hash and Nested Loops Join, the query optimizer can also perform a **Merge Join**. To seen an example of a Merge Join, we can run the following code in the AdventureWorks database:

```
SELECT  c.CustomerID
FROM    Sales.SalesOrderDetail od
        JOIN Sales.SalesOrderHeader oh
            ON od.SalesOrderID = oh.SalesOrderID
        JOIN Sales.Customer c
            ON oh.CustomerID = c.CustomerID
```

The above query produces an execution plan that looks as shown in figure 17.

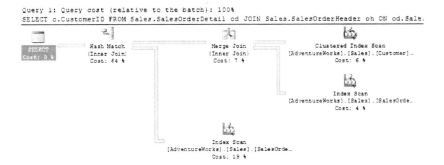

Query 1: Query cost (relative to the batch): 100%
SELECT c.CustomerID FROM Sales.SalesOrderDetail od JOIN Sales.SalesOrderHeader oh ON od.Sale.

Figure 17

According to the execution plan, the query optimizer performs a Clustered Index Scan on the **Customer** table and a non-clustered Index Scan on the **SalesOrderHeader** table. Since a **WHERE** clause was not specified in the query, a scan was performed on each table to return all the rows in each table.

Next, all the rows from both the **Customer** and **SalesOrderHeader** tables are joined using the **Merge Join** operator. A Merge Join occurs on tables where the join columns are presorted. For example, in the ToolTip window for the Merge Join, shown in figure 18, we see that the join columns are **Sales** and **CustomerID**. In this case, the data in the join columns are presorted in order. A Merge Join is an efficient way to join two tables, when the join columns are presorted but if the join columns are not presorted, the query optimizer has the option of a) sorting the join columns first, then performing a Merge Join, or b) performing a less efficient Hash Join. The query optimizer considers all the options and generally chooses the execution plan that uses the least resources.

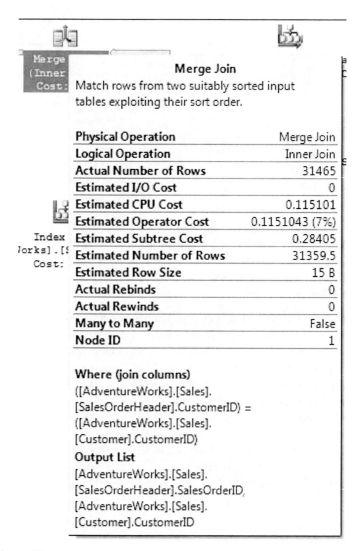

Figure 18

Once the Merge Join has joined two of the tables, the third table is joined to the first two using a Hash Match Join, which was discussed earlier. And finally, the joined rows are returned.

The key to performance of a Merge Join is that the joined columns are already presorted. If they are not, and the query optimizer chooses to sort the data before it performs a Merge Join, and this might be an indication that a Merge Join is not an ideal way to join the tables, or it might indicate that you need to consider some different indexes.

Adding a WHERE Clause

Only infrequently will queries run without some sort of conditional statements to limit the results set:; in other words, a **WHERE** clause. We'll investigate two multi-table, conditional queries using graphical execution plans.

Run the following query against AdventureWorks, and look at the actual execution plan. This query is the same as the one we saw at the start of the *Table Joins* section, but now has a **WHERE** clause.

```
SELECT   e.[Title],
         a.[City],
         c.[LastName] + ',' + c.[FirstName] AS EmployeeName
FROM     [HumanResources].[Employee] e
         JOIN [HumanResources].[EmployeeAddress] ed
            ON e.[EmployeeID] = ed.[EmployeeID]
         JOIN [Person].[Address] a
            ON [ed].[AddressID] = [a].[AddressID]
         JOIN [Person].[Contact] c
            ON e.[ContactID] = c.[ContactID]
WHERE    e.[Title] = 'Production Technician - WC20' ;
```

Figure 20 shows the actual execution plan for this query:

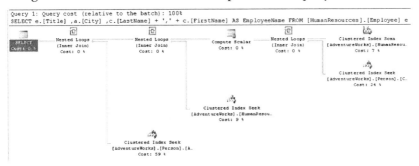

Figure 20

Starting from the right, we see that the optimizer has used the criteria from the **WHERE** clause to do a clustered index scan, using the primary key. The **WHERE** clause limited the number of rows to 22, which you can see by hovering your mouse pointer over the arrow coming out of the **Clustered Index Scan** operator (see figure 21).

Clustered Index Scan
[AdventureWorks].[HumanResources].[...
Cost: 7 %

Clustere
[AdventureWorks]
Cos

Clustered Index Scan

Scanning a clustered index, entirely or only a range.

Physical Operation	Clustered Index Scan
Logical Operation	Clustered Index Scan
Actual Number of Rows	22
Estimated I/O Cost	0.0075694
Estimated CPU Cost	0.000476
Estimated Operator Cost	0.0080454 (7%)
Estimated Subtree Cost	0.0080454
Estimated Number of Rows	22
Estimated Row Size	68 B
Actual Rebinds	0
Actual Rewinds	0
Ordered	False
Node ID	4

Predicate
[AdventureWorks].[HumanResources].[Employee].
[Title] as [e].[Title]=N'Production Technician - WC20'
Object
[AdventureWorks].[HumanResources].[Employee].
[PK_Employee_EmployeeID] [e]
Output List
[AdventureWorks].[HumanResources].
[Employee].EmployeeID, [AdventureWorks].
[HumanResources].[Employee].ContactID,
[AdventureWorks].[HumanResources].[Employee].Title

Figure 21

The optimizer, using the available statistics, was able to determine this up front, as we see by comparing the estimated and actual rows returned in the ToolTip.

Working with a smaller data set and a good index on the **Person.Contact** table, as compared to the previous query, the optimizer was able to use the more efficient **Nested Loop Join**. Since the optimizer changed where that table was joined, it also moved the scalar calculation right next to the join. Since it's still only 22 rows coming out of the scalar operation, a clustered index seek and another nested loop were used to join the data from the **HumanResources. EmployeeAddress** table. This then leads to a final clustered index seek and the final nested loop. All these more efficient joins are possible because we reduced the initial data set with the **WHERE** clause, as compared to the previous query which did not have a **WHERE** clause.

Frequently, developers who are not too comfortable with T-SQL will suggest that the "easiest" way to do things is to simply return all the rows to the application, either without joining the data between tables, or even without adding the **WHERE** clause. This was a very simple query with only a small set of data, but you can use this as an example, when confronted with this sort of argument. The final subtree cost for the optimizer for this query, when we used a **WHERE** clause, was 0.112425. Compare that to the 0.400885 of the previous query. That's four times faster even on this small, simple query. Just imagine what it might be like when the data set gets bigger and the query becomes more complicated.

Execution Plans with GROUP BY and ORDER BY

When other basic clauses are added to a query, different operators are displayed in the execution plans.

Sort

Take a simple select with an **ORDER BY** clause as an example:

```
SELECT   *
FROM     [Production].[ProductInventory]
ORDER BY [Shelf]
```

The execution plan is shown in figure 22.

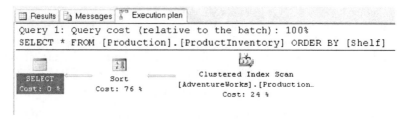

Figure 22

The **Clustered Index Scan** operator outputs into the **Sort** operator. Compared to many of the execution plan icons, the Sort operator is very straightforward. It literally is used to show when the query optimizer is sorting data within the execution plan. If an **ORDER BY** clause does not specify order, the default order is ascending, as you will see from the ToolTip for the **Sort** icon (see figure 23 below).

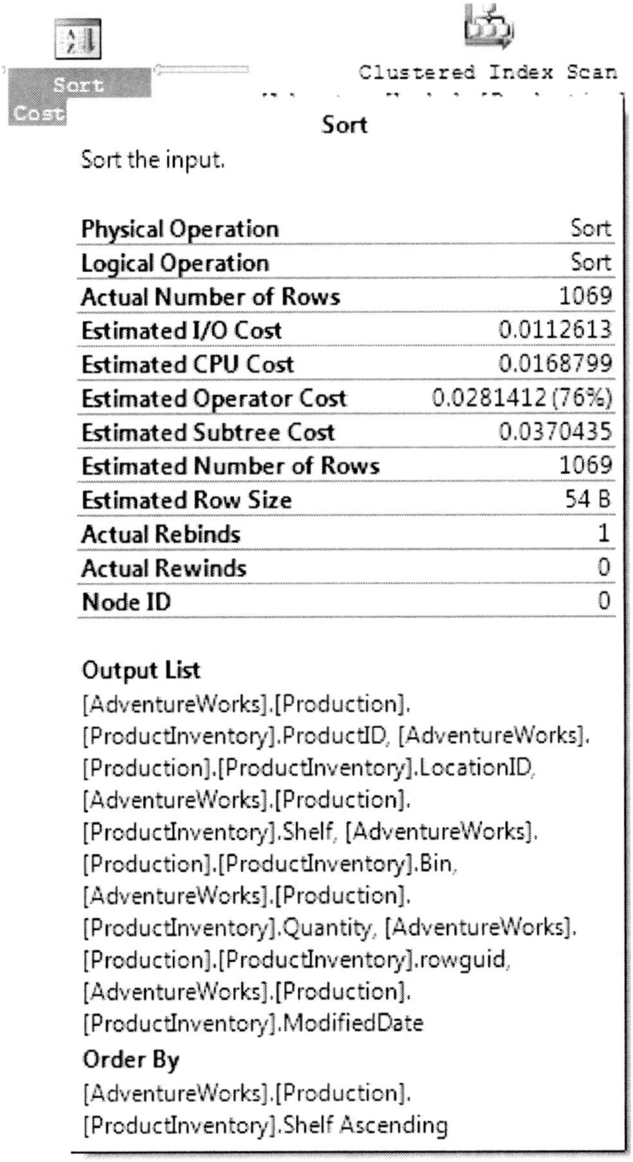

Sort

Sort the input.

Physical Operation	Sort
Logical Operation	Sort
Actual Number of Rows	1069
Estimated I/O Cost	0.0112613
Estimated CPU Cost	0.0168799
Estimated Operator Cost	0.0281412 (76%)
Estimated Subtree Cost	0.0370435
Estimated Number of Rows	1069
Estimated Row Size	54 B
Actual Rebinds	1
Actual Rewinds	0
Node ID	0

Output List
[AdventureWorks].[Production].
[ProductInventory].ProductID, [AdventureWorks].
[Production].[ProductInventory].LocationID,
[AdventureWorks].[Production].
[ProductInventory].Shelf, [AdventureWorks].
[Production].[ProductInventory].Bin,
[AdventureWorks].[Production].
[ProductInventory].Quantity, [AdventureWorks].
[Production].[ProductInventory].rowguid,
[AdventureWorks].[Production].
[ProductInventory].ModifiedDate
Order By
[AdventureWorks].[Production].
[ProductInventory].Shelf Ascending

Figure 23

If you pull up the ToolTip window for the Sort icon (see figure 24), you'll see that the Sort operator is being passed 1069 rows. The Sort operator takes these 1069 rows from the Clustered Index Scan, sorts them, and then passes the 1069 rows back in sorted order.

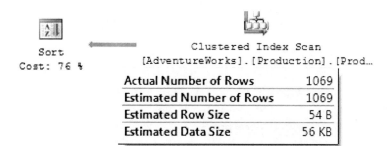

Figure 24

The most interesting point to note is that the Sort operation is 76% of the cost of the query. There is no index on this column, so the Sort operation is done within the query execution.

As a rule-of-thumb, I would say that when sorting takes more than 50% of a query's total execution time, then you need to carefully review it to ensure that it is optimized. In our case the reason why we are breaking this rule is fairly straightforward: we are missing a **WHERE** clause. Most likely, this query is returning more rows to be sorted than needs to be returned. However, even if a **WHERE** clause exists, you need to ensure that it limits the amount of rows to only the required number of rows to be sorted, not rows that will never be used.

Other things to consider are:

Is the sort really necessary? If not, remove it to reduce overhead.

Is it possible to have the data presorted so it doesn't have to be sorted? For example, can a clustered index be used that already sorts the data in the proper order? This is not always possible, but if it is, you will save sorting overhead if you create the appropriate clustered index.

If an execution plan has multiple Sort operators, review the query to see if they are all necessary, or if the code can be rewritten so that fewer sorts are needed to accomplish the goal of the query.

If we change the query to the following:

```
SELECT  *
FROM    [Production].[ProductInventory]
ORDER BY [ProductID]
```

We get the execution plan shown in figure 25:

```
Query 1: Query cost (relative to the batch): 100%
SELECT * FROM [Production].[ProductInventory] ORDER BY [ProductID]
```

```
                              Clustered Index Scan
SELECT              [AdventureWorks].[Production].[Prod...
Cost: 0 %                          Cost: 100 %
```

Figure 25

Although this query is almost identical to the previous query, and it includes an **ORDER BY** clause, we don't see a sort operator in the execution plan. This is because the column we are sorting by has changed, and this new column has a clustered index on it, which means that the returned data does not have to be sorted again, as it is already sorted as a byproduct of it being the clustered index. The query optimizer is smart enough to recognize that the data is already ordered, and does not have to order it again. If you have no choice but to sort a lot of data, you should consider using the SQL Server 2005 Profiler to see if any Sort Warnings are generated. To boost performance, SQL Server 2005 attempts to perform sorting in memory instead of disk. Sorting in RAM is much faster than sorting on disk. But if the sort operation is large, SQL Server may not be able to sort the data in memory, instead, having to write data to the tempdb database. Whenever this occurs, SQL Server generates a Sort Warning event, which can be captured by Profiler. If you see that your server is performing a lot of sorts, and many Sort Warnings are generated, then you may need to add more RAM to your server, or to speed up tempdb access.

Hash Match (Aggregate)

Earlier in this chapter, we took a look at the Hatch Match operator for joins. This same Hatch Match operator also can occur when aggregations occur within a query. Let's consider a simple aggregate query against a single table using the **COUNT** operator:

```
SELECT  [City],
        COUNT([City]) AS CityCount
FROM    [Person].[Address]
GROUP BY [City]
```

The actual execution plan is shown below.

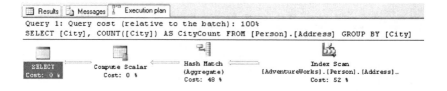

Figure 26

The query execution begins with an Index Scan, because all of the rows are returned for the query. There is no **WHERE** clause to filter the rows. These rows then need to be aggregated in order to perform the requested **COUNT** aggregate operation. In order for the query optimizer to count each row for each separate city, it must perform a Hatch Match operation. Notice that underneath Hatch Match in the execution plan that the word "aggregate" is put between parentheses. This is to distinguish it from a Hatch Match operation for a join. As with a Hatch Match with a join, a Hatch Match with an aggregate causes SQL Server to create a temporary hash table in memory in order to count the number of rows that match the **GROUP BY** column, which in this case is "City." Once the results are aggregated, then the results are passed back to us.

Quite often, aggregations with queries can be expensive operations. About the only way to "speed" the performance of an aggregation via code is to ensure that you have a restrictive **WHERE** clause to limit the number of rows that need to be aggregated, thus reducing the amount of aggregation that needs to be done.

Filter

If we add a simple **HAVING** clause to our previous query, our execution plan gets more complex

```
SELECT   [City],
         COUNT([City]) AS CityCount
FROM     [Person].[Address]
GROUP BY [City]
HAVING   COUNT([City]) > 1
```

The execution plan now looks as shown in figure 27:

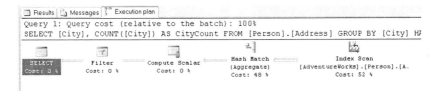

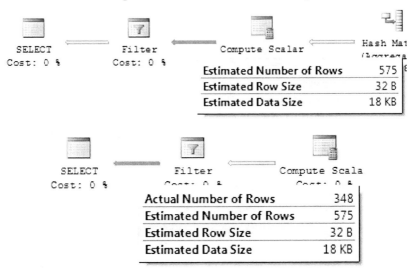

Figure 27

By adding the **HAVING** clause, the Filter operator has been added to the execution plan. We see that the **Filter** operator is applied to limit the output to those values of the column, **City**, that are greater than 1. One useful bit of knowledge to take away from this plan is that the **HAVING** clause is not applied until all the aggregation of the data is complete. We can see this by noting that the actual number of rows in the **Hash Match** operator is 575 and in the **Filter** operator it's 348.

Figure 28

While adding a **HAVING** clause reduces the amount of data returned, it actually adds to the resources needed to produce the query results, because the **HAVING** clause does not come into play until after the aggregation. This hurts performance. As with the previous example, if you want to speed the performance of a query with aggregations, the only way to do so in code is to add a **WHERE** clause to the query to limit the number of rows that need to be selected and aggregated.

Rebinds and Rewinds Explained

While examining the ToolTips for physical operators, throughout this chapter, you will have seen these terms several times:

- Actual Rebinds or Estimated Rebinds
- Actual Rewind or Estimated Rewinds

Most of the time in this chapter, the value for both the rebinds and rewinds has been zero, but for the Sort operator example, a little earlier, we saw that there was **one** actual rebind and **zero** actual rewinds.

In order to understand what these values mean, we need some background. Whenever a physical operator, such as the SORT operator in an execution plan occurs, three things happen.

- First, the physical operator is initialized and any required data structures are set up. This is called the **Init()** method. In all cases this happens once for an operator, although it is possible to happen many times.
- Second, the physical operator gets (or receives) the rows of data that it is to act on. This is called the **GetNext()** method. Depending on the type of operator, it may receive none, or many **GetNext()** calls.
- Third, once the operator is done performing its function, it needs to clean itself up and shut itself down. This is called the **Close()** method. A physical operator only ever receives a single **Close()** call.

A rebind or rewind is a count of the number of times the **Init()** method is called by an operator. A rebind and a rewind both count the number of times the **Init()** method is called, but do so under different circumstances.

A rebind count occurs when one or more of the correlated parameters of a join change and the inner side must be reevaluated. A rewind count occurs when none of the correlated parameters change and the prior inner result set may be reused. Whenever either of these circumstances occur, a rebind or rewind occurs, and increases their count.

Given the above information, you would expect to see a value of one or higher for the rebind or rewind in every ToolTips or Properties screen for a physical operator. But you don't. What is odd is that the rebind and rewind count values are only populated when particular physical operators occur, and are not populated when other physical operators occur. For example, if any of the following six operators occur, the rebind and rewind counts are populated:

- Nonclustered Index Spool
- Remote Query
- Row Count Spool
- Sort
- Table Spool
- Table-Valued Function

If the following operators occur, the rebind and rewind counts will only be populated when the **StartupExpression** for the physical operation is set to **TRUE**, which can vary depending on how the query optimizer evaluates the query. This is set by Microsoft in code and is something we have no control over.

- Assert
- Filter

And for all other physical operators, they are not populated. In these cases, the counts for rebind and rewind will be zero. This zero count does not mean that zero rebinds or rewinds occurred, just that these values were not populated. As you can imagine, this can get a little confusing. This also explains why most of the time you see zero values for rebind and rewind.

So, what does it mean when you see a value for either rebind or rewind for the eight operators where rebind and rewind may be populated?

If you see an operator where rebind equals one and rewinds equals zero, this means that an **Init()** method was called one time on a physical operator that is NOT on the inner side of a loop join. If the physical operator is ON the inner side of a loop join used by an operator, then the sum of the rebinds and rewinds will equal the number of rows process on the outer side of a join used by the operator

So how is this helpful to the DBA? Generally speaking, it is ideal if the rebind and rewind counts are as low as possible, as higher counts indicate more disk I/O. If the counts are high, it might indicate that a particular operator is working harder than it needs to, hurting server performance. If this is the case, it might be possible to rewrite the query, or modify current indexing, to use a different query plan that uses fewer rebinds and rewinds, reducing I/O and boosting performance.

Insert, Update and Delete Execution Plans

Execution plans are generated for all queries against the database in order for the engine to figure out how best to undertake the request you've submitted. While the previous examples have been for **SELECT** queries, in this section we will take a look at the execution plans of **INSERT**, **UPDATE**, and **DELETE** queries.

Insert Statements

Here is a very simple **INSERT** statement:

```
INSERT  INTO [AdventureWorks].[Person].[Address]
        (
            [AddressLine1],
            [AddressLine2],
            [City],
            [StateProvinceID],
            [PostalCode],
            [rowguid],
            [ModifiedDate]
        )
VALUES  (
            '1313 Mockingbird Lane',
            'Basement',
            'Springfield',
            '79',
            '02134',
            NEWID(),
            GETDATE()
        ) ;
```

This statement generates this rather interesting estimated plan (so that I don't actually affect the data within the system), shown in Figure 29.

Figure 29

The execution plan starts off, reading right to left, with an operator that is new to us: **Constant Scan**. This operator introduces a constant number of rows into a query. In our case, it's building a row in order for the next two operators to have a place to add their output. The first of these is a **Compute Scalar** operator to call a function called **getidentity**. This is the moment within the query plan when an identity value is generated for the data to follow. Note that this is the first thing done within the plan, which helps explain why, when an insert fails, you get a gap in the identity values for a table.

Another scalar operation occurs which outputs a series of placeholders for the rest of the data and creates the new **uniqueidentifier** value, and the date and time from the **GETDATE** function. All of this is passed to the **Clustered Index Insert** operator, where the majority of the cost of this plan is realized. Note the output value from the INSERT statement, the **Person.Address.StateProvinceId**. This is passed to the next operator, the **Nested Loop** join, which also gets input from the **Clustered Index Seek** against the **Person.StateProvince** table. In other words, we had a read during the INSERT to check for referential integrity on the foreign key of **StateProvinceId**. The join then outputs a new expression which is tested by the next operator, **Assert**. An **Assert** verifies that a particular condition exists. This one checks that the value of Expr1014 equals zero. Or, in other words, that the data that was attempted to be inserted into the **Person.Address.StateProvinceId** field matched a piece of data in the **Person.StateProvince** table; this was the referential check.

Update Statements

Consider the following update statement:

```
UPDATE    [Person].[Address]
SET       [City] = 'Munro',
          [ModifiedDate] = GETDATE()
WHERE     [City] = 'Monroe' ;
```

The estimated execution plan is shown below:

Figure 30

Let's begin reading this execution plan, from right to left. The first operator is a non-clustered Index Scan, which retrieves all of the necessary rows from a non-clustered index, scanning through them, one row at a time. This is not particular efficient and should be a flag to you that perhaps the table needs better indexes to speed performance. The purpose of this operator is to identify all the rows **WHERE [City] = 'Monroe'**, and then send them to the next operator.

The next operator is **TOP**. In an **UPDATE** execution plan, it is used to enforce row count limits, if there are any. In this case, no limits have been enforced because the **TOP** clause was not used in the **UPDATE** query.

Note: If the **TOP** operator is found in a **SELECT** statement, not an **UPDATE** statement, it indicates that a specified number, or percent, of rows have been returned, based on the **TOP** command used in the **SELECT** statement.

The next operator is an **Eager Spool** (a form of a Table Spool). This obscure sounding operator essentially takes each of the rows to be updated and stores them in a hidden temporary object stored in the tempdb database. Later in the execution plan, if the operator is rewound (say due to the use of a Nested Loops operator in the execution plan) and no rebinding is required, the spooled data can be reused instead of having to rescan the data again (which means the non-clustered Index Scan has to be repeated, which would be an expensive option). In this particular query, no rewind operation was required.

The next three operators are all Compute Scalar operators, which we have seen before. In this case, they are used to evaluate expressions and to produce a computed scalar value, such as the **GETDATE()** function used in the query.

Now we get to the core of the **UPDATE** statement, the Clustered Index Update operator. In this case, the values being updated are part of a clustered index. So this operator identifies the rows to be updated, and updates them.

And last of all, we see the generic T-SQL Language Element Catchall operator, which tells us that an **UPDATE** operation has been completed.

From a performance perspective, one of the things to watch for is how the rows to be updated are retrieved. In this example, an non-clustered Index Scan was performed, which is not very efficient. Ideally, a clustered or non-clustered index seek would be preferred from a performance standpoint, as either one of them would use less I/O to perform the requested **UPDATE**.

Delete Statements

What kind of execution plan is created with a **DELETE** statement? For example, let's run the following code and check out the execution plan.

```
DELETE   FROM [Person].[Address]
WHERE    [AddressID] = 52;
```

Figure 31 shows the estimated execution plan:

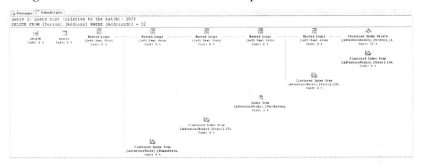

Figure 31

I know this is a bit difficult to read. I just wanted to show how big a plan is necessary to delete data within a relational database. Remember, removing a row, or rows, is not an event isolated to the table in question. Any tables related to the primary key of the table where we are removing data will need to be checked, to see if removing this piece of data affects their integrity. To a large degree, this plan looks more like a **SELECT** statement than a **DELETE** statement.

Starting on the right, and reading top to bottom, we immediately get a Clustered Index Delete operator. There are a couple of interesting points in this operation. The fact that the delete occurs at the very beginning of the process is good to know. The second interesting fact is that the Seek Predicate on this **Clustered Index Seek To Delete** operation was:

Prefix: [AdventureWorks].[Person].[Address].AddressID   =   Scalar Operator(CONVERT_IMPLICIT(int,[@1],0)).

This means that a parameter, **@1**, was used to look up the **AddressId**. If you'll notice in the code, we didn't use a parameter, but rather used a constant value, 52. Where did the parameter come from? This is an indication of the query engine generating a reusable query plan, as per the rules of simple parameterization.

Clustered Index Delete

Delete rows from a clustered index.

Physical Operation	Clustered Index Delete
Logical Operation	Delete
Estimated I/O Cost	0.04
Estimated CPU Cost	0.000004
Estimated Operator Cost	0.0432871 (72%)
Estimated Subtree Cost	0.0432871
Estimated Number of Rows	1
Estimated Row Size	11 B
Node ID	7

Object
[AdventureWorks].[Person].[Address].
[PK_Address_AddressID], [AdventureWorks].[Person].
[Address].[AK_Address_rowguid], [AdventureWorks].
[Person].[Address].
[IX_Address_AddressLine1_AddressLine2_City_StateProvi
nceID_PostalCode], [AdventureWorks].[Person].
[Address].[IX_Address_StateProvinceID]
Output List
[AdventureWorks].[Person].[Address].AddressID
Seek Predicate
Prefix: [AdventureWorks].[Person].[Address].AddressID
= Scalar Operator(CONVERT_IMPLICIT(int,[@1],0))

Figure 32

After the delete, a series of Index and Clustered Index Seeks and Scans are combined through a series of Nested Loop Join operators. These are specifically Left Semi Joins. These operators return a value if the join predicate between the two tables in question matches or if there is no join predicate supplied. Each one returns a value. Finally, at the last step, an Assert operator, the values returned from each Join, all the tables related to the table from which we're attempting to delete data, are checked to see if referential data exists. If there is none, the delete is completed. If they do return a value, an error would be generated, and the **DELETE** operation aborted.

Assert

Used to verify that a specified condition exists.

Physical Operation	Assert
Logical Operation	Assert
Estimated I/O Cost	0
Estimated CPU Cost	0.0000002
Estimated Operator Cost	0.0000002 (0%)
Estimated Subtree Cost	0.060231
Estimated Number of Rows	1
Estimated Row Size	9 B
Node ID	1

Predicate

CASE WHEN NOT [Expr1021] IS NULL THEN (0)
ELSE CASE WHEN NOT [Expr1022] IS NULL THEN
(1) ELSE CASE WHEN NOT [Expr1023] IS NULL
THEN (2) ELSE CASE WHEN NOT [Expr1024] IS
NULL THEN (3) ELSE CASE WHEN NOT [Expr1025]
IS NULL THEN (4) ELSE NULL END END END END
END

Figure 33

Summary

This chapter represents a major step in learning how to read graphical execution plans. However, as we discussed at the beginning of this chapter, we only focused on the most common type of operators and we only looked at simple queries. So if you decide to analyze a 200-line query and get a graphical execution plan that is just about as long, don't expect to be able to analyze it immediately. Learning how to read and analyze execution plans takes time and effort. But once you gain some experience, you will find that it becomes easier and easier to read and analyze, even for the most complex of execution plans.

CHAPTER 3: TEXT AND XML EXECUTION PLANS FOR BASIC QUERIES

The added bonus of learning how to read graphical execution plans, in Chapter 2, is that what you learned there also applies to reading Text and XML execution plans. While text and XML execution plans don't have icons, they still include the same operators. So by learning how to read graphical execution plans, you also learn how to read text and XML execution plans.

In early versions of SQL Server, only text-based execution plans were available and many people found them hard to read, especially with complex plans. Microsoft eventually relented and introduced graphical execution plans, in addition to offering text execution plans. I find graphical execution plans much easier to read than text plan and I guess I'm not the only DBA who feels this way, as text-based execution plans have been added to the SQL Server deprecation list and will eventually go away.

To replace text-based execution plans[7], Microsoft introduced XML Plans in SQL Server 2005.

Like text-based plans, XML Plans can be difficult to read and analyze if you look at the raw XML code only. So why did Microsoft decide to replace text-based execution plans with XML Plans if both of them are difficult to read? There are several reasons for the change. Essentially, XML is a common file format that can be used programmatically, unlike text-based execution plans. XML Plans also provide a much richer environment to store more execution plan details than ever before. In addition, XML Plans are stored in a portable format that makes them easy to share with others. For example, I can send an XML Plan to a fellow DBA, and she can use Management Console to graphically display and analyze it. Text-based plans, on the other hand, don't offer any of these benefits.

---

[7] SQL Server 2005 still offers text-based execution plans, but only for backward-compatibility.

Text Execution Plans

So why should you even bother to learn about text execution plans if this feature is being deprecated? That's only a question you can answer. If you are working with SQL Server 2005 for the most part, I suggest you focus your efforts on learning graphical execution plans, and understanding the benefits and uses of the XML Plan file format. On the other hand, if you are still managing many older versions of SQL Server, you might, but not necessarily, want to learn how to read text plans because they are still often seen in books and articles about SQL Server, and knowing how to read them might prove useful.

A Text Plan for a Simple Query

Let's start by examining the text plan for a query we saw in the previous chapter. First, as a reminder, we'll capture the graphical plan:

```
SELECT   ContactID,
         LastName,
         Phone
FROM     Person.Contact
WHERE    EmailAddress LIKE 'sab%'
```

Query 1: Query cost (relative to the batch): 100%
SELECT ContactID, LastName, Phone FROM Person.Contact where EmailAddress LIKE 'sab%'

Figure 1

Now, we'll capture the equivalent text plan. Remember that turning on **SHOWPLAN_ALL** will allow you to collect *estimated* execution plans. No T-SQL code submitted after this statement is actually executed, until you turn **SHOWPLAN_ALL** off again:

```
SET SHOWPLAN_ALL ON ;
GO

SELECT   ContactID,
         LastName,
         Phone
FROM     Person.Contact
WHERE    EmailAddress LIKE 'sab%'
```

```
GO

SET SHOWPLAN_ALL OFF ;
GO
```

The results are returned in a spreadsheet-style grid format, as shown in figure 2[8]:

	StmtText	StmtId	Nod...	Parent	PhysicalOp	LogicalOp	Argument	DefinedValues	Estimate
1	SELECT ContactID, LastName, Phone FRO...	1	1	0	NULL	NULL	1	NULL	19.8134
2	I-Nested Loops(Inner Join, OUTER REFERE...	1	2	1	Nested Loops	Inner Join	OUTER REFERENCES:([Adv...	NULL	19.8134
3	I-Index Seek(OBJECT:([AdventureWorks]...	1	3	2	Index Seek	Index Seek	OBJECT:([AdventureWorks].[...	[AdventureWorks].[Pers...	19.8134
4	I-Clustered Index Seek(OBJECT:([Advent...	1	5	2	Clustered Index Seek	Clustered Index Seek	OBJECT:([AdventureWorks].[...	[AdventureWorks].[Pers...	1

Figure 2

Row 1 is the parent node, and the **StmtText** column for this row contains the text for the TSQL statement that was executed. If you scroll right through the results, you'll find a column called **Type**, which describes the node type.

EstimateRows	EstimateIO	EstimateCPU	AvgRowSize	TotalSubtreeCost	OutputList	Warnings	Type	Parallel	EstimateExecutions
19.81349	NULL	NULL	NULL	0.06441426	NULL	NULL	SELECT	0	NULL
19.81349	0	8.28204E-05	92	0.06441426	[AdventureWorks].[Person].[Contact].[ContactID]...	NULL	PLAN_ROW	0	1
19.81349	0.003125	0.0001787948	70	0.003303795	[AdventureWorks].[Person].[Contact].[ContactID]...	NULL	PLAN_ROW	0	1
1	0.003125	0.0001581	88	0.0610102	[AdventureWorks].[Person].[Contact].[LastName]...	NULL	PLAN_ROW	0	19.81349

Figure 3

For the parent node this will contain the type of SQL statement that was executed (SELECT, in this case). For all other rows the type is **PLAN_ROW**. For all **PLAN_ROW** nodes, the **StmtText** column describes the type of operation that took place.

A quick glance at the **StmtText** column for the remaining rows reveals that three operations took place: a Nested Loops inner join, an index seek, and a clustered index seek.

Unlike for graphical plans, there's no easy "right to left and top to bottom" route through the text-based plans. In order to understand the flow of operations, we are helped by the indentation of the data and the use of pipe (|) to connect the statements, parent-to-child. We can also refer to the **NodeID** and **Parent** columns, which indicate the IDs of

---

[8] If you right-click in the query window of SSMS, you can select Results To | Results to Text, which offers a more conventional view of the text execution plan.

the current node and its parent node, respectively. Within each indentation, or for every row that has the same Parent number, the operators execute from top to bottom. In this example, the Index Seek occurs before the Clustered Index Seek.

Moving to the two most-indented rows, we start at row 3 (NodeId 3) with the Index Seek operation. By extending the **StmtText** column (or examining the **Argument** column) we can see that the index seek was against the **Person.Contact** table:

```
OBJECT:([AdventureWorks].[Person].[Contact].[IX_Contact_EmailAdd
ress]), SEEK:([AdventureWorks].[Person].[Contact].[EmailAddress]
>= N'sab' AND [AdventureWorks].[Person].[Contact].[EmailAddress]
< N'saC'),
WHERE:([AdventureWorks].[Person].[Contact].[EmailAddress] like
N'sab%') ORDERED FORWARD
```

The **DefinedValues** column for a given **PLAN_ROW** contains a comma-delimited list of the values that the operator introduces. These may be values that were present in the current query (in the SELECT or WHERE clauses), as in this case:

```
[AdventureWorks].[Person].[Contact].[ContactID],
[AdventureWorks].[Person].[Contact].[EmailAddress]
```

Or they could be internal (intermediate) values that the query processor needs in order to process the query. Think of a DefineValues as a temporary holding place for values used by the query optimizer as the operators execute.

Finally, note from the **EstimateRows** column in Figure 3, that this Index seek operation produces an estimated 19.8 rows.

Next we move on to line 4 (NodeID 5), which is a Clustered Index Seek against **Person.Contact**. This immediately illustrates what I would regard as a weakness with text plan format. It is not immediately obvious, as it was with the graphical plan, that this operation is, in fact, a key lookup operation. We need to scan through the whole contents of the **StmtText** column to find this out:

```
          |--Clustered Index
Seek(OBJECT:([AdventureWorks].[Person].[Contact].[PK_Contact_Con
tactID]),
SEEK:([AdventureWorks].[Person].[Contact].[ContactID]=[Adventure
Works].[Person].[Contact].[ContactID]) LOOKUP ORDERED FORWARD)
```

Notice this time, from the **EstimateRows** column, that this operation produces only 1 row. However, if you examine the final column in the result grid, **EstimateExecutions**, you'll see that the operator is called an estimated 19.8 times a while running the query.

The **EstimateExecutions** column does not have a direct parallel in the graphical execution plan. If you capture the graphical plan for this query and examined the properties of the Key LookUp Operator, rather than the number of executions, you will see values for the number of rebinds and rewinds. In this case 18.8 rebinds and 0 rewinds. As you may remember from chapter one, a rebind or rewind occurs each time an operator is reinitialized.

We then move up and out one Node to row 2 (NodeID 2) where we see the Nested Loop inner join that combines the results from the previous two operations. In this case the **DefinedValues** displays Null, meaning that the operation introduces no new values, and the **OutputList** shows the **ContactID**, **LastName** and **Phone** columns required by our query.

The remainder of the columns in the results grid, Such as **EstimateRows**, **EstimateIO**, **TotalSubTreeCost** and so on, mirror the information found in the ToolTips for graphical plans, and we won't cover them again here.

A Slightly more Complex Query

The text-based plan for the previous simple query was straightforward to read. However, with slightly more-complex queries, it quickly gets more taxing. Let's look at the Estimated text plan for the following query, containing a couple of joins and a **WHERE** clause:

```
SET SHOWPLAN_ALL ON ;
GO

SELECT   c.[LastName],
         a.[City],
         cu.[AccountNumber],
         st.[Name] AS TerritoryName
FROM     [Person].[Contact] c
JOIN [Sales].[Individual] i
    ON c.[ContactID] = i.[ContactID]
JOIN [Sales].[CustomerAddress] ca
    ON i.[CustomerID] = ca.[CustomerID]
JOIN Person.Address a
    ON [ca].[AddressID] = [a].[AddressID]
JOIN [Sales].Customer cu
    ON cu.[CustomerID] = i.[CustomerID]
JOIN [Sales].[SalesTerritory] st
    ON [cu].[TerritoryID] = [st].[TerritoryID]
WHERE    st.[Name] = 'Northeast'
         AND a.[StateProvinceID] = 55 ;
GO
```

```
SET SHOWPLAN_ALL OFF ;
GO
```

When you execute this query, the estimated plan is shown in the results pane. Figure 4 shows the StmtTexfirst column of the results.

StmtText
SELECT c.[LastName], .a.[City], .cu.[AccountNumber], .st.[Name] AS TerritoryName FROM [Person].[Contact] c JOIN [Sales].[Individual] i ON
|--Nested Loops(Inner Join, OUTER REFERENCES:([cu].[TerritoryID]))
|--Nested Loops(Inner Join, OUTER REFERENCES:([i].[ContactID]))
		--Nested Loops(Inner Join, OUTER REFERENCES:([cu].[CustomerID]) OPTIMIZED)
		--Compute Scalar(DEFINE:([cu].[AccountNumber]=[AdventureWorks].[Sales].[Customer].[AccountNumber] as [cu].[AccountNumber]))
			--Nested Loops(Inner Join, OUTER REFERENCES:([ca].[CustomerID]))
			--Hash Match(Inner Join, HASH:([a].[AddressID])=([ca].[AddressID]))
				--Nested Loops(Inner Join, OUTER REFERENCES:([a].[AddressID]))
				|--Index Seek(OBJECT:([AdventureWorks].[Person].[Address].[IX_Address_StateProvinceID] AS [a]), SEEK:([a].[StateProvinceID]=(55)) ORDERED F...
				|--Clustered Index Seek(OBJECT:([AdventureWorks].[Person].[Address].[PK_Address_AddressID] AS [a]), SEEK:([a].[AddressID]=[AdventureWorks].[...
				--Index Scan(OBJECT:([AdventureWorks].[Sales].[CustomerAddress].[AK_CustomerAddress_rowguid] AS [ca]))
			--Compute Scalar(DEFINE:([cu].[AccountNumber]=isnull('AW'+[AdventureWorks].[dbo].[ufnLeadingZeros]([AdventureWorks].[Sales].[Customer].[CustomerI...
			--Clustered Index Seek(OBJECT:([AdventureWorks].[Sales].[Customer].[PK_Customer_CustomerID] AS [cu]), SEEK:([cu].[CustomerID]=[AdventureWork...
		--Clustered Index Seek(OBJECT:([AdventureWorks].[Sales].[Individual].[PK_Individual_CustomerID] AS [i]), SEEK:([i].[CustomerID]=[AdventureWorks].[Sales].[Cu...
|--Clustered Index Seek(OBJECT:([AdventureWorks].[Person].[Contact].[PK_Contact_ContactID] AS [c]), SEEK:([c].[ContactID]=[AdventureWorks].[Sales].[Individual]...
|--Clustered Index Seek(OBJECT:([AdventureWorks].[Sales].[SalesTerritory].[PK_SalesTerritory_TerritoryID] AS [st]), SEEK:([st].[TerritoryID]=[AdventureWorks].[Sales]...

Figure 4

This is where the indentation of the data, and the use of pipe (|) character to connect parent to child, really starts to be useful. Tracking to the most internal set of statements, we see an index seek operation against **IX_Address_StateProvinceId** on the **Address** table.

	StmtText	StmtId	Nod...	Parent	PhysicalOp	LogicalOp	Argument	DefinedValues
1	SELECT c.[LastName], .a.[City], .cu.[AccountN...	1	1	0	NULL	NULL	1	NULL
2	|--Nested Loops(Inner Join, OUTER REFERENCES:([c...	1	2	1	Nested Loops	Inner Join	OUTER REFERENCES:([cu].[TerritoryID])	NULL
3	|--Nested Loops(Inner Join, OUTER REFERENCES:...	1	3	2	Nested Loops	Inner Join	OUTER REFERENCES:([i].[ContactID])	NULL
4			--Nested Loops(Inner Join, OUTER REFERENC...	1	4	3	Nested Loops	Inner Join	OUTER REFERENCES:([cu].[CustomerID]) OPTIMIZED	NULL
5			--Compute Scalar(DEFINE:([cu].[AccountNum...	1	6	4	Compute Scalar	Compute Scalar	DEFINE:([cu].[AccountNumber]=[AdventureWorks].[S...	[cu].[AccountNu...
6				--Nested Loops(Inner Join, OUTER REFE...	1	7	6	Nested Loops	Inner Join	OUTER REFERENCES:([ca].[CustomerID])	NULL
7				--Hash Match(Inner Join, HASH:([a].[Ad...	1	8	7	Hash Match	Inner Join	HASH:([a].[AddressID])=([ca].[AddressID])	NULL
8				--Nested Loops(Inner Join, OUTER ...	1	9	8	Nested Loops	Inner Join	OUTER REFERENCES:([a].[AddressID])	NULL
9				|--Index Seek(OBJECT:([Adventu...	1	10	9	Index Seek	Index Seek	OBJECT:([AdventureWorks].[Person].[Address].[IX_Ad...	[a].[AddressID]
10				|--Clustered Index Seek(OBJECT:([...	1	12	9	Clustered Index Seek	Clustered Index Seek	OBJECT:([AdventureWorks].[Person].[Address].[PK_A...	[a].[City]
11				--Index Scan(OBJECT:([AdventureW...	1	16	8	Index Scan	Index Scan	OBJECT:([AdventureWorks].[Sales].[CustomerAddress...	[ca].[CustomerID
12				--Compute Scalar(DEFINE:([cu].[Accou...	1	18	7	Compute Scalar	Compute Scalar	DEFINE:([cu].[AccountNumber]=isnull('AW'+[Adventu...	[cu].[AccountNu...
13				--Clustered Index Seek(OBJECT:([Ad...	1	19	18	Clustered Index Seek	Clustered Index Seek	OBJECT:([AdventureWorks].[Sales].[Customer].[PK_C...	[cu].[CustomerID
14			--Clustered Index Seek(OBJECT:([Adventure...	1	26	4	Clustered Index Seek	Clustered Index Seek	OBJECT:([AdventureWorks].[Sales].[Individual].[PK_In...	[i].[ContactID]
15	|--Clustered Index Seek(OBJECT:([AdventureWor...	1	27	3	Clustered Index Seek	Clustered Index Seek	OBJECT:([AdventureWorks].[Person].[Contact].[PK_C...	[c].[LastName]
16	|--Clustered Index Seek(OBJECT:([AdventureWorks]...	1	28	2	Clustered Index Seek	Clustered Index Seek	OBJECT:([AdventureWorks].[Sales].[SalesTerritory].[P...	[st].[Name]

Figure 5

This is how the plan displays the **WHERE** clause statement that limits the number of rows returned.

```
--Index Seek(
OBJECT:([AdventureWorks].[Person].[Address].[IX_Address_StatePro
vinceID] AS [a]), SEEK:([a].[StateProvinceID]=(55)) ORDERED
FORWARD)
```

The output from this operator is the **AddressId**, not a part of the **SELECT** list, but necessary for the operators that follow. This operator starts the query with a minimum number of rows to be used in all the subsequent processing.

The index seek is followed by a clustered index seek against the **PersonAddress** table clustered index, using the **AddressId** from the index seek. Again, in the **StmtText** column, we see that the clustered index seek operation is actually a key lookup operation.

```
--Clustered Index Seek
(OBJECT:([AdventureWorks].[Person].[Address].[PK_Address_Address
ID] AS [a]),
SEEK:([a].[AddressID]=[AdventureWorks].[Person].[Address].[Addre
ssID] as [a].[AddressID]) LOOKUP ORDERED FORWARD)
```

Stepping out one level, the output from these two operations is joined via a nested loop join (row 8).

	StmtText	StmtId	Nod..	Parent	PhysicalOp	LogicalOp	Argument	DefinedValues
1	SELECT c.[LastName] ,a.[City] ,cu.[AccountN..	1	1	0	NULL	NULL	1	NULL
2	|-Nested Loops(Inner Join, OUTER REFERENCES:([c..	1	2	1	Nested Loops	Inner Join	OUTER REFERENCES:([cu].[TerritoryID])	NULL
3	|-Nested Loops(Inner Join, OUTER REFERENCES:..	1	3	2	Nested Loops	Inner Join	OUTER REFERENCES:([f].[ContactID])	NULL
4	|-Nested Loops(Inner Join, OUTER REFERENC..	1	4	3	Nested Loops	Inner Join	OUTER REFERENCES:([cu].[CustomerID]) OPTIMIZED	NULL
5	| |-Compute Scalar(DEFINE:([cu].[AccountNum..	1	6	4	Compute Scalar	Compute Scalar	DEFINE:([cu].[AccountNumber]=[AdventureWorks].[S..	[cu].[AccountNu..
6	| | |-Nested Loops(Inner Join, OUTER REFE..	1	7	6	Nested Loops	Inner Join	OUTER REFERENCES:([cu].[CustomerID])	NULL
7	| | | |-Hash Match(Inner Join, HASH:([a].[Ad..	1	8	7	Hash Match	Inner Join	HASH:([a].[AddressID])=([ca].[AddressID])	NULL
8	| | | | |-Nested Loops(Inner Join, OUTER..	1	9	8	Nested Loops	Inner Join	OUTER REFERENCES:([a].[AddressID])	NULL
9	| | | | |-Index Seek(OBJECT:([Adventur..	1	10	9	Index Seek	Index Seek	OBJECT:([AdventureWorks].[Person].[Address].[IX_Ad..	[a].[AddressID]
10	| | | | |-Clustered Index Seek(OBJECT:([..	1	12	9	Clustered Index Seek	Clustered Index Seek	OBJECT:([AdventureWorks].[Person].[Address].[PK_A..	[a].[City]
11	| | | | |-Index Scan(OBJECT:([AdventureW..	1	16	8	Index Scan	Index Scan	OBJECT:([AdventureWorks].[Sales].[CustomerAddress..	[ca].[CustomerID]
12	| | | |-Compute Scalar(DEFINE:([cu].[Accou..	1	18	7	Compute Scalar	Compute Scalar	DEFINE:([cu].[AccountNumber]=isnull('AW'+[Adventur..	[cu].[AccountNu..
13	| | | |-Clustered Index Seek(OBJECT:([Ad..	1	19	18	Clustered Index Seek	Clustered Index Seek	OBJECT:([AdventureWorks].[Sales].[Customer].[PK_C..	[cu].[CustomerID]
14	| | |-Clustered Index Seek(OBJECT:([Adventure..	1	26	4	Clustered Index Seek	Clustered Index Seek	OBJECT:([AdventureWorks].[Sales].[Individual].[PK_In..	[i].[ContactID]
15	|-Clustered Index Seek(OBJECT:([AdventureWor..	1	27	3	Clustered Index Seek	Clustered Index Seek	OBJECT:([AdventureWorks].[Person].[Contact].[PK_C..	[c].[LastName]
16	|-Clustered Index Seek(OBJECT:([AdventureWorks]..	1	28	2	Clustered Index Seek	Clustered Index Seek	OBJECT:([AdventureWorks].[Sales].[SalesTerritory].[P..	[st].[Name]

Figure 6

Following the pipes down from this row, we reach row 11, which holds one of the costliest operations in this query, an index scan against the entire **CustomerAddress** index, **AK_CustomerAddress_rowguid**

```
--Index Scan(
OBJECT:([AdventureWorks].[Sales].[CustomerAddress].[AK_CustomerA
ddress_rowguid] AS [ca]))
```

This processes 19,000 + rows in order to provide output for the next step out, a Hash Match join between **Address** and **CustomerAddress**.

	StmtText	StmtId	Nod..	Parent	PhysicalOp	LogicalOp	Argument	DefinedValues
1	SELECT c.[LastName] ,a.[City] ,cu.[AccountN..	1	1	0	NULL	NULL	1	NULL
2	|-Nested Loops(Inner Join, OUTER REFERENCES:([c..	1	2	1	Nested Loops	Inner Join	OUTER REFERENCES:([cu].[TerritoryID])	NULL
3	|-Nested Loops(Inner Join, OUTER REFERENCES:..	1	3	2	Nested Loops	Inner Join	OUTER REFERENCES:([f].[ContactID])	NULL
4	|-Nested Loops(Inner Join, OUTER REFERENC..	1	4	3	Nested Loops	Inner Join	OUTER REFERENCES:([cu].[CustomerID]) OPTIMIZED	NULL
5	| |-Compute Scalar(DEFINE:([cu].[AccountNum..	1	6	4	Compute Scalar	Compute Scalar	DEFINE:([cu].[AccountNumber]=[AdventureWorks].[S..	[cu].[AccountNu..
6	| | |-Nested Loops(Inner Join, OUTER REFE..	1	7	6	Nested Loops	Inner Join	OUTER REFERENCES:([cu].[CustomerID])	NULL
7	| | | |-Hash Match(Inner Join, HASH:([a].[Ad..	1	8	7	Hash Match	Inner Join	HASH:([a].[AddressID])=([ca].[AddressID])	NULL
8	| | | | |-Nested Loops(Inner Join, OUTER..	1	9	8	Nested Loops	Inner Join	OUTER REFERENCES:([a].[AddressID])	NULL
9	| | | | |-Index Seek(OBJECT:([Adventur..	1	10	9	Index Seek	Index Seek	OBJECT:([AdventureWorks].[Person].[Address].[IX_Ad..	[a].[AddressID]
10	| | | | |-Clustered Index Seek(OBJECT:([..	1	12	9	Clustered Index Seek	Clustered Index Seek	OBJECT:([AdventureWorks].[Person].[Address].[PK_A..	[a].[City]
11	| | | | |-Index Scan(OBJECT:([AdventureW..	1	16	8	Index Scan	Index Scan	OBJECT:([AdventureWorks].[Sales].[CustomerAddress..	[ca].[CustomerID]
12	| | | |-Compute Scalar(DEFINE:([cu].[Accou..	1	18	7	Compute Scalar	Compute Scalar	DEFINE:([cu].[AccountNumber]=isnull('AW'+[Adventur..	[cu].[AccountNu..
13	| | | |-Clustered Index Seek(OBJECT:([Ad..	1	19	18	Clustered Index Seek	Clustered Index Seek	OBJECT:([AdventureWorks].[Sales].[Customer].[PK_C..	[cu].[CustomerID]
14	| | |-Clustered Index Seek(OBJECT:([Adventure..	1	26	4	Clustered Index Seek	Clustered Index Seek	OBJECT:([AdventureWorks].[Sales].[Individual].[PK_In..	[i].[ContactID]
15	|-Clustered Index Seek(OBJECT:([AdventureWor..	1	27	3	Clustered Index Seek	Clustered Index Seek	OBJECT:([AdventureWorks].[Person].[Contact].[PK_C..	[c].[LastName]
16	|-Clustered Index Seek(OBJECT:([AdventureWorks]..	1	28	2	Clustered Index Seek	Clustered Index Seek	OBJECT:([AdventureWorks].[Sales].[SalesTerritory].[P..	[st].[Name]

Figure 7

Following the pipe characters down from the hash Match, we arrive at a Computer Scalar operation (row 12). If we step back in for one step, we see that the Computer Scalar is fed by a Clustered Index Seek operation against the **Pk_Customer_CustomerId**. Its output then goes to the scalar operator, which is a function to format the column with leading zeros.

This scalar operation's output is combined with the hash match in another Nested Loop.

	StmtText	StmtId	Nod...	Parent	PhysicalOp	LogicalOp	Argument	DefinedValues
1	SELECT c.[LastName] .a.[City] .cu.[AccountN...	1	1	0	NULL	NULL	1	NULL
2	|-Nested Loops(Inner Join, OUTER REFERENCES:([c...	1	2	1	Nested Loops	Inner Join	OUTER REFERENCES:([cu].[TerritoryID])	NULL
3	|-Nested Loops(Inner Join, OUTER REFERENCES:...	1	3	2	Nested Loops	Inner Join	OUTER REFERENCES:([i].[ContactID])	NULL
4	| |-Nested Loops(Inner Join, OUTER REFERENC...	1	4	3	Nested Loops	Inner Join	OUTER REFERENCES:([cu].[CustomerID]) OPTIMIZED	NULL
5	| |-Compute Scalar(DEFINE:([cu].[AccountNum...	1	6	4	Compute Scalar	Compute Scalar	DEFINE:([cu].[AccountNumber]=[AdventureWorks].[S...	[cu].[AccountNu
6	| | |-Nested Loops(Inner Join, OUTER REFE...	1	7	6	Nested Loops	Inner Join	OUTER REFERENCES:([cu].[CustomerID])	NULL
7	| | |-Hash Match(Inner Join, HASH:([a].[Ad...	1	8	7	Hash Match	Inner Join	HASH:([a].[AddressID])=([ca].[AddressID])	NULL
8	| | | |-Nested Loops(Inner Join, OUTER ...	1	9	8	Nested Loops	Inner Join	OUTER REFERENCES:([a].[AddressID])	NULL
9	| | | | |-Index Seek(OBJECT:([Adventu...	1	10	9	Index Seek	Index Seek	OBJECT:([AdventureWorks].[Person].[Address].[IX_Ad...	[a].[AddressID]
10	| | | | | |-Clustered Index Seek(OBJECT:([...	1	12	9	Clustered Index Seek	Clustered Index Seek	OBJECT:([AdventureWorks].[Person].[Address].[PK_A...	[a].[City]
11	| | | | |-Index Scan(OBJECT:([AdventureW...	1	16	8	Index Scan	Index Scan	OBJECT:([AdventureWorks].[Sales].[CustomerAddress...	[ca].[CustomerID
12	| | | |-Compute Scalar(DEFINE:([cu].[Accou...	1	18	7	Compute Scalar	Compute Scalar	DEFINE:([cu].[AccountNumber]=isnull('AW'+[Adventur...	[cu].[AccountNu
13	| | | |-Clustered Index Seek(OBJECT:([Ad...	1	19	18	Clustered Index Seek	Clustered Index Seek	OBJECT:([AdventureWorks].[Sales].[Customer].[PK_C...	[cu].[CustomerID
14	| | |-Clustered Index Seek(OBJECT:([Adventure...	1	26	4	Clustered Index Seek	Clustered Index Seek	OBJECT:([AdventureWorks].[Sales].[Individual].[PK_In...	[i].[ContactID]
15	|-Clustered Index Seek(OBJECT:([AdventureWor...	1	27	3	Clustered Index Seek	Clustered Index Seek	OBJECT:([AdventureWorks].[Person].[Contact].[PK_C...	[c].[LastName]
16	|-Clustered Index Seek(OBJECT:([AdventureWorks]...	1	28	2	Clustered Index Seek	Clustered Index Seek	OBJECT:([AdventureWorks].[Sales].[SalesTerritory].[P...	[st].[Name]

Figure 8

Stepping up one more time, we have to compute a scalar for the **AccountNumber** column, since it is a calculated column using the function listed above.

	StmtText	StmtId	Nod...	Parent	PhysicalOp	LogicalOp	Argument	DefinedValues
1	SELECT c.[LastName] .a.[City] .cu.[AccountN...	1	1	0	NULL	NULL	1	NULL
2	|-Nested Loops(Inner Join, OUTER REFERENCES:([c...	1	2	1	Nested Loops	Inner Join	OUTER REFERENCES:([cu].[TerritoryID])	NULL
3	|-Nested Loops(Inner Join, OUTER REFERENCES:...	1	3	2	Nested Loops	Inner Join	OUTER REFERENCES:([i].[ContactID])	NULL
4	| |-Nested Loops(Inner Join, OUTER REFERENC...	1	4	3	Nested Loops	Inner Join	OUTER REFERENCES:([cu].[CustomerID]) OPTIMIZED	NULL
5	| |-Compute Scalar(DEFINE:([cu].[AccountNum...	1	6	4	Compute Scalar	Compute Scalar	DEFINE:([cu].[AccountNumber]=[AdventureWorks].[S...	[cu].[AccountNu
6	| | |-Nested Loops(Inner Join, OUTER REFE...	1	7	6	Nested Loops	Inner Join	OUTER REFERENCES:([cu].[CustomerID])	NULL
7	| | |-Hash Match(Inner Join, HASH:([a].[Ad...	1	8	7	Hash Match	Inner Join	HASH:([a].[AddressID])=([ca].[AddressID])	NULL
8	| | | |-Nested Loops(Inner Join, OUTER ...	1	9	8	Nested Loops	Inner Join	OUTER REFERENCES:([a].[AddressID])	NULL
9	| | | | |-Index Seek(OBJECT:([Adventu...	1	10	9	Index Seek	Index Seek	OBJECT:([AdventureWorks].[Person].[Address].[IX_Ad...	[a].[AddressID]
10	| | | | |-Clustered Index Seek(OBJECT:([...	1	12	9	Clustered Index Seek	Clustered Index Seek	OBJECT:([AdventureWorks].[Person].[Address].[PK_A...	[a].[City]
11	| | | |-Index Scan(OBJECT:([AdventureW...	1	16	8	Index Scan	Index Scan	OBJECT:([AdventureWorks].[Sales].[CustomerAddress...	[ca].[CustomerID
12	| | |-Compute Scalar(DEFINE:([cu].[Accou...	1	18	7	Compute Scalar	Compute Scalar	DEFINE:([cu].[AccountNumber]=isnull('AW'+[Adventur...	[cu].[AccountNu
13	| | |-Clustered Index Seek(OBJECT:([Ad...	1	19	18	Clustered Index Seek	Clustered Index Seek	OBJECT:([AdventureWorks].[Sales].[Customer].[PK_C...	[cu].[CustomerID
14	| |-Clustered Index Seek(OBJECT:([Adventure...	1	26	4	Clustered Index Seek	Clustered Index Seek	OBJECT:([AdventureWorks].[Sales].[Individual].[PK_In...	[i].[ContactID]
15	|-Clustered Index Seek(OBJECT:([AdventureWo...	1	27	3	Clustered Index Seek	Clustered Index Seek	OBJECT:([AdventureWorks].[Person].[Contact].[PK_C...	[c].[LastName]
16	|-Clustered Index Seek(OBJECT:([AdventureWorks]...	1	28	2	Clustered Index Seek	Clustered Index Seek	OBJECT:([AdventureWorks].[Sales].[SalesTerritory].[P...	[st].[Name]

Figure 9

Following down on the same level, using the pipe (|) connectors, the next operator is the clustered index seek against the **PK_Individual_CustomerId**.

Stepping out and up again, the output from these operators is combined using a Nested Loop, and following the pipes down, through an increasing number of rows in the text plan's result set from Row 4 to Row 15, we get a clustered index seek against the **Person.Contact** table.

StmtText	StmtId	Nod..	Parent	PhysicalOp	LogicalOp	Argument	DefinedValues
1	SELECT c.[LastName] ,a.[City] ,cu.[AccountN...	1	1	0	NULL	NULL	1	NULL
2	I-Nested Loops[Inner Join, OUTER REFERENCES:[(c...	1	2	1	Nested Loops	Inner Join	OUTER REFERENCES:[[cu].[TerritoryID]]	NULL
3	I-Nested Loops[Inner Join, OUTER REFERENCES:...	1	3	2	Nested Loops	Inner Join	OUTER REFERENCES:[[i].[ContactID]]	NULL
4	I I-Nested Loops[Inner Join, OUTER REFEREN...	1	4	3	Nested Loops	Inner Join	OUTER REFERENCES:[[cu].[CustomerID]] OPTIMIZED	NULL
5	I I I-Compute Scalar[DEFINE:([cu].[AccountNum...	1	6	4	Compute Scalar	Compute Scalar	DEFINE:([cu].[AccountNumber]=[AdventureWorks].[S...	[cu].[AccountNu
6	I I I-Nested Loops[Inner Join, OUTER REFE...	1	7	6	Nested Loops	Inner Join	OUTER REFERENCES:[[ca].[CustomerID]]	NULL
7	I I I I-Hash Match[Inner Join, HASH:([a].[Ad...	1	8	7	Hash Match	Inner Join	HASH:([a].[AddressID])=([ca].[AddressID])	NULL
8	I I I I I-Nested Loops[Inner Join, OUTER ...	1	9	8	Nested Loops	Inner Join	OUTER REFERENCES:[[a].[AddressID]]	NULL
9	I I I I I I-Index Seek[OBJECT:([Adventur...	1	10	9	Index Seek	Index Seek	OBJECT:([AdventureWorks].[Person].[Address].[IX_Ad...	[a].[AddressID]
10	I I I I I I-Clustered Index Seek[OBJECT:[[...	1	12	9	Clustered Index Seek	Clustered Index Seek	OBJECT:([AdventureWorks].[Person].[Address].[PK_A...	[a].[City]
11	I I I I I-Index Scan[OBJECT:([AdventureW...	1	16	8	Index Scan	Index Scan	OBJECT:([AdventureWorks].[Sales].[CustomerAddress...	[ca].[CustomerID
12	I I I I-Compute Scalar[DEFINE:([cu].[Accou...	1	18	7	Compute Scalar	Compute Scalar	DEFINE:([cu].[AccountNumber]=isnull('AW'+[Adventur...	[cu].[AccountNu
13	I I I I-Clustered Index Seek[OBJECT:([Ad...	1	19	18	Clustered Index Seek	Clustered Index Seek	OBJECT:([AdventureWorks].[Sales].[Customer].[PK_C...	[cu].[CustomerID
14	I I I-Clustered Index Seek[OBJECT:([Adventure...	1	26	4	Clustered Index Seek	Clustered Index Seek	OBJECT:([AdventureWorks].[Sales].[Individual].[PK_In...	[i].[ContactID]
15	I I-Clustered Index Seek[OBJECT:([AdventureWor...	1	27	3	Clustered Index Seek	Clustered Index Seek	OBJECT:([AdventureWorks].[Person].[Contact].[PK_C...	[c].[LastName]
16	I-Clustered Index Seek[OBJECT:([AdventureWorks]...	1	28	2	Clustered Index Seek	Clustered Index Seek	OBJECT:([AdventureWorks].[Sales].[SalesTerritory].[P...	[st].[Name]

Figure 10

Stepping out again, and back up to Row 3, we see that the output of the Nested Loop join in row 4 and the Clustered Index seek in row 15 are combined once again in a Nested Loop join.

StmtText	StmtId	Nod..	Parent	PhysicalOp	LogicalOp	Argument	DefinedValues
1	SELECT c.[LastName] ,a.[City] ,cu.[AccountN...	1	1	0	NULL	NULL	1	NULL
2	I-Nested Loops[Inner Join, OUTER REFERENCES:[(c...	1	2	1	Nested Loops	Inner Join	OUTER REFERENCES:[[cu].[TerritoryID]]	NULL
3	I-Nested Loops[Inner Join, OUTER REFERENCES:...	1	3	2	Nested Loops	Inner Join	OUTER REFERENCES:[[i].[ContactID]]	NULL
4	I I-Nested Loops[Inner Join, OUTER REFEREN...	1	4	3	Nested Loops	Inner Join	OUTER REFERENCES:[[cu].[CustomerID]] OPTIMIZED	NULL
5	I I I-Compute Scalar[DEFINE:([cu].[AccountNum...	1	6	4	Compute Scalar	Compute Scalar	DEFINE:([cu].[AccountNumber]=[AdventureWorks].[S...	[cu].[AccountNu
6	I I I-Nested Loops[Inner Join, OUTER REFE...	1	7	6	Nested Loops	Inner Join	OUTER REFERENCES:[[ca].[CustomerID]]	NULL
7	I I I I-Hash Match[Inner Join, HASH:([a].[Ad...	1	8	7	Hash Match	Inner Join	HASH:([a].[AddressID])=([ca].[AddressID])	NULL
8	I I I I I-Nested Loops[Inner Join, OUTER ...	1	9	8	Nested Loops	Inner Join	OUTER REFERENCES:[[a].[AddressID]]	NULL
9	I I I I I I-Index Seek[OBJECT:([Adventur...	1	10	9	Index Seek	Index Seek	OBJECT:([AdventureWorks].[Person].[Address].[IX_Ad...	[a].[AddressID]
10	I I I I I I-Clustered Index Seek[OBJECT:[[...	1	12	9	Clustered Index Seek	Clustered Index Seek	OBJECT:([AdventureWorks].[Person].[Address].[PK_A...	[a].[City]
11	I I I I I-Index Scan[OBJECT:([AdventureW...	1	16	8	Index Scan	Index Scan	OBJECT:([AdventureWorks].[Sales].[CustomerAddress...	[ca].[CustomerID
12	I I I I-Compute Scalar[DEFINE:([cu].[Accou...	1	18	7	Compute Scalar	Compute Scalar	DEFINE:([cu].[AccountNumber]=isnull('AW'+[Adventur...	[cu].[AccountNu
13	I I I I-Clustered Index Seek[OBJECT:([Ad...	1	19	18	Clustered Index Seek	Clustered Index Seek	OBJECT:([AdventureWorks].[Sales].[Customer].[PK_C...	[cu].[CustomerID
14	I I I-Clustered Index Seek[OBJECT:([Adventure...	1	26	4	Clustered Index Seek	Clustered Index Seek	OBJECT:([AdventureWorks].[Sales].[Individual].[PK_In...	[i].[ContactID]
15	I I-Clustered Index Seek[OBJECT:([AdventureWor...	1	27	3	Clustered Index Seek	Clustered Index Seek	OBJECT:([AdventureWorks].[Person].[Contact].[PK_C...	[c].[LastName]
16	I-Clustered Index Seek[OBJECT:([AdventureWorks]...	1	28	2	Clustered Index Seek	Clustered Index Seek	OBJECT:([AdventureWorks].[Sales].[SalesTerritory].[P...	[st].[Name]

Figure 11

Following the pipes down to Row 16, we get a final clustered index seek on the **Sales.SalesTerritory** table. Stepping out for the last time, the last operator performs the final Nested Loop join in this query, with the final output list showing the columns necessary for generating the actual result set.

As you see for yourself, reading text-based execution plans is not easy, and we have only taken a brief look at a couple of very simple queries. Longer queries generate much more complicated plans, sometimes running to dozens of pages long. While it's sometimes handy to know how to read text-based execution plans, I would suggest you focus on graphical execution plans, unless you have some special need where only text-based execution plans will meet your needs.

XML Execution Plans

I think it's safe to say that most DBAs would prefer to view execution plans in graphical format. However, the big drawback in SQL Server 2000 and earlier, was that there was no "file format" for graphical execution plans, so they could not easily be exchanged between people.

This limitation was removed in SQL Server 2005, with the introduction of the XML Plan. To most people, an XML Plan is simply a common file format in which to store a graphical execution plan, so that it can be shared with other DBAs and developers.

I would imagine that very few people would actually prefer to read execution plans in XML format. Having said that, here are two reasons why you might want to do so.

Firstly, there is undocumented data stored in an XML Plan that is not available when it is displayed as a graphical execution plan. For example, XML Plans include such additional data as cached plan size, memory fractions (how memory grant is to be distributed across operators in a query plan), parameter list with values used during optimization, and missing indexes information. In most cases, the typical DBA won't be interested in this information, or there are easier ways to gather this same information, such as using Database Engine Tuning Wizard to identify missing indexes.

Secondly, XML plans display a lot of details, and its inherent search capabilities make it relatively easy for an experienced DBA to track down specific, potentially problematic aspects of the query, by doing a search on specific terms, such as "index scan".

XML Plans can also be used in Plan Forcing, covered in Chapter 7, whereby you essentially dictate to the query optimizer that it should use only the plan you specify to execute the query.

In the following section, we take a brief look at the structure of XML Plans.

An Estimated XML Plan

So, let's take a look at an example. In order not to over-complicate things, let's look at the same execution plan as we evaluated with the text plan.

We issue the **SHOWPLAN_XML** command in order to start capturing the estimated execution plan in XML format (remember that any statements that follow the command will not be executed). We then execute the required statement and then immediately deactivate **SHOWPLAN_XML** so that any subsequent statements we issue will actually be executed.

```
SET SHOWPLAN_XML ON ;

GO

SELECT    c.[LastName],
          a.[City],
          cu.[AccountNumber],
          st.[Name] AS TerritoryName
FROM      [Person].[Contact] c
          JOIN [Sales].[Individual] i
               ON c.[ContactID] = i.[ContactID]
          JOIN [Sales].[CustomerAddress] ca
               ON i.[CustomerID] = ca.[CustomerID]
          JOIN Person.Address a
               ON [ca].[AddressID] = [a].[AddressID]
          JOIN [Sales].Customer cu
               ON cu.[CustomerID] = i.[CustomerID]
          JOIN [Sales].[SalesTerritory] st
               ON [cu].[TerritoryID] = [st].[TerritoryID]
WHERE     st.[Name] = 'Northeast'
          AND a.[StateProvinceID] = 55 ;
GO

SET SHOWPLAN_XML OFF ;
```

Click on the link to the XML document, and the plan will open up in a new tab:

Figure 12

The results are far too large to output here, but Figure 12 shows the opening portion of the resulting XML file. XML data is more difficult to take in all at once than the graphical execution plans but, with the ability to expand and collapse elements, using the "+" and "-" nodules down the left hand side, the hierarchy of the data being processed quickly becomes clearer.

A review of some of the common elements and attributes and the full schema is available here:

http://schemas.microsoft.com/sqlserver/2004/07/showplan/

The information at this link is designed for those familiar with XML and who want to learn more about the schema in order to use the data programmatically.[9]

After the familiar **BatchSequence**, **Batch**, **Statements** and **Stmt Simple** elements (described in Chapter 1), the first point of real interest in the physical attributes of the **QueryPlan**:

```
<QueryPlan CachedPlanSize="52" CompileTime="29293"
          CompileCPU="6277" CompileMemory="520">
```

This describes the size of the plan in the cache, along with the amount of time, CPU cycles and memory used by the plan.

Next in the execution plan, we see an element labeled **MissingIndexes**. This contains information about tables and columns that did not have an index available to the execution plan created by the optimizer. While the information about missing indexes can sometimes be useful, it is generally easier to identify missing index using a tool, such as the Database Engine Tuning Wizards, which not only uses this information, but uses additional information to identify potentially missing indexes.

---

[9] As described in Chapter 1, we can also generate XML plans from the Profiler events Showplan XML, Showplan XML for Query Compile, and Showplan XML Statistics Profile. You will also get XML plans from the dynamic management view sys.dm_exec_query_plan.

```
<MissingIndexes>
  <MissingIndexGroup Impact="30.8535">
    <MissingIndex Database="[AdventureWorks]"
Schema="[Sales]" Table="[CustomerAddress]">
      <ColumnGroup Usage="EQUALITY">
        <Column Name="[AddressID]" ColumnId="2" />
      </ColumnGroup>
      <ColumnGroup Usage="INCLUDE">
        <Column Name="[CustomerID]" ColumnId="1" />
      </ColumnGroup>
    </MissingIndex>
  </MissingIndexGroup>
</MissingIndexes>
```

The execution plan then lists, via the RelOP nodes, the various physical operations that it anticipates performing, according to the data supplied by the optimizer. The first node, with **NodeId=0**, refers to the final **NestedLoop** operation:

```
<RelOp NodeId="0" PhysicalOp="Nested Loops"
    LogicalOp="Inner Join" EstimateRows="1.94953"
    EstimateIO="0" EstimateCPU="6.37415e-005"
    AvgRowSize="119" EstimatedTotalSubtreeCost="0.376226"
    Parallel="0" EstimateRebinds="0" EstimateRewinds="0">
```

The information that is displayed here will be familiar to you from the ToolTip window for the graphical plans. Notice that, unlike for the text plans, which just displayed **EstimateExecutions**, the XML plan the estimated number of rebinds and rewinds. This can often give you a more accurate idea of what occurred within the query, such as how many times the operator was executed.

For example, for NodeId=26, the final clustered index seek, associated with the Nested Loops join in NodeId=0, we see:

```
<RelOp NodeId="26" PhysicalOp="Clustered Index Seek"
    LogicalOp="Clustered Index Seek" EstimateRows="1"
    EstimateIO="0.003125" EstimateCPU="0.0001581"
    AvgRowSize="28" EstimatedTotalSubtreeCost="0.00553589"
    Parallel="0" EstimateRebinds="12.7784"
    EstimateRewinds="1.47074">
```

Whereas in the text plan for this query, we simply saw "Estimate Executions=15.24916".

Returning to Node 0, the next element listed is the **OutputList** element with a list of **ColumnReference** elements, each containing a set of attributes to describe that column:

```
<OutputList>
    <ColumnReference Database="[AdventureWorks]"
Schema="[Person]" Table="[Contact]" Alias="[c]"
Column="LastName" />
    <ColumnReference Database="[AdventureWorks]"
Schema="[Person]" Table="[Address]" Alias="[a]"
Column="City" />
    <ColumnReference Table="[cu]" Column="AccountNumber"
ComputedColumn="1" />
    <ColumnReference Database="[AdventureWorks]"
Schema="[Sales]" Table="[SalesTerritory]" Alias="[st]"
Column="Name" />
</OutputList>
```

This makes XML not only easier to read, but much more readily translated directly back to the original query. The output described above is from the references to the schema "Person" and the tables "Contact" (aliased as "c"), "Address" (aliased as "a") and "SalesTerritory" (aliased as "st"), in order to output the required columns (LastName, City, AccountNumber and Name). The names of the operator elements are the same as the operators you would see in the graphical plans and the details within the attributes are usually those represented in the ToolTip windows or in the Properties window.

Finally for Node 0, in the estimated plan, we see some more information about the Nested Loops operation, such as the table involved, along with the table's alias.

```
<NestedLoops Optimized="0">
<OuterReferences>
<ColumnReference Database="[AdventureWorks]"
Schema="[Sales]" Table="[Customer]" Alias="[cu]"
Column="TerritoryID" />
</OuterReferences>
```

An Actual XML Plan

We can use the same query, but this time execute it and collect the actual XML plan, as follows. We won't go through the plan in detail again, just highlight the main differences.

```
SET STATISTICS XML ON ;
GO
```

```
SELECT   c.[LastName],
         a.[City],
         cu.[AccountNumber],
         st.[Name] AS TerritoryName
FROM     [Person].[Contact] c
         JOIN [Sales].[Individual] i
             ON c.[ContactID] = i.[ContactID]
         JOIN [Sales].[CustomerAddress] ca
             ON i.[CustomerID] = ca.[CustomerID]
         JOIN Person.Address a
             ON [ca].[AddressID] = [a].[AddressID]
         JOIN [Sales].Customer cu
             ON cu.[CustomerID] = i.[CustomerID]
         JOIN [Sales].[SalesTerritory] st
             ON [cu].[TerritoryID] = [st].[TerritoryID]
WHERE    st.[Name] = 'Northeast'
         AND a.[StateProvinceID] = 55 ;
GO

SET STATISTICS XML OFF ;
GO
```

When we look at the Actual plan, we see that the **QueryPlan** has some additional information such as the **DegreeOfParallelism** (more on parallelism in Chapter 7) and the **MemoryGrant**, the amount of memory needed for the execution of the query:

```
<QueryPlan DegreeOfParallelism="0" MemoryGrant="82"
    CachedPlanSize="57" CompileTime="29293"
    CompileCPU="6277" CompileMemory="520">
```

The other major difference between the Actual XML execution plan and the estimated one is that the actual plan includes an element called **RunTimeInformation**, showing the thread, actual rows and number of executions prior to the same final nested loop information. While this additional information can sometimes be interesting, it generally is not relevant to most query performance analysis.

```
<RunTimeInformation>
 <RunTimeCountersPerThread Thread="0" ActualRows="4"
ActualEndOfScans="1" ActualExecutions="1" />
</RunTimeInformation>
<NestedLoops Optimized="0">...
```

Summary

As you can see, trying to read an XML plan not an easy task, and one that most DBA's won't want to spend their time mastering, unless you are the kind of DBA who likes to know every internal detail, or who wants to learn how to access the data programmatically. If this is really the case, you need to first master XML before you take on learning the specifics of XML plans.

Instead, DBAs should focus on understanding the benefits of having an execution plan in a portable format such as an XML plan, and how it can be shared among other DBAs and applications. This is practical knowledge that you can use almost every day in your DBA work.

CHAPTER 4: UNDERSTANDING MORE COMPLEX QUERY PLANS

As we've seen, even simple queries can generate somewhat complicated execution plans. So, what about complex T-SQL statements? These generate ever-expanding execution plans that become more and more time consuming to decipher. However, just as a large T-SQL statement can be broken down into a series of simple steps, so large execution plans are simply extensions of the same simple plans we have already examined.

The previous chapter we dealt with single statement T-SQL queries. In this chapter we'll extend that to consider stored procedures, temp tables, table variables, **APPLY** statements, and more.

Please bear in mind that the plans you see may vary slightly from what's shown in the text, due to different service pack levels, hotfixes, differences in the AdventureWorks database and so on.

Stored Procedures

The best place to get started is with stored procedures. We'll create a new one for AdventureWorks:

```
CREATE PROCEDURE [Sales].[spTaxRateByState]
    @CountryRegionCode NVARCHAR(3)
AS
    SET NOCOUNT ON ;

    SELECT   [st].[SalesTaxRateID],
             [st].[Name],
             [st].[TaxRate],
             [st].[TaxType],
             [sp].[Name] AS StateName
    FROM     [Sales].[SalesTaxRate] st
             JOIN [Person].[StateProvince] sp
                 ON [st].[StateProvinceID] =
                    [sp].[StateProvinceID]
    WHERE    [sp].[CountryRegionCode] = @CountryRegionCode
    ORDER BY [StateName]
GO
```

Which we can then execute:

```
EXEC [Sales].[spTaxRateByState] @CountryRegionCode = 'US'
```

The resulting actual execution plan is quite simple, as shown in Figure 1:

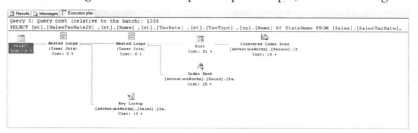

Figure 1

Starting from the right, as usual, we see a **Clustered Index Scan** operator, which gets the list of States based on the parameter, **@CountryRegionCode**, visible in the ToolTip or the Properties window. This data is then placed into an ordered state by the **Sort** operator. Data from the **SalesTaxRate** table is gathered using an **Index Seek** operator as part of the **Nested Loop** join with the sorted data from the **States** table.

Next, we have a **Key Lookup** operator. This operator takes a list of keys, like those supplied from **Index Seek** on the **AK_CountryRegion _Name** index from the **SalesTaxRate** table, and gets the data from where it is stored, on the clustered index. This output is joined to the output from the previous **Nested Loop** within another **Nested Loop** join for the final output to the user.

While this plan isn't complex, the interesting point is that we don't have a stored procedure in sight. Instead, the T-SQL within the stored procedure is treated in the same way as if we had written and run the **SELECT** statement through the Query window.

Derived Tables

One of the ways that data is accessed through T-SQL is via a **derived table**. If you are not familiar with derived tables, think of a derived table as a virtual table that's created on the fly from within a **SELECT** statement.

You create derived tables by writing a second **SELECT** statement within a set of parentheses in the **FROM** clause of an outer **SELECT** query. Once you apply an alias, this **SELECT** statement is treated as a table. In my own code, one place where I've come to use derived tables frequently is when dealing with data that changes over time, for which I have to maintain history.

A Subselect without a Derived Table

Using AdventureWorks as an example, the **Production.Production ListPriceHistory** table maintains a running list of changes to product price. To start with, we want to see what the execution plan looks like not using a derived table so, instead of a derived table, we'll use a subselect within the **ON** clause of the join to limit the data to only the latest versions of the **ListPrice**.

```
SELECT   [p].[Name],
         [p].[ProductNumber],
         [ph].[ListPrice]
FROM     [Production].[Product] p
         INNER JOIN [Production].[ProductListPriceHistory] ph
ON [p].[ProductID] = ph.[ProductID]
           AND ph.[StartDate] = ( SELECT TOP ( 1 )
[ph2].[StartDate]
               FROM      [Production].[ProductListPriceHistory]
ph2
               WHERE     [ph2].[ProductID] = [p].[ProductID]
               ORDER BY [ph2].[StartDate] DESC
```

```
)
```

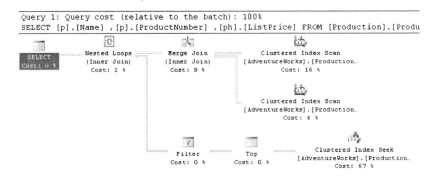

Query 1: Query cost (relative to the batch): 100%
SELECT [p].[Name] ,[p].[ProductNumber] ,[ph].[ListPrice] FROM [Production].[Produ

Figure 2

What appears to be a somewhat complicated query turns out to have a fairly straightforward execution plan. First, we get the two Clustered Index Scans against **Production.Product** and **Production.Product ListPriceHistory**. These two data streams are combined using the **Merge Join** operator.

The Merge Join requires that both data inputs be ordered on the join key, in this case, **ProductId**. The data resulting from a clustered index is always ordered, so no additional operation is required here.

A Merge Join takes a row each from the two ordered inputs and compares them. Because the inputs are sorted, the operation will only scan each input one time (except in the case of a many-to-many join; more on that further down). The operation will scan through the right side of the operation until it reaches a row that is different from the row on the left side. At that point it will progress the left side forward a row and begin scanning the right side until it reaches a changed data point. This operation continues until all the rows are processed. With the data already sorted, as in this case, it makes for a very fast operation.

Although we don't have this situation in our example, Merge Joins that are many-to-many create a worktable to complete the operation. The creation of a worktable adds a great deal of cost to the operation although it will generally still be less costly than the use of a Hash Join, which is the other choice the query optimizer can make. We can see that no worktable was necessary here because the ToolTips property labeled **Many-To-Many** (see figure below) that is set to "False".

Merge Join

Match rows from two suitably sorted input tables
exploiting their sort order.

Physical Operation	Merge Join
Logical Operation	Inner Join
Estimated I/O Cost	0
Estimated CPU Cost	0.0075174
Estimated Operator Cost	0.0075204 (9%)
Estimated Subtree Cost	0.0254437
Estimated Number of Rows	294.969
Estimated Row Size	108 B
Many to Many	False
Node ID	1

Where (join columns)

([AdventureWorks].[Production].
[ProductListPriceHistory].ProductID) =
([AdventureWorks].[Production].
[Product].ProductID)

Output List

[AdventureWorks].[Production].
[Product].ProductID, [AdventureWorks].
[Production].[Product].Name, [AdventureWorks].
[Production].[Product].ProductNumber,
[AdventureWorks].[Production].
[ProductListPriceHistory].StartDate,
[AdventureWorks].[Production].
[ProductListPriceHistory].ListPrice

Figure 3

Next, we move down to the Clustered Index Seek operation in the lower right. Interestingly enough, this process accounts for 67% of the cost of the query because the seek operation returned all 395 rows from the query, only limited to the **TOP (1)** after the rows were returned. A scan in this case may have worked better because all the rows were returned. The only way to know for sure would be to add a hint to the query to force a table scan and see if performance is better or worse.

The **Top** operator simply limits the number of returned rows to the value supplied within the query, in this case "1."

The **Filter** operator is then applied to limit the returned values to only those where the dates match the main table. In other words, a join occurred between the **[Production].[Product]** table and the **[Production].[ProductListPriceHistory]** table, where the column **[StartDate]** is equal in each. See the ToolTip in Figure 4:

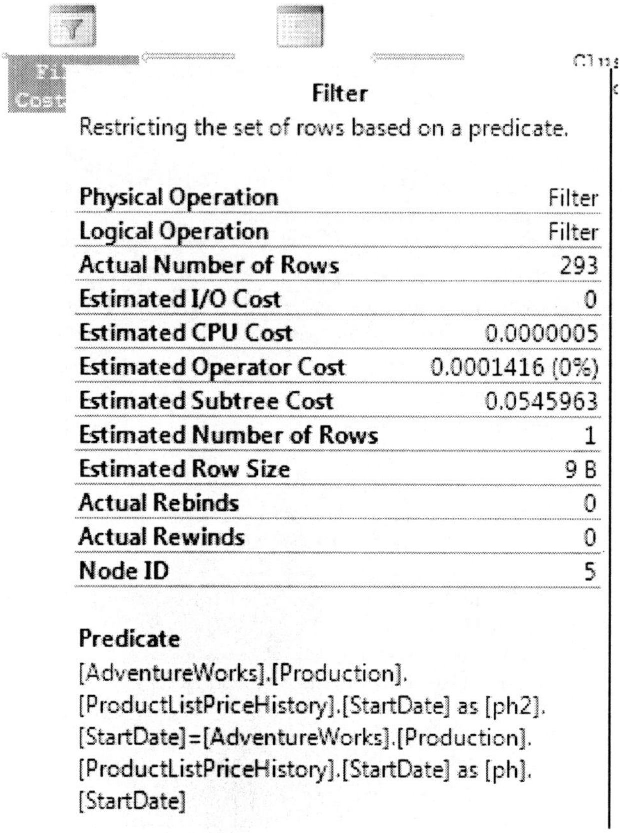

Filter	
Restricting the set of rows based on a predicate.	
Physical Operation	Filter
Logical Operation	Filter
Actual Number of Rows	293
Estimated I/O Cost	0
Estimated CPU Cost	0.0000005
Estimated Operator Cost	0.0001416 (0%)
Estimated Subtree Cost	0.0545963
Estimated Number of Rows	1
Estimated Row Size	9 B
Actual Rebinds	0
Actual Rewinds	0
Node ID	5

Predicate
[AdventureWorks].[Production].
[ProductListPriceHistory].[StartDate] as [ph2].
[StartDate]=[AdventureWorks].[Production].
[ProductListPriceHistory].[StartDate] as [ph].
[StartDate]

Figure 4

The two data feeds are then joined through a Nested Loops operator, to produce the final result.

A Derived Table using APPLY

Now that we have seen what kind of execution plan is created when using a subselect, we can rewrite the query to use a derived table instead. There are several different ways to do this, but we'll look at how the SQL Server 2005 **APPLY** operator can be used to rewrite the above subselect into a derived query, and then see how this affects the execution plan.

SQL Server 2005 introduces a new type of derived table, created using one of the two forms of the **APPLY** operator, **CROSS APPLY** or **OUTER APPLY**. The **APPLY** operator allows you to use a table valued function, or a derived table, to compare values between the function and each row of the table to which the function is being "applied".

If you are not familiar with the APPLY operator, check out:

http://technet.microsoft.com/en-us/library/ms175156.aspx

Below is an example of the rewritten query. Remember, both queries return identical data, they are just written differently.

```
SELECT    [p].[Name],
          [p].[ProductNumber],
          [ph].[ListPrice]
FROM      [Production].[Product] p
          CROSS APPLY ( SELECT TOP ( 1 )
                                   [ph2].[ProductID],
                                   [ph2].[ListPrice]
                        FROM
          [Production].[ProductListPriceHistory] ph2
                        WHERE      [ph2].[ProductID] =
          [p].[ProductID]
                        ORDER BY   [ph2].[StartDate] DESC
                      ) ph
```

The introduction of this new functionality changes the execution plan substantially, as shown in Figure 5:

```
Query 1: Query cost (relative to the batch): 100%
SELECT [p].[Name] ,[p].[ProductNumber] ,[ph].[ListPrice] FROM [Production].
```

Figure 5

The **TOP** statement is now be applied row-by-row within the control of the **APPLY** functionality, so the second index scan against the **ProductListPriceHistory** table, and the merge join that joined the tables together, are no longer needed. Furthermore, only the **Index Seek** and **Top** operations are required to provide data back for the **Nested Loops** operation.

So which method of writing this query is more efficient? One way to find out is to run each query with the **SET STATISTICS IO** option set to **ON**. With this option set, IO statistics are displayed as part of the Messages returned by the query.

When we run the first query, which uses the subselect, the results are:

```
(293 row(s) affected)
Table 'ProductListPriceHistory'. Scan count 396, logical reads
795, physical reads 0, read-ahead reads 0, lob logical reads 0,
lob physical reads 0, lob read-ahead reads 0.
Table 'Product'. Scan count 1, logical reads 15, physical reads
0, read-ahead reads 0, lob logical reads 0, lob physical reads
0, lob read-ahead reads 0.
```

If we run the query using a derived table, the results are:

```
(293 row(s) affected)
Table 'ProductListPriceHistory'. Scan count 504, logical reads
1008, physical reads 0, read-ahead reads 0, lob logical reads 0,
lob physical reads 0, lob read-ahead reads 0.
Table 'Product'. Scan count 1, logical reads 15, physical reads
0, read-ahead reads 0, lob logical reads 0, lob physical reads
0, lob read-ahead reads 0.
```

Although both queries returned identical result sets, the query with the subselect query uses fewer logical reads (795) verses the query written using the derived table (1008 logical reads).

This gets more interesting if we add the following **WHERE** clause to each of the previous queries:

```
WHERE [p].[ProductID] = '839'
```

When we re-run the original query with the added **WHERE** clause, we get the plan shown in Figure 6:

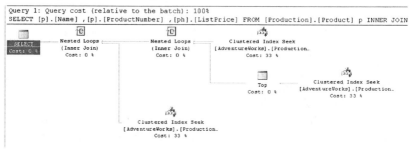

Figure 6

The **Filter** operator is gone but, more interestingly, the costs have changed. Instead of index scans and the inefficient (in this case) index seeks mixed together, we have three, clean **Clustered Index Seeks** with an equal cost distribution.

If we add the **WHERE** clause to the derived table query, we see the plan shown in Figure 7:

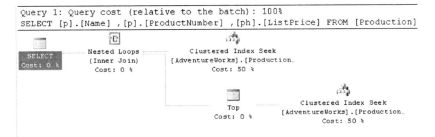

```
Query 1: Query cost (relative to the batch): 100%
SELECT [p].[Name] ,[p].[ProductNumber] ,[ph].[ListPrice] FROM [Production]
```

Figure 7

The plan is almost identical to the one seen in Figure 5, with the only change being that the **Clustered Index Scan** has changed to a **Clustered Index Seek**, because the inclusion of the **WHERE** clause allows the optimizer to take advantage of the clustered index to identify the rows needed, rather than having to scan through them all in order to find the correct rows to return.

Now, let's compare the IO statistics for each of the queries, which return the same physical row.

When we run the query with the subselect, we get:

```
(1 row(s) affected)
Table 'ProductListPriceHistory'. Scan count 1, logical reads 4,
physical reads 0, read-ahead reads 0, lob logical reads 0, lob
physical reads 0, lob read-ahead reads 0.
Table 'Product'. Scan count 0, logical reads 2, physical reads
0, read-ahead reads 0, lob logical reads 0, lob physical reads
0, lob read-ahead reads 0.
```

When we run the query with the derived query, we get:

```
(1 row(s) affected)
Table 'ProductListPriceHistory'. Scan count 1, logical reads 2,
physical reads 0, read-ahead reads 0, lob logical reads 0, lob
physical reads 0, lob read-ahead reads 0.
Table 'Product'. Scan count 0, logical reads 2, physical reads
0, read-ahead reads 0, lob logical reads 0, lob physical reads
0, lob read-ahead reads 0.
```

Now, with the addition of a **WHERE** clause, the derived query is more efficient, with only 2 logical reads, versus the subselect query with 4 logical reads.

The lesson to learn here is that in one set of circumstances a particular T-SQL method may be exactly what you need, and yet in another circumstance that same syntax impacts performance. The **Merge join** made for a very efficient query when we were dealing with inherent scans of the data, but was not used, nor applicable, when the introduction of the **WHERE** clause reduced the data set. With the **WHERE** clause in place the subselect became, relatively, more costly to maintain when compared to the speed provided by the **APPLY** functionality. Understanding the execution plan makes a real difference in deciding which of these to apply.

Common Table Expressions

SQL Server 2005 introduced a T-SQL command, whose behavior appears similar to derived tables, called a common table expression (CTE). A CTE is a "temporary result set" that exists only within the scope of a single SQL statement. It allows access to functionality within that single SQL statement that was previously only available through use of functions, temp tables, cursors, and so on. Unlike derived tables, a CTE can be self referential and can be referenced repeatedly within a single query. [10]

One of the classic use cases for a CTE is to create a **recursive query**. AdventureWorks takes advantage of this functionality in a classic recursive exercise, listing employees and their managers. The procedure in question, **uspGetEmployeeManagers**, is as follows:

```
ALTER PROCEDURE [dbo].[uspGetEmployeeManagers]
    @EmployeeID [int]
AS
BEGIN
    SET NOCOUNT ON;

    -- Use recursive query to list out all Employees
required for a particular Manager
    WITH [EMP_cte]([EmployeeID], [ManagerID], [FirstName],
[LastName], [Title], [RecursionLevel])
-- CTE name and columns
    AS (
        SELECT e.[EmployeeID], e.[ManagerID], c.[FirstName],
c.[LastName], e.[Title], 0
-- Get the initial Employee
        FROM [HumanResources].[Employee] e
            INNER JOIN [Person].[Contact] c
```

---

[10] For more details on the CTE check out this article in Simple-Talk: http://www.simple-talk.com/sql/sql-server-2005/sql-server-2005-common-table-expressions/.

```
            ON e.[ContactID] = c.[ContactID]
        WHERE e.[EmployeeID] = @EmployeeID
        UNION ALL
        SELECT e.[EmployeeID], e.[ManagerID], c.[FirstName],
c.[LastName], e.[Title], [RecursionLevel] + 1
    -- Join recursive member to anchor
        FROM [HumanResources].[Employee] e
            INNER JOIN [EMP_cte]
            ON e.[EmployeeID] = [EMP_cte].[ManagerID]
            INNER JOIN [Person].[Contact] c
            ON e.[ContactID] = c.[ContactID]
        )
    -- Join back to Employee to return the manager name
    SELECT [EMP_cte].[RecursionLevel],
[EMP_cte].[EmployeeID], [EMP_cte].[FirstName],
[EMP_cte].[LastName],
        [EMP_cte].[ManagerID], c.[FirstName] AS
'ManagerFirstName', c.[LastName] AS 'ManagerLastName'
-- Outer select from the CTE
    FROM [EMP_cte]
        INNER JOIN [HumanResources].[Employee] e
        ON [EMP_cte].[ManagerID] = e.[EmployeeID]
        INNER JOIN [Person].[Contact] c
        ON e.[ContactID] = c.[ContactID]
    ORDER BY [RecursionLevel], [ManagerID], [EmployeeID]
    OPTION (MAXRECURSION 25)
END;
```

Let's execute this procedure, capturing the actual XML plan:

```
SET STATISTICS XML ON;
GO
EXEC [dbo].[uspGetEmployeeManagers] @EmployeeID = 9;
GO
SET STATISTICS XML OFF;
GO
```

We get a fairly complex execution plan so let's break it down into sections in order to evaluate it. We will examine the XML plan alongside the graphical plan.

The top-right hand section of the graphical plan is displayed in Figure 8:

Figure 8

A **Nested Loops** join takes the data from **Clustered Index Seeks** against **HumanResources.Employee** and **Person.Contact**. The **Scalar** operator puts in the constant "0" from the original query for the derived column, **RecursionLevel**, since this is the core query for the common table expression. The second scalar, which is only carried to a later operator, is an identifier used as part of the **Concatenation** operation.

This data is fed into a **Concatenation** operator. This operator scans multiple inputs and produces one output. It is most-commonly used to implement the **UNION ALL** operation from T-SQL.

The bottom right hand section of the plan is displayed in Figure 9:

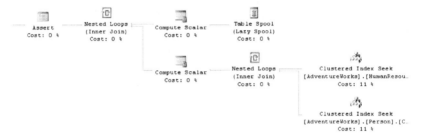

Figure 9

This is where things get interesting. The recursion methods are implemented via the **Table Spool** operator. This operator provides the mechanism for looping through the records multiple times. As noted in chapter 2, this operator takes each of the rows and stores them in a hidden temporary object stored in the tempdb database. Later in the execution plan, if the operator is rewound (say due to the use of a Nested Loops operator in the execution plan) and no rebinding is required, the spooled data can be reused instead of having to rescan the data again. As the operator loops through the records they are joined to the data from the tables as defined in the second part of the **UNION ALL** definition within the CTE.

If you look up NodeId 19 in the XML plan, you can see the **RunTimeInformation** element.

```
<RunTimeInformation>
    <RunTimeCountersPerThread Thread="0" ActualRows="4"
    ActualRebinds="1" ActualRewinds="0"
    ActualEndOfScans="1" ActualExecutions="1" />
</RunTimeInformation>
```

This shows us that one rebind of the data was needed. The rebind, a change in an internal parameter, would be the second manager. From the results, we know that three rows were returned; the initial row and two others supplied by the recursion through the management chain of the data within Adventureworks.

The final section of the graphical plan is shown in Figure 10:

Figure 10

After the **Concatenation** operator we get an **Index Spool** operator. This operation aggregates the rows into a work table, within tempdb. The data gets sorted and then we just have the rest of the query, joining index seeks to the data put together by the recursive operation.

Views

A view is essentially just a "stored query" – a way of representing data as if it were a table, without actually creating a new table. The various uses of views are well documented (preventing certain columns being selected, reducing complexity for end users, and so on). Here, we will just focus on what happens within the execution plan when we're working with a view.

Standard Views

The view, **Sales.vIndividualCustomer**, provides a summary of customer data, displaying information such as their name, email address, physical address and demographic information. A very simple query to get a specific customer would look something like this:

```
SELECT    *
FROM      [Sales].[vIndividualCustomer]
WHERE     [CustomerID] = 26131 ;
```

The resulting graphical execution plan is shown in Figure 11:

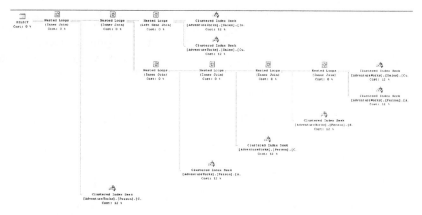

Figure 11

What happened to the view, **vIndividualCustomer**, which we referenced in this query? Remember that while SQL Server treats views similarly to tables, a view is just a named construct that sits on top of the component tables that make them up. The optimizer, during binding, resolves all those component parts in order to arrive at an execution plan to access the data. In effect, the query optimizer ignores the view object, and instead deals directly with the eight tables and the seven joins that are defined within this view.

This is important to keep in mind since views are frequently used to mask the complexity of a query. In short, while the view makes coding easier, it doesn't in any way change the necessities of the query optimizer to perform the actions defined within the view.

Indexed Views

An Indexed View, also called a materialized view, is essentially a "view plus a clustered index". A clustered index stores the column data as well as the index data, so creating a clustered index on a view results, essentially, in a new table in the database. Indexed views can often speed the performance of many queries, as the data is directly stored in the indexed view, negating the need to join and lookup the data from multiple tables each time the query is run.

Creating an indexed view is, to say the least, a costly operation. Fortunately, this is a one-time operation that can be scheduled to occur when your server is less busy.

Maintaining an index view is a different story. If the tables in the indexed view are relatively static, there is not much overhead associated with maintaining indexed views. On the other hand, if an indexed view is based on tables that are modified often, there can be a lot of overhead associated with maintaining the indexed view. For example, if one of the underlying tables is subject to a hundred **INSERT** statements a minute, then each **INSERT** will have to be updated in the indexed view. As a DBA, you have to decide if the overhead associated with maintaining an indexed view is worth the gains provided by creating the indexed view in the first place.

Queries that contain aggregates are a good candidate for indexed views because the creation of the aggregates can occur once, when the index is created, and the aggregated results can be returned with a simple **SELECT** query, rather than having the added overhead of running the aggregates through a **GROUP BY** each time the query runs.

For example, one of the indexed views supplied with AdventureWorks is **vStateProvinceCountryRegion**. This combines the **StateProvince** table and the **CountryRegion** table into a single entity for querying:

```
SELECT    *
FROM      [Person].[vStateProvinceCountryRegion]
```

The execution plan is shown in Figure 12:

Figure 12

From our previous experience with execution plans containing views, you might have expected to see two tables and the join in the execution plan. Instead, we see a single Clustered Index Scan operation: rather than execute each step of the view, the optimizer went straight to the clustered index that makes this an indexed view.

Since these indexes are available to the optimizer, they can also be used by queries that don't refer to the indexed view at all. For example, the following query will result in the exact same execution plan as shown in Figure 12:

```
SELECT    sp.[Name] AS [StateProvinceName],
          cr.[Name] AS [CountryRegionName]
FROM      [Person].[StateProvince] sp
          INNER JOIN [Person].[CountryRegion] cr ON
                     sp.[CountryRegionCode] =
cr.[CountryRegionCode] ;
```

This is because the optimizer recognizes the index as the best way to access the data.

However, this behavior is neither automatic nor guaranteed as execution plans become more complicated. For example, take the following query:

```
SELECT  a.[City],
        v.[StateProvinceName],
        v.[CountryRegionName]
FROM    [Person].[Address] a
        JOIN [Person].[vStateProvinceCountryRegion] v
            ON [a].[StateProvinceID] = [v].[StateProvinceID]
WHERE   [a].[AddressID] = 22701 ;
```

If you expected to see a join between the indexed view and the **Person.Address** table, you will be disappointed:

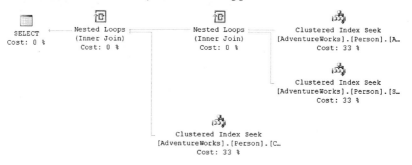

Figure 13

Instead of using the clustered index that defines the materialized view, as we saw in figure 12, the optimizer performs the same type of index expansion as it did when presented with a regular view. The query that defines the view is fully resolved, substituting the tables that make it up instead of using the clustered index provided with the view.[11]

---

[11] There is a way around this, which will be explained when we encounter the NOEXPAND hint, in the Table Hints section of Chapter 5.

Indexes

A big part of any tuning effort revolves around choosing the right indexes to include in a database. In most peoples' minds, the importance of using indexes is already well established. A frequently asked question however, is "how come some of my indexes are used and others are not?"

The availability of an index directly affects the choices made by the query optimizer. The right index leads the optimizer to the selection of the right plan. However, a lack of indexes or, even worse, a poor choice of indexes, can directly lead to poor execution plans and inadequate query performance.

Included Indexes: Avoiding Bookmark Lookups

One of the more pernicious problems when attempting to tune a query is the **Bookmark Lookup**. Type "avoid bookmark lookup" into Google and you'll get quite a few hits. As we discovered in Chapter 2, SQL Server 2005 no longer refers directly to bookmark lookup operators, although it does use the same term for the operation within its documentation.

To recap, a Bookmark Lookup occurs when a non-clustered index is used to identify the row, or rows, of interest, but the index is not covering (does not contain all the columns requested by the query). In this situation, the Optimizer is forced to send the Query Engine to a clustered index, if one exists (a **Key Lookup**), otherwise, to the heap, or table itself (a **RID Lookup**), in order to retrieve the data.

A Bookmark Lookup is not necessarily a bad thing, but the operation required to first read from the index followed by an extra read to retrieve the data from the clustered index, or heap, can lead to performance problems.

We can demonstrate this with a very simple query:

```
SELECT    [sod].[ProductID],
          [sod].[OrderQty],
          [sod].[UnitPrice]
FROM      [Sales].[SalesOrderDetail] sod
WHERE     [sod].[ProductID] = 897
```

This query returns an execution plan, shown in Figure 14, which fully demonstrates the cost of lookups.

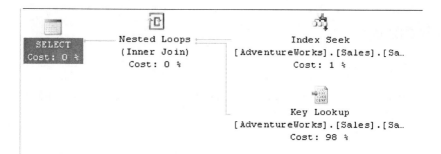

Figure 14

The **Index Seek** operator pulls back the four rows we need, quickly and efficiently. Unfortunately, the only data available on that index is the **ProductId**.

Index Seek

Scan a particular range of rows from a nonclustered index.

Physical Operation	Index Seek
Logical Operation	Index Seek
Estimated I/O Cost	0.003125
Estimated CPU Cost	0.0002402
Estimated Operator Cost	0.0033652 (1%)
Estimated Subtree Cost	0.0033652
Estimated Number of Rows	75.6667
Estimated Row Size	19 B
Ordered	True
Node ID	2

Object
[AdventureWorks].[Sales].[SalesOrderDetail].
[IX_SalesOrderDetail_ProductID] [sod]
Output List
[AdventureWorks].[Sales].
[SalesOrderDetail].SalesOrderID,
[AdventureWorks].[Sales].
[SalesOrderDetail].SalesOrderDetailID,
[AdventureWorks].[Sales].
[SalesOrderDetail].ProductID
Seek Predicates
Prefix: [AdventureWorks].[Sales].
[SalesOrderDetail].ProductID = Scalar Operator
((897))

Figure 15

As you can see from figure 15, the index seek also outputs columns that define the clustered index, in this case **SalesOrderId** and **SalesOrderDetailId**. These are used to keep the index synchronized with the clustered index and the data itself.

We then get the Key LookUp, whereby the optimizer retrieves the other columns required by the query, **OrderQty** and **UnitPrice**, from the clustered index.

In SQL Server 2000, the only way around this would be to modify the existing index used by this plan, **IX_SalesOrderDetail_ProductId**, to use all three columns. However, in SQL Server 2005, we have the additional option of using the **INCLUDE** attribute within the non-clustered index.

The **INCLUDE** attribute was added to indexes in SQL Server 2005 specifically to solve problems of this type. It allows you to add a column to the index, for storage only, not making it a part of the index itself, therefore not affecting the sorting or lookup values of the index. Adding the columns needed by the query can turn the index into a covering index, eliminating the need for the lookup operation. This does come at the cost of added disk space and additional overhead for the server to maintain the index, so due consideration must be paid prior to implementing this as a solution.

In the following code, we create a new index using the **INCLUDE** attribute. In order to get an execution plan focused on what we're testing, we set **STATISTICS XML** to on, and turn it off when we are done. The code that appears after we turn **STATISTICS XML** back off recreates the original index so that everything is in place for any further tests down the road.

```
IF EXISTS ( SELECT *
            FROM    sys.indexes
            WHERE   OBJECT_ID =
                    OBJECT_ID(N'[Sales].[SalesOrderDetail]')
                AND name = N'IX_SalesOrderDetail_ProductID' )
    DROP INDEX [IX_SalesOrderDetail_ProductID]
        ON [Sales].[SalesOrderDetail]
        WITH ( ONLINE = OFF ) ;
CREATE NONCLUSTERED INDEX [IX_SalesOrderDetail_ProductID]
                    ON [Sales].[SalesOrderDetail]
                        ([ProductID] ASC)
INCLUDE ( [OrderQty], [UnitPrice] ) WITH ( PAD_INDEX = OFF,
    STATISTICS_NORECOMPUTE = OFF, SORT_IN_TEMPDB = OFF,
IGNORE_DUP_KEY
    = OFF, DROP_EXISTING = OFF, ONLINE = OFF,
ALLOW_ROW_LOCKS = ON,
```

```
      ALLOW_PAGE_LOCKS = ON )
      ON [PRIMARY] ;
GO

SET STATISTICS XML ON ;
GO

SELECT  [sod].[ProductID],
        [sod].[OrderQty],
        [sod].[UnitPrice]
FROM    [Sales].[SalesOrderDetail] sod
WHERE   [sod].[ProductID] = 897 ;
GO
SET STATISTICS XML OFF ;
GO

--Recreate original index
IF EXISTS ( SELECT   *
           FROM    sys.indexes
           WHERE   OBJECT_ID =
                   OBJECT_ID(N'[Sales].[SalesOrderDetail]')
           AND name = N'IX_SalesOrderDetail_ProductID' )
   DROP INDEX [IX_SalesOrderDetail_ProductID]
             ON [Sales].[SalesOrderDetail]
             WITH ( ONLINE = OFF ) ;
CREATE NONCLUSTERED INDEX [IX_SalesOrderDetail_ProductID]
                    ON [Sales].[SalesOrderDetail]
                       ([ProductID] ASC)
   WITH ( PAD_INDEX = OFF, STATISTICS_NORECOMPUTE = OFF,
      SORT_IN_TEMPDB = OFF, IGNORE_DUP_KEY = OFF,
      DROP_EXISTING = OFF,
      ONLINE = OFF, ALLOW_ROW_LOCKS = ON,
      ALLOW_PAGE_LOCKS = ON ) ON [PRIMARY] ;
GO

EXEC sys.sp_addextendedproperty @name = N'MS_Description',
    @value = N'Nonclustered index.', @level0type =
              N'SCHEMA',
    @level0name = N'Sales', @level1type = N'TABLE',
    @level1name = N'SalesOrderDetail', @level2type =
              N'INDEX',
    @level2name = N'IX_SalesOrderDetail_ProductID' ;
```

Run this code in Management Studio with the "Include Actual Execution Plan" option turned on, and you will see the execution plan shown in Figure 16:

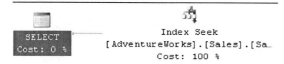

Figure 16

The execution plan is able to use a single operator to find and return all the data we need because the index is now covering, meaning it includes all the necessary columns.

Index Selectivity

Let's now move on to the question of which index is going to get used, and why the optimizer sometimes avoids using available indexes.

First, let's briefly review the definition of the two kinds of available indexes: the clustered and non-clustered index. A clustered index stores the data along with the lookup values of the index and it sorts the data, physically. A non-clustered index sorts the column, or columns, included in the index, but it doesn't sort the data.

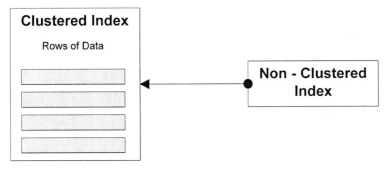

Figure 17

As described in Chapter 1, the utility of a given index is determined by the statistics generated automatically by the system for that index. The key indicator of the usefulness of the index is its **selectivity.**

An index's selectivity describes the distribution of the distinct values within a given data set. To put it more simply, you count the number of rows and then you count the number of unique values for a given column across all the rows. After that, divide the unique values by the number of rows. This results in a ratio that is expressed as the selectivity of the index. The better the selectivity, the more useful the index and the more likely it will be used by the optimizer.

For example, on the **Sales.SalesOrderDetail** table there is an index, **IX_SalesOrderDetail_ProductID**, on the **ProductID** column. To see the statistics for that index use the DBCC command, **SHOW_STATISTICS**:

```
DBCC SHOW_STATISTICS('Sales.SalesOrderDetail',
                     'IX_SalesOrderDetail_ProductID')
```

This returns three result sets with various amounts of data. Usually, the second result set is the most interesting one:

```
All density    Average Length Columns
-------------  -------------- -----------------------------------
--------
0.003759399    4              ProductID
8.242868E-06   8              ProductID, SalesOrderID
8.242868E-06   12             ProductID, SalesOrderID,
SalesOrderDetailID
```

The Density is inverse to the selectivity, meaning that the lower the density, the higher the selectivity. So an index like the one above, with a density of .003759399, will very likely be used by the optimizer. The other rows refer to the clustered index. Any index in the system that is not clustered will also have a pointer back to the clustered index since that's where the data is stored. If no clustered index is present then a pointer to the data itself, often referred to as a **heap**, is generated. That's why the columns of the clustered index are included as part of the selectivity of the index in question.

Selectivity can affect the use of an index negatively as well as positively. Let's assume that you've taken the time to create an index on a frequently-searched field, and yet you're not seeing a performance benefit. Let's create such a situation ourselves. The business represented in AdventureWorks has decided that they're going to be giving away prizes based on the quantity of items purchased. This means a query very similar to the one from the previous *Avoiding BookMark Lookups* section:

```
SELECT   sod.OrderQty,
         sod.[SalesOrderID],
         sod.[SalesOrderDetailID],
         sod.[LineTotal]
FROM     [Sales].[SalesOrderDetail] sod
WHERE    sod.[OrderQty] = 10
```

The execution plan for this query is shown in Figure 18:

Figure 18

We see a **Clustered Index Scan** against the entire table and then a simple **Filter** operation to derive the final results sets, where **OrderQty = 10**.

Let's now create an index that our query can use:

```
CREATE NONCLUSTERED INDEX [IX_SalesOrderDetail_OrderQty]
         ON [Sales].[SalesOrderDetail] ( [OrderQty] ASC )
   WITH ( PAD_INDEX = OFF, STATISTICS_NORECOMPUTE = OFF,
          SORT_IN_TEMPDB = OFF,IGNORE_DUP_KEY = OFF,
          DROP_EXISTING = OFF, ONLINE = OFF,
          ALLOW_ROW_LOCKS = ON,ALLOW_PAGE_LOCKS = ON )
      ON [PRIMARY]
```

Unfortunately, if you capture the plan again, you'll see that it's identical to the one shown in Figure 18; in other words, our new index is completely ignored. Since we know that selectivity determines when, or if, and index is used, let's examine the new index using **DBCC SHOW_STATISTICS**:

```
All density    Average Length Columns
------------- -------------- ------------------------------------
--------
0.02439024 2      OrderQty
2.18055E-05 6     OrderQty, SalesOrderID
8.242868E-06      10     OrderQty, SalesOrderID,
SalesOrderDetailID
```

We can see that the density of the **OrderQty** is 10 times less than for the **ProductId** column, meaning that our **OrderQty** index is ten times less selective. To see this in more quantifiable terms, there are 121317 rows in the **SalesOrderDetail** table on my system. There are only 41 distinct values for the **OrderQty** column. This column just isn't, by itself, an adequate index to make a difference in the query plan.

If we really had to make this query run well, the answer would be to make the index selective enough to be useful by the optimizer. You could also try forcing the optimizer to use the index we built by using a query hint, but in this case, it wouldn't help the performance of the query (hints are covered in detail in Chapter 5). Remember that adding an index, however selective, comes at a price during inserts, deletes and updates as the data within the index is reordered, added or removed based on the actions of the query being run.

If you're following along in AdventureWorks, you'll want to be sure to drop the index we created:

```
DROP INDEX
[Sales].[SalesOrderDetail].[IX_SalesOrderDetail_OrderQty]
```

Statistics and Indexes

The main cause of a difference between the plans lies in differences between the statistics and the actual data. Not only can this cause differences between the plans, but you can get bad execution plans because the statistical data is not up to date.

The following example is somewhat contrived, but it does demonstrate how, as the data changes, the exact same query will result in two different execution plans. In the example, the new table is created, along with an index:

```
IF EXISTS ( SELECT  *
            FROM    sys.objects
            WHERE   object_id = OBJECT_ID(N'[NewOrders]')
            AND type in ( N'U' ) )
    DROP TABLE [NewOrders]
GO
SELECT  *
INTO    NewOrders
FROM    Sales.SalesOrderDetail
GO
CREATE INDEX IX_NewOrders_ProductID on NewOrders ( ProductID
)
GO
```

I then capture the estimated plan (in MXL format). After that I run a query that updates the data, changing the statistics and then run another query, getting the actual execution plan

```
-- Estimated Plan
SET SHOWPLAN_XML ON
GO
SELECT  [OrderQty]
        ,[CarrierTrackingNumber]
FROM    NewOrders
WHERE   [ProductID] = 897
GO
SET SHOWPLAN_XML OFF
GO

BEGIN TRAN
UPDATE  NewOrders
SET     [ProductID] = 897
WHERE   [ProductID] between 800 and 900
GO

-- Actual Plan
SET STATISTICS XML ON
GO
SELECT  [OrderQty]
        ,[CarrierTrackingNumber]
```

```
FROM      NewOrders
WHERE     [ProductID]  = 897

ROLLBACK TRAN
GO
SET STATISTICS XML OFF
GO
```

I took the XML output and saved them to files (See *Saving XML Plans as Graphical Plans*, in Chapter 1), and then reopened the files in order to get an easy-to-read graphical plan. Breaking bits and pieces of SQL code apart and only showing plans for the pieces that you want is a big advantage to using XML plans. First the estimated plan:

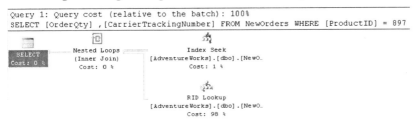

```
Query 1: Query cost (relative to the batch): 100%
SELECT [OrderQty] ,[CarrierTrackingNumber] FROM NewOrders WHERE [ProductID] = 897
```

Figure 19

Then the Actual execution plan:

```
Query 1: Query cost (relative to the batch): 100%
SELECT [OrderQty],[CarrierTrackingNumber] FROM [NewOrders] WHERE [ProductID]=@1
```

```
                         Table Scan
   SELECT        [AdventureWorks].[dbo].[NewO...
   Cost: 0 %              Cost: 100 %
```

Figure 20

Go to the top and right of Figure 19 to find the Index Seek operator. Clearly, prior to the updates, the data and statistics within the index were selective enough that the **SELECT** could use a seek operation. Then, because the data being requested is not included in the index itself, a **RID Lookup** operation is performed. This is a lookup against a heap table using the row identifier to bring back the data from the correct row.

However, after the data is updated, the query is much less selective and returns much more data, so that the actual plan does not use the index, but instead retrieves the data by scanning the whole table, as we can see from the Table Scan operator in Figure 20. The estimated cost is .243321 while the actual cost is 1.2434. Note that if you recapture the estimated plan, you'll see that the statistics have automatically updated, and the estimated plan will also show a table scan.

Summary

This chapter introduced various concepts that go a bit beyond the basics in displaying and understanding execution plans. Stored procedures, views, derived tables, and common table expressions were all introduced along with their attendant execution plans.

The most important point to take away from all of the various plans derived is that you have to walk through them all in the same way, working right to left, top to bottom, in order to understand the behavior implied by the plan. The importance of indexes and their direct impact on the execution of the optimizer and the query engine was introduced. The most important point to take away from here is that simply adding an index doesn't necessarily mean you've solved a performance problem. You need to ensure the selectivity of your data. You also need to make appropriate choices regarding the addition or inclusion of columns in your indexes, both clustered and non-clustered.

Chapter 5: Controlling Execution Plans with Hints

It is possible to impose your will on the optimizer and, to some degree, control its behavior. This is done through hints:

- **Query Hints** tell the optimizer to apply this hint throughout the execution of the entire query.
- **Join Hints** tell the optimizer to use a particular join at a particular point in the query
- **Table Hints** control table scans and the use of a particular index for a table

In this chapter I'll describe how to use each of the above types of hint, but I can't stress the following hard enough: these things are *dangerous*. Appropriate use of the right hint on the right query can save your application. The exact same hint used on another query can create more problems than it solves, slowing your query down radically and leading to severe blocking and timeouts in your application.

If you find yourself putting hints on a majority of your queries and procedures, then you're *doing something wrong*. Within the details of each of the hints described, I'll lay out the problem that you're hoping to solve by applying the hint. Some of the examples will improve performance or change the behavior in a positive manner, and some will negatively impact performance.

Query Hints

There are quite a number of query hints and they perform a variety of different duties. Some may be used somewhat regularly and a few are for rare circumstances.

Query hints are specified in the **OPTION** clause. The basic syntax is as follows:

```
SELECT ...
OPTION (<hint>,<hint>...)
```

Query hints can't be applied to **INSERT** statements except when used with a **SELECT** operation. You also can't use query hints in subselect statements.

Before we proceed, let me take this opportunity to warn you once again: injudicious use of these hints can cause you more problems than they solve!

HASH|ORDER GROUP

These two hints – **HASH GROUP** and **ORDER GROUP** – directly apply to a **GROUP BY** aggregate operation (as well as to **DISTINCT** or **COMPUTE** clauses). They instruct the optimizer to apply either hashing or grouping to the aggregation, respectively.

In the example below we have a simple **GROUP BY** query that is called frequently by the application to display the various uses of Suffix to people's names.

```
SELECT   [c].[Suffix],
         COUNT([c].[Suffix]) AS SuffixUsageCount
FROM     [Person].[Contact] c
GROUP BY [Suffix]
```

The business has instructed you to make this query run as fast as possible because you're maintaining a high-end shop with lots of queries from the sales force against an ever-changing set of data. The first thing you do, of course, is to look at the execution plan, as shown in Figure 1:

Figure 1

As you can see, by "default" the optimizer opts to use hashing. The unordered data from the clustered index scan is grouped within the Hash Match (Aggregate) operator. This operator will build a hash table, select distinct values from the data supplied by the Clustered Index Scan and then develop the counts based on the matched values. This plan has a cost of 0.590827, which you can see in the Tool Tip in Figure 2:

Hash Match

Use each row from the top input to build a hash
table, and each row from the bottom input to probe
into the hash table, outputting all matching rows.

Physical Operation	Hash Match
Logical Operation	Aggregate
Actual Number of Rows	7
Estimated I/O Cost	0
Estimated CPU Cost	0.146317
Estimated Operator Cost	0.146317 (25%)
Estimated Subtree Cost	0.590827
Estimated Number of Rows	7
Estimated Row Size	25 B
Actual Rebinds	0
Actual Rewinds	0
Node ID	1

Output List
[AdventureWorks].[Person].[Contact].Suffix,
Expr1005
Build Residual
[AdventureWorks].[Person].[Contact].[Suffix] as
[c].[Suffix] = [AdventureWorks].[Person].[Contact].
[Suffix] as [c].[Suffix]

Figure 2

Since it's not performing in the manner you would like, you decide that
the best solution would be to try to use the data from the Clustered
Scan in an ordered fashion rather than the unordered Hash Match. So
you add the **ORDER GROUP** hint to the query:

```
SELECT   [c].[Suffix],
         COUNT([c].[Suffix]) AS SuffixUsageCount
FROM     [Person].[Contact] c
GROUP BY [Suffix]
OPTION  ( ORDER GROUP )
```

The new plan is shown in Figure 3:

Figure 3

We've told the optimizer to use ordering rather than hashing, via the
ORDER GROUP hint, so instead of the hash table, it's been forced to

use a **SORT** operator to feed into the **Stream Aggregate** operator, which works with ordered data.

As per my repeated warning, this query had a cost of .590827 prior to applying the hint and a cost of 1.77745 after, a little more than three times the cost. The source of the increased cost is ordering the data as it comes out of the Clustered Index Scan.

Depending on your situation, you may find an instance where, using our example above, the data is already ordered yet the optimizer chose to use the Hash Match operator instead of the Stream Aggregate. In that case, the Query Engine would recognize that the data was ordered and accept the hint gracefully, increasing performance. While query hints allow you to control the behavior of the optimizer, it doesn't mean your choices are necessarily better than those provided to you. To optimize this query, you may want to consider adding a different index or modifying the clustered index.

MERGE |HASH |CONCAT UNION

These hints affect how UNION operations are carried out in your queries, instructing the optimizer to use either merging, hashing or concatenation of the data sets. The most likely reason to apply this hint would be with performance issues where you may be able to affect the behavior of how the UNION is executed.

The example query below is not running fast enough to satisfy the demands of the application:

```
SELECT   [pm1].[Name],
         [pm1].[ModifiedDate]
FROM     [Production].[ProductModel] pm1
UNION
SELECT   [pm2].[Name],
         [pm2].[ModifiedDate]
FROM     [Production].[ProductModel] pm2
```

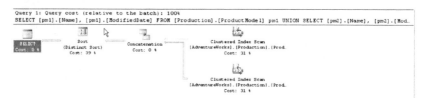

Figure 4

You can see that the Concatenation operation that the optimizer chooses to use is, in the context of the plan, very cheap, but the Sort operation that follows it is relatively expensive. The overall cost of the plan is 0.0377.

In a test to see if changing implementation of the UNION operation will affect overall performance, you apply the **MERGE UNION** hint:

```
SELECT    [pm1].[Name],
          [pm1].[ModifiedDate]
FROM      [Production].[ProductModel] pm1
UNION
SELECT    [pm2].[Name],
          [pm2].[ModifiedDate]
FROM      [Production].[ProductModel] pm2
OPTION  ( MERGE UNION )
```

Figure 5

You have forced the **UNION** operation to use the **Merge Join** instead of the **Concatenation** operator. However, since the Merge Join only works with sorted data feeds, we've also forced the optimizer to add two **Sort** operators. The estimated cost for the query has gone from 0.0377 to 0.0548. Clearly this didn't work.

What if you tried the other hint, **HASH UNION**:

```
SELECT    [pm1].[Name],
          [pm1].[ModifiedDate]
FROM      [Production].[ProductModel] pm1
UNION
SELECT    [pm2].[Name],
          [pm2].[ModifiedDate]
FROM      [Production].[ProductModel] pm2
OPTION  ( HASH UNION )
```

This results in a new execution plan, shown in Figure 6:

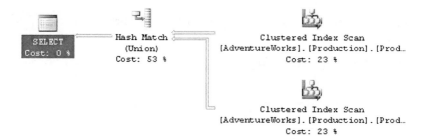

Figure 6

The execution plan is simplified, with the sort operations completely eliminated. However, the cost is still higher (0.0497) than for the original un-hinted query so clearly, for the amount of data involved in this query, the Hash Match operator doesn't offer a performance enhancement over the original Concatenation operator.

In this situation, the hints are working to modify the behavior of the query, but they are not helping you to increase performance of the query.

LOOP|MERGE|HASH JOIN

This makes all the join operations in a particular query use the method supplied by the hint. However, note that if a join hint (covered later in this chapter) is applied to a specific join, then the more granular join hint takes precedence over the general query hint.

You've found that your system is suffering from poor disk I/O, so you need to reduce the number of scans and reads that your queries generate. By collecting data from Profiler and Performance Monitor you're able to identify the following query as needing some work. Here is the query and the original execution plan:

```
SELECT  s.[Name] AS StoreName,
        ct.[Name] AS ContactTypeName,
        c.[LastName] + ', ' + c.[LastName]
FROM    [Sales].[Store] s
        JOIN [Sales].[StoreContact] sc
        ON [s].[CustomerID] = [sc].[CustomerID]
        JOIN [Person].[Contact] c
        ON [sc].[ContactID] = [c].[ContactID]
        JOIN [Person].[ContactType] ct
        ON [sc].[ContactTypeID] = [ct].[ContactTypeID]
```

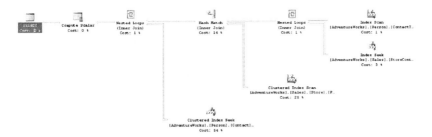

Figure 7

As you can see, the query uses a mix of **Nested Loop** and **Hash Match** operators to put the data together. Let's see the I/O output of the query. This can be done by navigating from the main menu, **Query | Query Options**, selecting the advanced tab and activating the "Set Statistics IO" check box.

```
Table 'Contact'. Scan count 0, logical reads 1586, …
Table 'Worktable'. Scan count 0, logical reads 0, …
Table 'Address'. Scan count 1, logical reads 216, …
Table 'CustomerAddress'. Scan count 753, logical reads
        1624, …
Table 'Store'. Scan count 1, logical reads 103, …
Table 'StoreContact'. Scan count 20, logical reads 42, …
Table 'ContactType'. Scan count 1, logical reads 2, …
```

From this data, you can see that the scans against the **CustomerAddress** table are causing a problem within this query. It occurs to you that allowing the query to perform all those Hash Join operations is slowing it down and you decide to change the behavior by adding the Loop Join hint to the end of the query:

```
OPTION ( LOOP JOIN )
```

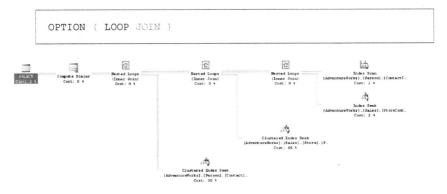

Figure 8

Now the **Hash Joins** are **Loop Joins**. This situation could be interesting. If you look at the operations that underpin the query execution plan you'll see that the second query, with the hint, eliminates the creation of a work table. While the estimated cost of the second query is a bit higher than the original, the addition of the query hint does, in this case, results in a negligible improvement in performance, going from about 172ms to about 148ms on average. However, when you look at the scans and reads, they tell a different story:

```
Table 'ContactType'. Scan count 0, logical reads 1530, …
Table 'Contact'. Scan count 0, logical reads 1586, …
Table 'StoreContact'. Scan count 712, logical reads 1432,
    …
Table 'Address'. Scan count 0, logical reads 1477, …
Table 'CustomerAddress'. Scan count 701, logical reads
    1512, …
Table 'Store'. Scan count 1, logical reads 103, …
```

Not only have we been unsuccessful in reducing the reads, despite the elimination of the work table, but we've actually increased the number of scans. What if we were to modify the query to use the **MERGE JOIN** hint instead? Change the final line of the query to read:

```
OPTION ( MERGE JOIN )
```

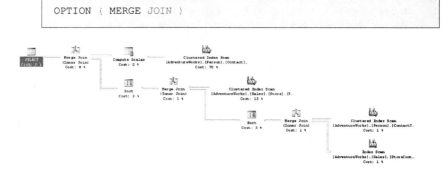

Figure 9

The execution of the plan was about as fast as the original, but did it solve our problem?

```
Table 'Worktable'. Scan count 11, logical reads 91, …
Table 'CustomerAddress'. Scan count 1, logical reads 6, …
Table 'StoreContact'. Scan count 1, logical reads 4, …
Table 'ContactType'. Scan count 1, logical reads 2, …
Table 'Store'. Scan count 1, logical reads 103, …
Table 'Address'. Scan count 1, logical reads 18, …
Table 'Contact'. Scan count 1, logical reads 33, …
```

We've re-introduced a worktable, but it does appear that the large number of scans has been eliminated. We may have a solution. However, before we conclude the experiment, we may as well as try out the **HASH JOIN** hint to see what it might do. Modify the final line of the query to read:

```
OPTION ( HASH JOIN )
```

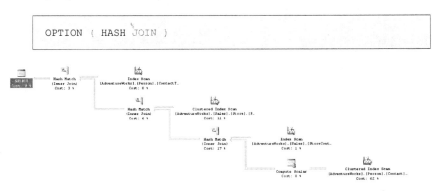

Figure 10

We're back to a simplified execution plan using only Hash Join operations. The execution time was about the same as the original query and the I/O looked like this:

```
Table 'Worktable'. Scan count 0, logical reads 0, ...
Table 'Contact'. Scan count 1, logical reads 569, ...
Table 'Store'. Scan count 1, logical reads 103, ...
Table 'Address'. Scan count 1, logical reads 216, ...
Table 'CustomerAddress'. Scan count 1, logical reads 67, ...
Table 'StoreContact'. Scan count 1, logical reads 4, ...
Table 'ContactType'. Scan count 1, logical reads 2, ...
```

For the example above, using the MERGE JOIN hint appears to be the best bet for reducing the I/O costs of the query, with only the added overhead of the creation of the worktable.

FAST n

This time, we're not concerned about performance of the database. This time, we're concerned about perceived performance of the application. The users would like an immediate return of data to the screen, even if it's not the complete result set, and even if they have to wait longer for the complete result set.

The **FAST n** hint provides that feature by getting the optimizer to focus on getting the execution plan to return the first 'n' rows as fast as possible, where 'n' has to be a positive integer value. Consider the following query and execution plan:

```
SELECT    *
FROM      [Sales].[SalesOrderDetail] sod
```

```
JOIN [Sales].[SalesOrderHeader] soh
  ON [sod].[SalesOrderID] = [soh].[SalesOrderID]
```

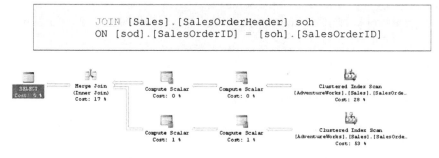

Figure 11

This query performs adequately, but there is a delay before the end users see any results, so we try to fix this by adding the Fast n hint to return the first 10 rows as quickly as possible:

```
OPTION ( FAST 10 )
```

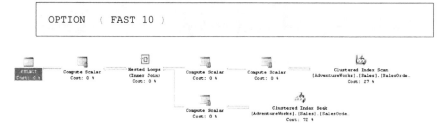

Figure 12

Instead of the **Hash Match** operator for the join, the optimizer attempted to use a **Nested Loop**. The loop join results in getting the first rows back very fast, but the rest of the processing was somewhat slower. So, because the plan will be concentrating on getting the first ten rows back as soon as possible, you'll see a difference in the cost and the performance of the query. The total cost for the original query was 1.973. The hint reduced that cost to 0.012 (for the first 10 rows). The number of logical reads increases dramatically, 1238 for the un-hinted query to 101,827 for the hinted query, but the actual speed of the execution of the query increases only marginally, from around 4.2 seconds to 5 seconds. This slight slow-down in performance was accepted by the end-users since they got what they really wanted, a very fast display to the screen.

If you want to see the destructive as well as beneficial effects that hints can have, try applying the **LOOP JOIN** hint, from the previous section. It increases the cost by a factor of five!

FORCE ORDER

You've identified a query that is performing poorly. It's a somewhat long query with a few tables. Normally, the optimizer will determine the order in which the joins occur but using the **FORCE ORDER** hint you can make the optimizer use the order of joins as listed in the query itself. This would be done if you've got a fairly high degree of certainty that your join order is better than that supplied by the optimizer. The optimizer can make incorrect choices when the statistics are not up to date, when the data distribution is less than optimal or if the query has a high degree of complexity. Here is the query in question:

```
SELECT   pc.[Name] ProductCategoryName,
         psc.[Name] ProductSubCategoryName,
         p.[Name] ProductName,
         pd.[Description],
         pm.[Name] ProductModelName,
         c.[Name] CultureName,
         d.[FileName],
         pri.[Quantity],
         pr.[Rating],
         pr.[Comments]
FROM     [Production].[Product] p
LEFT JOIN [Production].[ProductModel] pm
ON [p].[ProductModelID] = [pm].[ProductModelID]
LEFT JOIN [Production].[ProductDocument] pdo
ON p.[ProductID] = pdo.[ProductID]
LEFT JOIN [Production].[ProductSubcategory] psc
ON [p].[ProductSubcategoryID] =
   [psc].[ProductSubcategoryID]
LEFT JOIN [Production].[ProductInventory] pri
ON p.[ProductID] = pri.[ProductID]
LEFT JOIN [Production].[ProductReview] pr
ON p.[ProductID] = pr.[ProductID]
LEFT JOIN [Production].[Document] d
ON pdo.[DocumentID] = d.[DocumentID]
LEFT JOIN [Production].[ProductCategory] pc
ON [pc].[ProductCategoryID] =
   [psc].[ProductCategoryID]
LEFT JOIN
[Production].[ProductModelProductDescriptionCulture]
   pmpd
ON pmpd.[ProductModelID] = pm.[ProductModelID]
LEFT JOIN [Production].[ProductDescription] pd
ON pmpd.[ProductDescriptionID] =
   pd.[ProductDescriptionID]
LEFT JOIN [Production].[Culture] c
ON c.[CultureID] = pmpd.[CultureID]
```

Based on your knowledge of the data, you're fairly certain that you've put the joins in the correct order. Here is the execution plan as it exists:

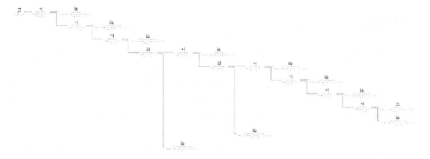

Figure 3

Obviously this is far too large to review on the page. The main point to showing the graphic is really for you to get a feel for the shape of the plan. The estimated cost as displayed in the tool tip is 0.5853.

Take the same query and apply the **FORCE ORDER** query hint:

```
OPTION (FORCE ORDER)
```

It results in the plan shown in Figure 14.

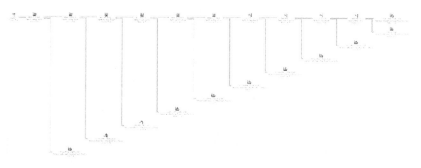

Figure 4

Don't try to read the plan in Figure 14; simply notice that the overall shape has changed radically from the execution plan in Figure 13. All the joins are now in the exact order listed in the SELECT statement of the query. Unfortunately, our choice of order was not as efficient as the choices made by the optimizer. The estimated cost for the query displayed on the ToolTip is 1.1676. The added cost is caused by the fact that our less efficient join order is filtering less data from the early parts of the query. Instead, we're force to carry more data between each operation.

MAXDOP

You have one of those really nasty problems, a query that sometimes runs just fine, but sometimes runs incredibly slowly. You investigate the issue, and use SQL Server Profiler to capture the execution of this procedure, over time, with various parameters. You finally arrive at two execution plans. The execution plan when the query runs quickly looks like this:

Figure 5

When the execution is slow, the plan looks this way (note that this image was split in order to make it more readable):

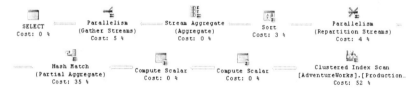

Figure 6

Here, you're seeing a situation where the parallelism (covered in Chapter 8) that should be helping the performance of your system is, instead, hurting that performance. Since parallelism is normally turned on and off at the server level, and other procedures running on the server are benefiting from it, you can't simply turn it off. That's where the **MAXDOP** hint becomes useful.

The **MAXDOP** query hint can control the use of parallelism within an individual query, rather than working with the server-wide setting of "Max Degree of Parallelism".

In order to get this to fire on a system with only a single processor, I'm going to reset the threshold for my system as part of the query:

```
sp_configure 'cost threshold for parallelism', 1 ;
GO

RECONFIGURE WITH OVERRIDE ;
GO

SELECT   wo.[DueDate],
         MIN(wo.[OrderQty]) MinOrderQty,
         MIN(wo.[StockedQty]) MinStockedQty,
         MIN(wo.[ScrappedQty]) MinScrappedQty,
```

```
              MAX(wo.[OrderQty]) MaxOrderQty,
              MAX(wo.[StockedQty]) MaxStockedQty,
              MAX(wo.[ScrappedQty]) MaxScrappedQty
FROM       [Production].[WorkOrder] wo
GROUP BY wo.[DueDate]
ORDER BY wo.[DueDate]
GO

sp_configure 'cost threshold for parallelism', 5 ;
GO

RECONFIGURE WITH OVERRIDE ;
GO
```

This will result in an execution plan that takes full advantage of parallel processing, looking like figure 16 above. The optimizer chooses a parallel execution for this plan. Look at the properties of the **Clustered Index Scan** operator by selecting that icon on the plan in Management Studio. The property **Actual Number of Rows** can be expanded by clicking on the plus (+) icon. It will show three different threads, the number of threads spawned by the parallel operation.

However, we know that when our query uses parallel processing, it is running slowly. We have no desire to change the overall behavior of parallelism within the server itself, so we directly affect the query that is causing problems by adding this code:

```
SELECT   wo.[DueDate],
          MIN(wo.[OrderQty]) MinOrderQty,
          MIN(wo.[StockedQty]) MinStockedQty,
          MIN(wo.[ScrappedQty]) MinScrappedQty,
          MAX(wo.[OrderQty]) MaxOrderQty,
          MAX(wo.[StockedQty]) MaxStockedQty,
          MAX(wo.[ScrappedQty]) MaxScrappedQty
FROM     [Production].[WorkOrder] wo
GROUP BY wo.[DueDate]
ORDER BY wo.[DueDate]
OPTION  ( MAXDOP 1 )
```

The new execution plan is limited, in this case, to a single processor, so no parallelism occurs at all. In other instances you would be limiting the degree of parallelism (e.g. two processors instead of four):

Figure 7

As you can see, limiting parallelism didn't fundamentally change the execution plan since it's still using a **Clustered Index Scan** to get the initial data set. The plan still puts the data set through two Compute Scalar operators to deal with the **StockedQty** column, a calculated column. The same **Hash Match** join operator is performed between the table and itself as part of aggregating the data, and then finally a **Sort** operator puts the data into the correct order before the **Select** operator adds the column aliases back in. The only real changes are the removal of the operators necessary for the parallel execution. The reason, in this instance, that the performance was worse on the production machine was due to the extra steps required to take the data from a single stream to a set of parallel streams and then bring it all back together again. While the optimizer may determine this should work better, it's not always correct.

OPTIMIZE FOR

You have identified a query that will run at an adequate speed for hours, or days, with no worries and then suddenly it performs horribly. With a lot of investigation and experimentation, you find that most of the time, the parameters being supplied by the application to run the procedure, result in an execution plan that performs very well. Sometimes, a certain value, or subset of values, is supplied to the parameter when the plan is recompiling and the execution plan stored in the cache with this parameter performs very badly indeed.

The **OPTIMIZE FOR** hint was introduced with SQL Server 2005. It allows you to instruct the optimizer to optimize query execution for the particular parameter value that you supply, rather than for the actual value of a parameter supplied within the query.

This can be an extremely useful hint. Situations can arise whereby the data distribution of a particular table, or index, is such that most parameters will result in a good plan, but some parameters can result in a bad plan. Since plans can age out of the cache, or events can be fired that cause plan recompilation, it becomes, to a degree, a gamble as to where and when the problematic execution plan is the one that gets created and cached.

In SQL Server 2000, only two options were available:

1. Recompile the plan every time using the RECOMPILE hint
2. Get a good plan and keep it using the **KEEPFIXED PLAN** hint

Both of these solutions (covered later in this chapter) could create as many problems as they solved since the **RECOMPILE** of the query, depending on the complexity and size of the query, could be longer than the execution itself or the **KEEPFIXED PLAN** hint could be applied to the problematic values as well as the useful ones.

In SQL Server 2005, when such a situation is identified that leads you to desire that one parameter be used over another, you can use the **OPTIMIZE FOR** hint.

We can demonstrate the utility of this hint with a very simple set of queries:

```
SELECT    *
FROM      [Person].[Address]
WHERE     [City] = 'Newark'

SELECT    *
FROM      [Person].[Address]
WHERE     [City] = 'London'
```

We'll run these at the same time and we'll get two different execution plans:

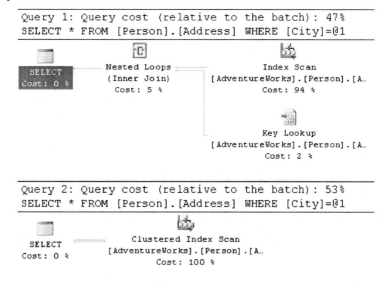

Figure 8

If you look at the cost relative to the Batch of each of these queries, the first query is just a little less expensive than the second, with costs of 0.194 compared to 0.23. This is primarily because the second query is doing a clustered index scan, which walks through all the rows available.

If we modify our T-SQL so that we're using parameters, like this:

```
DECLARE @City NVARCHAR(30)

SET @City = 'Newark'
SELECT  *
FROM    [Person].[Address]
WHERE   [City] = @City

SET @City = 'London'
SELECT  *
FROM    [Person].[Address]
WHERE   [City] = @City
```

We'll get a standard execution plan for both queries that looks like this:

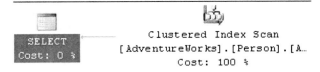

Figure 9

It's using the clustered index for both queries now because it's not sure which of the values available in the table is most likely going to be passed in as **@City**.

Let's make one more modification. In the second query, we instruct the optimizer to optimize for Newark:

```
DECLARE @City NVARCHAR(30)

SET @City = 'London'
SELECT  *
FROM    [Person].[Address]
WHERE   [City] = @City

SET @City = 'London'
SELECT  *
FROM    [Person].[Address]
WHERE   [City] = @City
OPTION  ( OPTIMIZE FOR ( @City = 'Newark' ) )
```

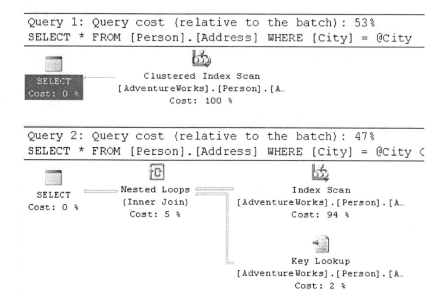

```
Query 1: Query cost (relative to the batch): 53%
SELECT * FROM [Person].[Address] WHERE [City] = @City
```

```
Query 2: Query cost (relative to the batch): 47%
SELECT * FROM [Person].[Address] WHERE [City] = @City (
```

Figure 20

The value 'London' has very low level of selectivity (there are a lot of values equal to 'London') within the index and this is displayed by the Clustered Index Scan in the first query. Despite the fact that the second query looks up the same value, it's now the faster of the two queries. The **OPTIMIZE FOR** operator was able to focus the optimizer to create a plan that counted on the fact that the data was highly selective, even though it was not. The execution plan created was one for the more selective value, 'Newark', yet that plan helped the performance for the other value, 'London.'

Use of this hint requires intimate knowledge of the underlying data. Choosing the wrong value to supply **OPTIMIZE FOR** will not only fail to help performance, but could have a very serious negative impact. You can set as many hints as you use parameters within the query.

PARAMETERIZATION SIMPLE | FORCED

Parameterization, forced and simple, is covered in a lot more detail in the section on Plan Guides, in Chapter 8. It's covered in that section because you can't actually use this query hint by itself within a query, but must use it only with a plan guide.

RECOMPILE

You have yet another problem query that performs slowly in an intermittent fashion. Investigation and experimentation with the query leads you to realize that the very nature of the query itself is the problem. It just so happens that this query is a built-in, ad hoc (using SQL statements or code to generate SQL statements) query of the application you support. Each time the query is passed to SQL Server, it has slightly different parameters, and possibly even a slightly different structure. So, while plans are being cached for the query, many of these plans are either useless or could even be problematic. The execution plan that works well for one set of parameter values may work horribly for another set. The parameters passed from the application in this case are highly volatile. Due to the nature of the query and the data, you don't really want to keep all of the execution plans around. Rather than attempting to create a single perfect plan for the whole query, you identify the sections of the query that can benefit from being recompiled regularly.

The **RECOMPILE** hint was introduced in SQL 2005. It instructs the optimizer to mark the plan created so that it will be discarded by the next execution of the query. This hint might be useful when the plan created, and cached, isn't likely to be useful to any of the following calls. For example, as described above, there is a lot of ad hoc SQL in the query, or the data is relatively volatile, changing so much that no one plan will be optimal. Regardless of the cause, the determination has been made that the cost of recompiling the procedure each time it is executed is worth the time saved by that recompile.

You can also add the instruction to recompile the plan to stored procedures, when they're created, but the **RECOMPILE** query hint offers greater control. The reason for this is that statements within a query or procedure can be recompiled independently of the larger query or procedure. This means that if only a section of a query uses ad hoc SQL, you can recompile just that statement as opposed to the entire procedure. When a statement recompiles within a procedure, all local variables are initialized and the parameters used for the plan are those supplied to the procedure.

If you use local variables in your queries, the optimizer makes a guess as to what value may work best. This guess is kept in the cache. Consider the following pair of queries:

```
DECLARE @PersonId INT
SET @PersonId = 277
SELECT  [soh].[SalesOrderNumber],
        [soh].[OrderDate],
        [soh].[SubTotal],
        [soh].[TotalDue]
```

```
FROM      [Sales].[SalesOrderHeader] soh
WHERE     [soh].[SalesPersonID] = @PersonId

SET @PersonId = 288
SELECT    [soh].[SalesOrderNumber],
          [soh].[OrderDate],
          [soh].[SubTotal],
          [soh].[TotalDue]
FROM      [Sales].[SalesOrderHeader] soh
WHERE     [soh].[SalesPersonID] = @PersonId
```

These result in an identical pair of execution plans:

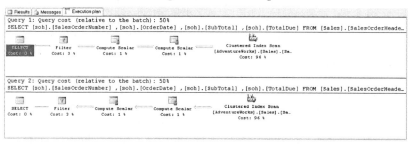

Figure 21

With a full knowledge of your system, you know that the plan for the second query should be completely different because the value passed is much more selective, and a useful index exists on that column. So, you modify the queries using the **RECOMPILE** hint. In this instance, I'm adding it to both queries so that you can see that the performance gain in the second query is due to the **RECOMPILE** leading to a better plan, while the same **RECOMPILE** on the first query leads to the original plan.

```
DECLARE @PersonId INT
SET @PersonId = 277
SELECT    [soh].[SalesOrderNumber],
          [soh].[OrderDate],
          [soh].[SubTotal],
          [soh].[TotalDue]
FROM      [Sales].[SalesOrderHeader] soh
WHERE     [soh].[SalesPersonID] = @PersonId
OPTION  ( RECOMPILE )

SET @PersonId = 288
SELECT    [soh].[SalesOrderNumber],
          [soh].[OrderDate],
          [soh].[SubTotal],
          [soh].[TotalDue]
FROM      [Sales].[SalesOrderHeader] soh
WHERE     [soh].[SalesPersonID] = @PersonId
```

```
OPTION  ( RECOMPILE )
```

This results in the following mismatched set of query plans:

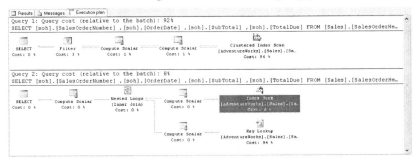

Figure 22

Note that the second query is now using our **IX_SalesOrderHeader_SalesPersonID** index and accounts for 8% of the combined cost of both queries, instead of 50%. This is because the **Index Seek** and **Key Lookup** operators with the **Nested Loop** are faster and less costly than the Clustered Index Scan since they will only work with a subset of the rows.

ROBUST PLAN

This hint is used when you need to work with very wide rows. For example:

1. A row that contains one or more variable length columns set to very large size or even the MAX size allowed in 2005

2. A row that contains one or more large objects (LOB) such as **BINARY**, **XML** or **TEXT** data types.

Sometimes, when processing these rows, it's possible for some operators to encounter errors, usually when creating worktables as part of the plan. The **ROBUST PLAN** hint ensures that a plan that could cause errors won't be chosen by the optimizer. While this will eliminate errors, it will almost certainly result in longer query times since the optimizer won't be able to choose the optimal plan over the "robust" plan. This is a very rare event so this hint should only be used if you actually have a set of wide rows that cause the error condition.

KEEP PLAN

As the data in a table changes, gets inserted or deleted, the statistics describing the data also change. As these statistics change, queries get marked for recompile. Setting the **KEEP PLAN** hint doesn't prevent recompiles, but it does cause the optimizer to use less stringent rules when determining the need for a recompile. This means that, with more volatile data, you can keep recompiles to a minimum. The hint causes the optimizer to treat temporary tables within the plan in the same way as permanent tables, reducing the number of recompiles caused by the temp table. This reduces the time and cost of recompiling a plan, which, depending on the query, can be quite large.

However, problems may arise because the old plans might not be as efficient as newer plans could be.

KEEPFIXED PLAN

The **KEEPFIXED PLAN** query hint is similar to **KEEP PLAN**, but instead of simply limiting the number of recompiles, **KEEPFIXED PLAN** eliminates any recompile due to changes in statistics.

Use this hint with extreme caution. The whole point of letting SQL Server maintain statistics is to aid the performance of your queries. If you prevent these changed statistics from being used by optimizer, it can lead to severe performance issues.

As with **KEEP PLAN**, this will keep the plan in place unless the schema of the tables referenced in the query changes or **sp_recompile** is run against the query, forcing a recompile.

EXPAND VIEWS

Your users come to you with a complaint. One of the queries they're running isn't returning correct data. Checking the execution plan you find that the query is running against a materialized, or indexed, view. While the performance is excellent, the view itself is only updated once a day. Over the day the data referenced by the view ages, or changes, within the table where it is actually stored. Several queries that use the view are not affected by this aging data, so changing the refresh times for the view isn't necessary. Instead, you decide that you'd like to get directly at the data, but without completely rewriting the query.

The **EXPAND VIEWS** query hint eliminates the use of the index views within a query and forces the optimizer to go to the tables for the data. The optimizer replaces the indexed view being referenced with the view definition (in other words, the query used to define the view) just like it normally does with a view. This behavior can be overridden on a view-by-view basis by adding the **WITH (NOEXPAND)** clause to any indexed views within the query.

In some instances, the indexed view performs worse than the view definition. In most cases, the reverse is true. However, if the data in the indexed view is not up to date, this hint can address that issue, usually at the cost of performance. Test this hint to ensure its use doesn't negatively impact performance.

Using one of the indexed views supplied with AdventureWorks, we can run this simple query:

```
SELECT  *
FROM    [Person].[vStateProvinceCountryRegion]
```

Figure 23 shows the resulting execution plan:

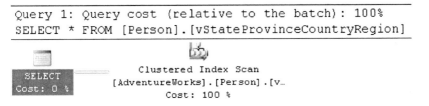

Figure 23

An indexed view is simply a clustered index, so this execution plan makes perfect sense. If we add the query hint, **OPTION (EXPAND VIEWS)**, things change as we see in Figure 24:

Figure 24

Now we're no longer scanning the clustered index. Within the Optimizer, the view has been expanded into its definition so we see the **Clustered Index Scan** against the **Person.CountryRegion** and **Person.StateProvince** tables. These are then joined using the **Merge Join**, after the data in the **StateProvince** stream is run through a **Sort** operation. The first query has a cost estimate of .004221 as opposed to the expanded view which is estimated to cost .02848, but the data being referenced is straight from the source tables as opposed to be pulled from the clustered index that defines the materialized view.

MAXRECURSION

With the addition of the Common Table Expression to SQL Server, a very simple method for calling recursive queries was created. The **MAXRECURSION** hint places an upper limit on the number of recursions within a query.

Valid values are between 0 and 32,767. Setting the value to zero allows for infinite recursion. The default number of recursions is 100. When the number is reached, an error is returned and the recursive loop is exited. This will cause any open transactions to be rolled back. Using the option doesn't change the execution plan but, because of the error, an actual execution plan might not be returned.

USE PLAN

This hint simply substitutes any plan the optimizer may have created with the XML plan supplied with the hint. This is covered in great detail in Chapter 8.

Join Hints

A **join hint** provides a means to force SQL Server to use one of the three join methods that we've encountered previously, in a given part of a query. To recap, these join methods are:

- **Nested Loop join**: compares each row from one table ("outer table") to each row in another table ("inner table") and returns rows that satisfy the join predicate. Cost is proportional to the product of the rows in the two tables. Very efficient for smaller data sets.
- **Merge join**: compares two **sorted** inputs, one row at a time. Cost is proportional to the sum of the total number of rows. Requires an equi-join condition. Efficient for larger data sets
- **Hash Match join**: reads rows from one input, hashes the rows, based on the equi-join condition, into an in-memory hash table. Does the same for the second input and then returns matching rows. Most useful for very large data sets (especially data warehouses)

By incuding one of the join hints in your T-SQL you will potentially override the optimizer's choice of the most efficent join method. In general, this is not a good idea and if you're not careful you could seriously impede performance[12].

Application of the join hint applies to any query (select, insert, or delete) where joins can be applied. Join hints are specified between two tables.

Consider a simple report that lists Product Models, Products and Illustrations from Adventure works:

```
SELECT    [pm].[Name],
          [pm].[CatalogDescription],
          p.[Name] AS ProductName,
          i.[Diagram]
FROM      [Production].[ProductModel] pm
          LEFT JOIN [Production].[Product] p
          ON [pm].[ProductModelID] = [p].[ProductModelID]
          LEFT JOIN [Production].[ProductModelIllustration]
                    pmi
          ON [pm].[ProductModelID] = [pmi].[ProductModelID]
          LEFT JOIN [Production].[Illustration] i
          ON [pmi].[IllustrationID] = [i].[IllustrationID]
WHERE     [pm].[Name] LIKE '%Mountain%'
ORDER BY [pm].[Name] ;
```

We'll get the following execution plan:

---

[12] There is a fourth join method, the Remote join, that is used when dealing with data from a remote server. It forces the join operation from your local machine onto the remote server. This has no affects on execution plans, so we won't be drilling down on this functionality here.

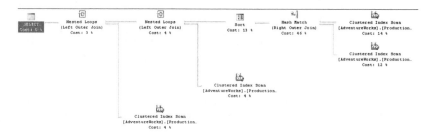

Figure 25

This is a fairly straightforward plan. The presence of the **WHERE** clause using the **LIKE '%Mountain%'** condition means that there won't be any seek on an index; and so the Clustered Index Scan operators on the **Product** and **ProductModel** table make sense. They're then joined using a **Hash Match** operator, encompassing 46% of the cost of the query. Once the data is joined, the **ORDER BY** command is implemented by the **Sort** operator. The plan continues with the **Clustered Index Scan** against the **ProductModelIllustration** table that joins to the data stream with a Loop operator. This is repeated with another Clustered Index Scan against the **Illustration** table and a join to the data stream with a Loop operator. The total estimated cost for these operations comes to 0.09407.

What happens if we decide that we're smarter than the optimizer and that it really should be using a Nested Loop join instead of that Hash Match join? We can force the issue by adding the **LOOP** hint to the join condition between **Product** and **ProductModel**:

```
SELECT    [pm].[Name],
          [pm].[CatalogDescription],
          p.[Name] AS ProductName,
          i.[Diagram]
FROM      [Production].[ProductModel] pm
          LEFT LOOP JOIN [Production].[Product] p
          ON [pm].[ProductModelID] = [p].[ProductModelID]
          LEFT JOIN [Production].[ProductModelIllustration]
                  pmi
          ON [pm].[ProductModelID] = [pmi].[ProductModelID]
          LEFT JOIN [Production].[Illustration] i
          ON [pmi].[IllustrationID] = [i].[IllustrationID]
WHERE     [pm].[Name] LIKE '%Mountain%'
ORDER BY [pm].[Name] ;
```

If we execute this new query, we'll see the following plan:

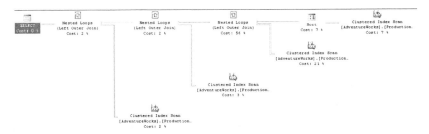

Figure 26

Sure enough, where previously we saw a Hash Match operator, we now see the Nested Loop operator. Also, the sort moved before the join in order to feed ordered data into the Loop operation, which means that the original data is sorted instead of the joined data. This adds to the overall cost. Also, note that the Nested Loop join accounts for 56% of the cost, whereas the original Hash Match accounted for only 46%. All this resulted in a total, higher cost of 0.16234.

If you replace the previous **LOOP** hint with the **MERGE** hint, you'll see the following plan:

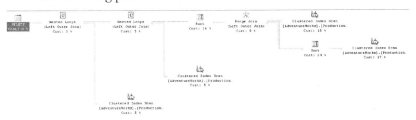

Figure 27

The Nested Loop becomes a Merge Join operator and the overall cost of the plan drops to 0.07647, apparently offering us a performance benefit.

The Merge Join plus the Sort operator, which is required to make sure it uses ordered data, turns out to cost less than the Hash Match or the Nested Loop.

In order to verify the possibility of a performance increase, we can change the query options so that it shows us the I/O costs of each query. The output of all three queries is listed, in part, here:

```
Original (Hash)
Table 'Illustration'. Scan count 1, logical reads 273
Table 'ProductModelIllustration'. Scan count 1, logical
      reads 183
Table 'Worktable'. Scan count 0, logical reads 0
Table 'ProductModel'. Scan count 1, logical reads 14
Table 'Product'. Scan count 1, logical reads 15
```

```
       Loop
Table 'Illustration'. Scan count 1, logical reads 273
Table 'ProductModelIllustration'. Scan count 1, logical
       reads 183
Table 'Product'. Scan count 1, logical reads 555
Table 'ProductModel'. Scan count 1, logical reads 14
       Merge
Table 'Illustration'. Scan count 1, logical reads 273
Table 'ProductModelIllustration'. Scan count 1, logical
       reads 183
Table 'Product'. Scan count 1, logical reads 15
Table 'ProductModel'. Scan count 1, logical reads 14
```

This shows us that the Merge and Loop joins required almost exactly the same number of reads to arrive at the data set needed as the original Hash join. The differences come when we see that, in order to support the Loop join, 555 reads were required instead of 15 for both the Merge and Hash joins. The other difference, probably the clincher in this case, is the work table that the Hash creates to support the query. This was eliminated with the Merge join. This illustrates the point that the optimizer does not always choose an optimal plan. Based on the statistics in the index and the amount of time it had to calculate its results, it must have decided that the Hash join would perform faster. In fact, as the data changes within the tables, it's possible that the Merge join will cease to function better over time, but because we've hard coded the join, no new plan will be generated by the optimizer as the data changes, as would normally be the case.

Table Hints

Table hints enable you to specifically control how the optimizer "uses" a particular table when generating an execution plan. For example, you can force the use of a table scan, or specify a particular index that you want used on that table.

As with the query and join hints, using a table hint circumvents the normal optimizer processes and could lead to serious performance issues. Further, since table hints can affect locking strategies, they possibly affect data integrity leading to incorrect or lost data. These must be used judiciously.

Some of the table hints are primarily concerned with locking strategies. Since some of these don't affect execution plans, we won't be covering them. The three table hints covered below have a direct impact on the execution plans. For a full list of table hints, please refer to the Books Online supplied with SQL Server 2005.

Table Hint Syntax

The correct syntax in SQL Server 2005 is to use the **WITH** keyword and list the hints within a set of parenthesis like this:

```
FROM TableName WITH (hint, hint,…)
```

The **WITH** keyword is not required in all cases, nor are the commas required in all cases, but rather than attempt to guess or remember which hints are the exceptions, all hints can be placed within the **WITH** clause and separated by commas as a best practice to ensure consistent behavior and future compatibility. Even with the hints that don't require the **WITH** keyword, it must be supplied if more than one hint is to be applied to a given table.

NOEXPAND

When multiple indexed views are referenced within the query, use of the **NOEXPAND** table hint will override the **EXPAND VIEWS** query hint and prevent the indexed view to which the table hint applies from being "expanded" into its underlying view definition. This allows for a more granular control over which of the indexed views is forced to resolve to its base tables and which simply pull their data from the clustered index that defines it.

SQL 2005 Enterprise and Developer editions will use the indexes in an indexed view if the optimizer determines that index will be best for the query. This is called indexed view matching. It requires the following settings for the connection:

- ANSI_NULL set to on
- ANSI_WARNINGS set to on
- CONCAT_NULL_YIELDS_NULL set to on
- ANSI_PADDING set to on
- ARITHABORT set to on
- QUOTED_IDENTIFIERS set to on
- NUMERIC_ROUNDABORT set to off

Using the **NOEXPAND** hint can force the optimizer to use the index from the indexed view. In Chapter 4, we used a query that referenced one of the Indexed Views, **vStateProvinceCountryRegion,** in AdventureWorks. The optimizer expanded the view and we saw an execution plan that featured a 3-table join. We change that behavior using the **NOEXPAND** hint

```
SELECT   a.[City],
         v.[StateProvinceName],
         v.[CountryRegionName]
FROM     [Person].[Address] a
         JOIN [Person].[vStateProvinceCountryRegion] v WITH (
NOEXPAND )
         ON [a].[StateProvinceID] = [v].[StateProvinceID]
WHERE    [a].[AddressID] = 22701 ;
Now, instead of a 3- table join, we get the following
execution plan:
```

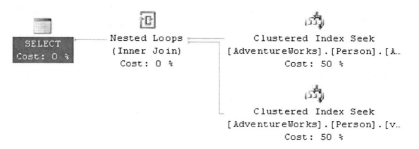

Figure 28

Now, not only are we using the clustered index defined on the view, but we're seeing a performance increase, with the estimated cost decreasing from .00985 to .00657.

INDEX()

The **index()** table hint allows you to define the index to be used when accessing the table. The syntax supports either numbering the index, starting at 0 with the clustered index, if any, and proceeding one at a time through the rest of the indexes:

```
FROM TableName WITH (INDEX(0))
```

However, I recommend that you simply refer to the index by name because the order in which indexes are applied to a table can change (although the clustered index will always be 0):

```
FROM TableName WITH (INDEX ([IndexName]))
```

You can only have a single index hint for a given table, but you can define multiple indexes within that one hint.

Let's take a simple query that lists Department Name, Title and Employee Name:

```
SELECT   [de].[Name],
         [e].[Title],
         [c].[LastName] + ', ' + [c].[FirstName]
FROM     [HumanResources].[Department] de
         JOIN [HumanResources].[EmployeeDepartmentHistory]
edh
         ON [de].[DepartmentID] = [edh].[DepartmentID]
         JOIN [HumanResources].[Employee] e
         ON [edh].[EmployeeID] = [e].[EmployeeID]
         JOIN [Person].[Contact] c
         ON [e].[ContactID] = [c].[ContactID]
WHERE    [de].[Name] LIKE 'P%'
```

We get a standard execution plan:

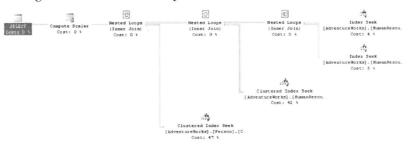

Figure 29

We see a series of Index Seek and Cluster Index Seek operations joined together by Nested Loop operations. Suppose we're convinced that we can get better performance if we could eliminate the Index Seek on the **HumanResources.Department** table and instead use that table's clustered index, **PK_Department_DepartmentID**. We could accomplish this using the **INDEX** hint, as follows:

```
SELECT   [de].[Name],
         [e].[Title],
         [c].[LastName] + ', ' + [c].[FirstName]
FROM     [HumanResources].[Department] de
         WITH ( INDEX ( PK_Department_DepartmentID ) )
         JOIN [HumanResources].[EmployeeDepartmentHistory]
             edh
         ON [de].[DepartmentID] = [edh].[DepartmentID]
         JOIN [HumanResources].[Employee] e
         ON [edh].[EmployeeID] = [e].[EmployeeID]
```

```
                JOIN [Person].[Contact] c
                ON [e].[ContactID] = [c].[ContactID]
    WHERE       [de].[Name] LIKE 'P%'
```

This results in the following execution plan:

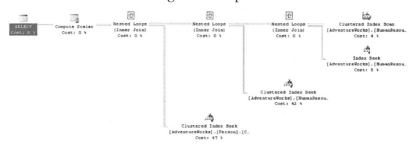

Figure 30

We can see the **Clustered Index Scan** in place of the **Index Seek**. This change causes a marginally more expensive query, with the cost coming in at 0.0739643 as opposed to 0.0739389. While the index seek is certainly faster than the scan, the difference at this time is small because the scan is only hitting a few more rows than the seek, in such a small table. However, using the clustered index didn't improve the performance of the query as we originally surmised because the query used it within a scan instead of the more efficient seek operation.

FASTFIRSTROW

Just like the FAST n query hint, outlined above, **FASTFIRSTROW** forces the optimizer to choose a plan that will return the first row as fast as possible for the table in question. Functionally, **FASTFIRSTROW** is equivalent to the FAST n query hint, but it is more granular in its application.

Microsoft recommends against using **FASTFIRSTROW** as it may be removed in future versions of SQL Server. Nevertheless, we'll provide a simple example. The following query is meant to get a summation of the available inventory by product model name and product name:

```
    SELECT  [pm].[Name] AS ProductModelName,
            [p].[Name] AS ProductName,
            SUM([pin].[Quantity])
    FROM    [Production].[ProductModel] pm
            JOIN [Production].[Product] p
            ON [pm].[ProductModelID] = [p].[ProductModelID]
            JOIN [Production].[ProductInventory] pin
            ON [p].[ProductID] = [pin].[ProductID]
```

```
GROUP BY [pm].[Name],
         [p].[Name] ;
```

It results in this execution plan:

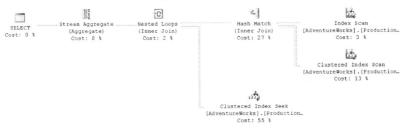

Figure 31

As you can see, an **Index Scan** operation against the **ProductModel** database returns the first stream of data. This is joined against a **Clustered Index Scan** operation from the **Product** table, through a **Hash Match** operator. The data from the **ProductInventory** table can be retrieved through a **Clustered Index Seek** and this is then joined to the other data through a **Nested Loop**. Finally, the summation information is built through a **Stream Aggregate** operator.

If we decided that we thought that getting the Product information a bit quicker might make a difference in the behavior of the query we could add the table hint, only to that table:

```
SELECT    [pm].[Name] AS ProductModelName,
          [p].[Name] AS ProductName,
          SUM([pin].[Quantity])
FROM      [Production].[ProductModel] pm
          JOIN [Production].[Product] p WITH ( FASTFIRSTROW )
          ON [pm].[ProductModelID] = [p].[ProductModelID]
          JOIN [Production].[ProductInventory] pin
          ON [p].[ProductID] = [pin].[ProductID]
GROUP BY [pm].[Name],
         [p].[Name]
```

This gives us the following execution plan:

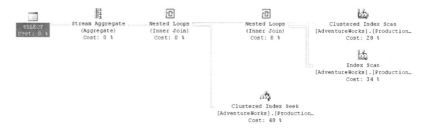

Figure 32

This makes the optimizer choose a different path through the data. Instead of hitting the **ProductModel** table first, it's now collecting the **Product** information first. This is being passed to a **Nested Loop** operator that will loop through the smaller set of rows from the **Product** table and compare them to the larger data set from the **ProductModel** table.

The rest of the plan is the same. The net result is that, rather than building the worktable to support the hash match join, most of the work occurs in accessing the data through the index scans and seeks, with cheap nested loop joins replacing the hash joins. The cost estimate decreases from .101607 in the original query to .011989 in the second.

One thing to keep in mind, though, is that while the performance win seems worth it in this query, it comes at the cost of a change in the scans against the **ProductModel** table. Instead of one scan and two reads, the second query has 504 scans and 1008 reads against the **ProductModel** table. This appears to be less costly than creating the worktable, but you need to remember these tests are being run against a server in isolation. I'm running no other database applications or queries against my system at this time. That kind of additional I/O could cause this process, which does currently run faster ~130ms vs. ~200ms, to slow down significantly.

Summary

While the Optimizer makes very good decisions most of the time, at times it may make less than optimal choices. Taking control of the queries using Table, Join and Query hints where appropriate can be the right choice. Remember that the data in your database is constantly changing. Any choices you force on the Optimizer through these hints today to achieve whatever improvement you're hoping for may become a major pain in your future. Test the hints prior to applying them and remember to document their use in some manner so that you can come back and test them again periodically as your database grows. As

Microsoft releases patches and service packs, behavior of the optimizer can change. Be sure to retest any queries using hints after an upgrade to your server. I intentionally found about as many instances where the query hints would help and where the query hints hurt to put the point across; use of these hints should be considered as a last resort, not a standard method of operation.

CHAPTER 6: CURSOR OPERATIONS

Most operations within a SQL Server database should be set-based rather than use the procedural, row-by-row processing embodied by cursors. However, there may still be occasions when a cursor is the more appropriate or more expedient way to resolve a problem. Certainly, most query processing for application behavior, reporting and other uses, will be best solved by concentrating on set-based solutions. However, certain maintenance routines will be more easily implemented using cursors (although even these may need to be set based in order to reduce the maintenance footprint in a production system).

There are a specific set of operators that describe the effects of the operations of a cursor, within execution plans. The operators, similar to those for data manipulation, are split between logical (or estimated) and physical (or actual) operators. In the case of the data manipulation operators, these represented the possible path and the actual path through the query, respectively. For cursors, there are bigger differences between the logical and physical operators. The logical operators give more information about the actions that will occur while the cursor is created, opened, fetched, closed and de-allocated. The physical operators show the functions that are part of the actual execution.

As with all the previous execution plans, the plans for cursors can be output as text, graphically or as XML through the appropriate methods for displaying each of these types of execution plans. This chapter will use only graphical plans and will describe all of the operators that represent the action of cursors, in these plans.

Simple Cursors

In this example, the cursor is declared with no options, accepting all defaults, and then it is traversed straight through using the **FETCH NEXT** method, returning a list of all the CurrencyCodes used in the AdventureWorks database. I'm going to continue working with the same basic query throughout the section on cursors because it returns a small number of rows and because we can easily see how changes to cursor properties affect the execution plans.

```
DECLARE CurrencyList CURSOR FOR
SELECT CurrencyCode FROM [Sales].[Currency]
WHERE Name LIKE '%Dollar%'
```

```
OPEN CurrencyList

FETCH NEXT FROM CurrencyList

WHILE @@FETCH_STATUS = 0
BEGIN
        -- Normally there would be operations here using data
from cursor

    FETCH NEXT FROM CurrencyList
END

CLOSE CurrencyList
DEALLOCATE CurrencyList
GO
```

The data is returned as multiple result sets, as pictured below in Figure 1:

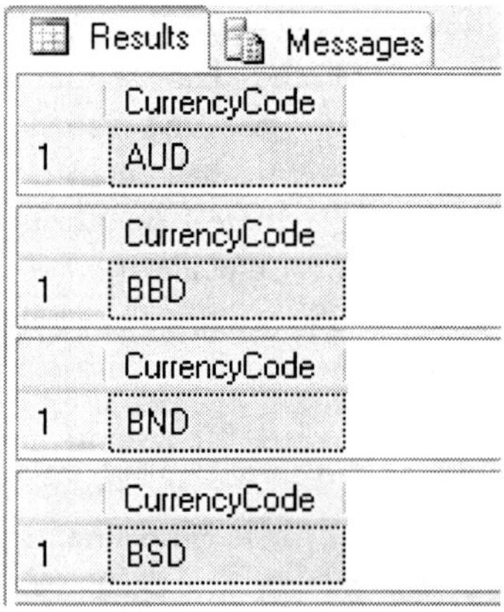

Figure 1

Logical Operators

Use the "Display Estimated Execution Plan" option to generate the graphical estimated execution plan for the above code. The query consists of six distinct statements and therefore six distinct plans, as shown in Figure 2:

Query 1: Query cost (relative to the batch): 100%
--SET STATISTICS XML ON --SET SHOWPLAN_XML ON --GO DECLARE CurrencyList CURSOR FOR SELECT Currer

Dynamic Cost: 0 %	Fetch Query Cost: 0 %	Clustered Index Insert [tempdb].[dbo].[CWT_PrimaryK_ Cost: 75 %	Compute Scalar Cost: 0 %	Clustered Index Scan [AdventureWorks].[Sales].[Cu_ Cost: 25 %

Query 2: Query cost (relative to the batch): 0%
OPEN CurrencyList

OPEN CURSOR
Cost: 0 %

Query 3: Query cost (relative to the batch): 0%
FETCH NEXT FROM CurrencyList

FETCH CURSOR
Cost: 0 %

Query 4: Query cost (relative to the batch): 0%
WHILE @@FETCH_STATUS = 0

COND Cost: 0 %	FETCH CURSOR Cost: 0 %

Query 5: Query cost (relative to the batch): 0%
END CLOSE CurrencyList

CLOSE CURSOR
Cost: 0 %

Query 6: Query cost (relative to the batch): 0%
DEALLOCATE CurrencyList

DEALLOCATE CURSOR
Cost: 0 %

Figure 2

We'll split this plan into it component parts. The top section shows the definition of the cursor:

```
DECLARE CurrencyList CURSOR FOR
SELECT CurrencyCode FROM [Sales].[Currency]
WHERE Name LIKE '%Dollar%'
```

Query 1: Query cost (relative to the batch): 100%
DECLARE CurrencyList CURSOR FOR SELECT CurrencyCode FROM [Sales].[Currency] WHERE Name LIKE '%Dollar%'

Dynamic Cost: 0 %	Fetch Query Cost: 0 %	Clustered Index Insert [tempdb].[dbo].[CWT_PrimaryKey] Cost: 75 %	Compute Scalar Cost: 0 %	Clustered Index Scan [AdventureWorks].[Sales].[Currency]_ Cost: 25 %

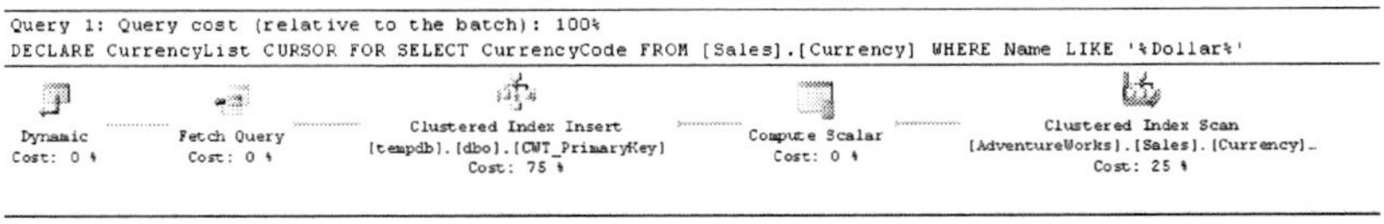

Figure 3

This definition in the header includes the select statement that will provide the data that the cursor uses. This plan contains our first two cursor-specific operators but, as usual, we'll read this execution plan starting on the right. First, we have a Clustered Index Scan against the **Sales.Currency** table.

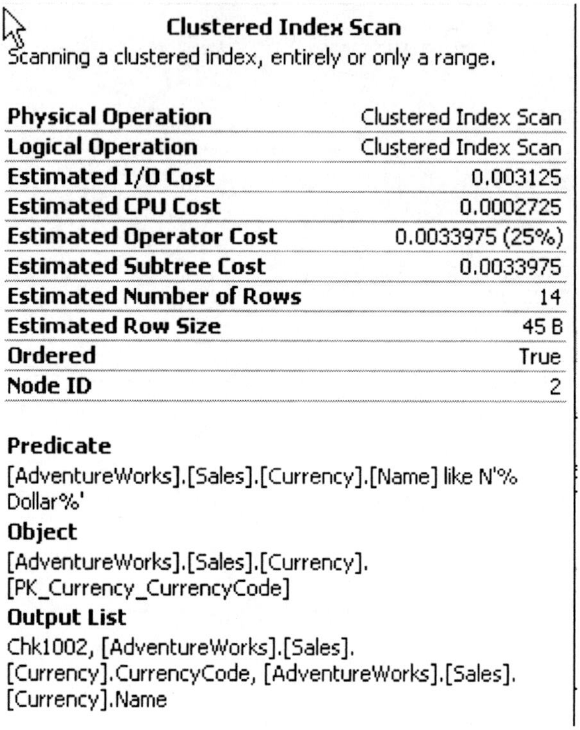

Clustered Index Scan

Scanning a clustered index, entirely or only a range.

Physical Operation	Clustered Index Scan
Logical Operation	Clustered Index Scan
Estimated I/O Cost	0.003125
Estimated CPU Cost	0.0002725
Estimated Operator Cost	0.0033975 (25%)
Estimated Subtree Cost	0.0033975
Estimated Number of Rows	14
Estimated Row Size	45 B
Ordered	True
Node ID	2

Predicate
[AdventureWorks].[Sales].[Currency].[Name] like N'%
Dollar%'
Object
[AdventureWorks].[Sales].[Currency].
[PK_Currency_CurrencyCode]
Output List
Chk1002, [AdventureWorks].[Sales].
[Currency].CurrencyCode, [AdventureWorks].[Sales].
[Currency].Name

Figure 4

The clustered index scan retrieves an estimated 14 rows. This is
followed by the Compute Scalar operator, which creates a unique
identifier to identify the data returned by the query, independent of any
unique keys on the table or tables from which the data was selected (see
Figure 5, below).

Compute Scalar

Compute new values from existing values in a row.

Physical Operation	Compute Scalar
Logical Operation	Compute Scalar
Estimated I/O Cost	0
Estimated CPU Cost	0.0000014
Estimated Operator Cost	0.0000203 (0%)
Estimated Subtree Cost	0.0034178
Estimated Number of Rows	14
Estimated Row Size	21 B
Node ID	1

Output List

Chk1002, [AdventureWorks].[Sales].
[Currency].CurrencyCode, Expr1005

Figure 5

With a new key value, these rows are then inserted into a temporary clustered index, created in tempdb. This clustered index is the mechanism by which the server is able to walk through a set of data as a cursor (Figure 5, below). It's commonly referred to as a "work table".

Clustered Index Insert

Insert rows in a clustered index.

Physical Operation	Clustered Index Insert
Logical Operation	Insert
Estimated I/O Cost	0.01
Estimated CPU Cost	0.000014
Estimated Operator Cost	0.010014 (75%)
Estimated Subtree Cost	0.0134318
Estimated Number of Rows	14
Estimated Row Size	17 B
Node ID	0

Object
[tempdb].[dbo].[CWT_PrimaryKey]
Output List
[AdventureWorks].[Sales].[Currency].CurrencyCode,
Expr1005
Predicate
[CWT].[COLUMN0] = [AdventureWorks].[Sales].
[Currency].[CurrencyCode],[CWT].[CHECKSUM1] =
[Chk1002],[CWT].[ROWID] = [Expr1005]

Figure 6

After that, we get our first cursor operation.

Fetch Query

The Fetch Query operation is the one that actually retrieves the rows from the cursor, the clustered index created above, when the FETCH command is issued. The ToolTip displays the following, familiar information (which doesn't provide much that's immediately useful):

Fetch Query	
The query used to retrieve rows when a fetch is issued against a cursor.	
Cached plan size	16 B
Estimated Operator Cost	0 (0%)
Estimated Subtree Cost	0.0134318

Figure 7

Finally, instead of yet another Select Operator, we finish with a Dynamic operator.

Dynamic

The Dynamic operator contains the definition of the cursor itself; in this case, the default cursor type is a dynamic cursor, which means that it sees data changes made by others to the underlying data, including inserts, as they occur. This means that the data within the cursor can change over the life of the cursor. The ToolTip, this time, shows some slightly different, more detailed and useful information:

Dynamic
Cursor that can see all changes made by others.

Estimated Operator Cost	0 (0%)
Estimated Subtree Cost	0.0134318

Statement
DECLARE CurrencyList CURSOR FOR
SELECT CurrencyCode FROM [Sales].
[Currency]
WHERE Name LIKE '%Dollar%'

Figure 8

Unlike the DML queries before, we see a view of the direct TSQL that defined the cursor, rather than the SQL statement after it had been bound by the optimization process.

Cursor Catchall

The next five sections of our original execution plan, from Figure 2, all feature a generic icon known as the **Cursor Catchall**. In general, a catch-all icon is used for operations that Microsoft determined didn't need their own special graphic.

In Query 2 and Query 3 we see catchall icons for the **OPEN CURSOR** operation, and the **FETCH CURSOR** operation:

```
OPEN CurrencyList

FETCH NEXT FROM CurrencyList
```

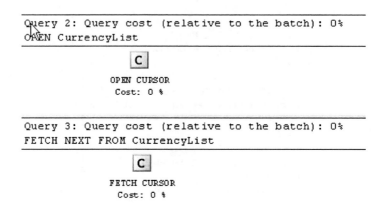

Query 2: Query cost (relative to the batch): 0%
OPEN CurrencyList

OPEN CURSOR
Cost: 0 %

Query 3: Query cost (relative to the batch): 0%
FETCH NEXT FROM CurrencyList

FETCH CURSOR
Cost: 0 %

Figure 9

Query 4 shows the next time within the T-SQL that the **FETCH CURSOR** command was used, and it shows a language element icon, for the **WHILE** loop, as a **COND** or conditional operator.

```
WHILE @@FETCH_STATUS = 0
BEGIN
    --Normally there would be operations here using data from
cursor
    FETCH NEXT FROM CurrencyList
END
```

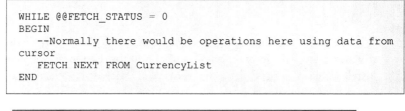

Query 4: Query cost (relative to the batch): 0%
WHILE @@FETCH_STATUS = 0

COND   FETCH CURSOR
Cost: 0 %   Cost: 0 %

Figure 10

Finally, Query 5 closes the cursor and Query 6 deallocates it, removing the cursor from the tempdb.

```
CLOSE CurrencyList
DEALLOCATE CurrencyList
```

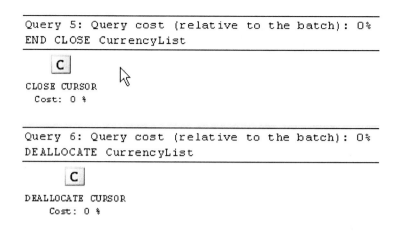

```
Query 5: Query cost (relative to the batch): 0%
END CLOSE CurrencyList
```

```
CLOSE CURSOR
  Cost: 0 %
```

```
Query 6: Query cost (relative to the batch): 0%
DEALLOCATE CurrencyList
```

```
DEALLOCATE CURSOR
    Cost: 0 %
```

Figure 11

Physical Operators

When we execute the same script, using the "Display Graphical Execution Plan" option, the actual execution plan doesn't mirror the estimated plan. Instead we see the following:

Figure 12

This simple plan is repeated fifteen times, once for each row of data added to the cursor (note the slight discrepancy between the actual number of rows, fifteen, and the estimated fourteen rows you'll see in the ToolTip).

One interesting thing to note is that there are no cursor icons present in the plan. Instead, the one cursor command immediately visible, **FETCH CURSOR**, is represented by the generic T-SQL operator icon. This is because all the physical operations that occur with a cursor are represented by the actual operations being performed, and the **FETCH** is roughly equivalent to the **SELECT** statement.

Hopefully, this execution plan demonstrates why a dynamic cursor may be costly to the system. It's performing a clustered index insert, as well as the reads necessary to return the data to the cursor, as each of the fifteen separate **FETCH** statements are called. The same query, outside a cursor, would return a very simple, one-step execution plan:

SELECT
Cost: 0 %

Index Scan
[AdventureWorks].[Sales].[Currency]...
Cost: 100 %

Figure 13

More Cursor Operations

Changing the settings and operations of the cursor results in differences in the plans generated. We've already seen the dynamic cursor; next we'll take a look at the other three cursor types.

STATIC Cursor

Unlike the Dynamic cursor, outlined above, the Static cursor is a temporary copy of the data, created when the cursor is called. This means that it doesn't get underlying changes to the data over the life of the cursor. To see this in action, change the cursor declaration as follows:

```
DECLARE CurrencyList CURSOR STATIC FOR
```

Logical Operators

Now generate an estimated execution plan. You should see six distinct plans again. Figure 14 shows the plan for the first query, which represents the cursor definition. The remaining queries in the estimated plan look just like the Dynamic query in Figure 2.

Figure 14

Starting at the top right, as usual, we see an **Index Scan** to get the data out of the **Sales.Currency** table. Data from here is passed to the **Segment** operator. The Segment operator divides the input into segments, based on a particular column, or columns. In this case, as you can see in the ToolTip, it's based on a derived column called **Segment1006**. The derived column splits the data up in order to pass it to the next operation, which will assign the unique key.

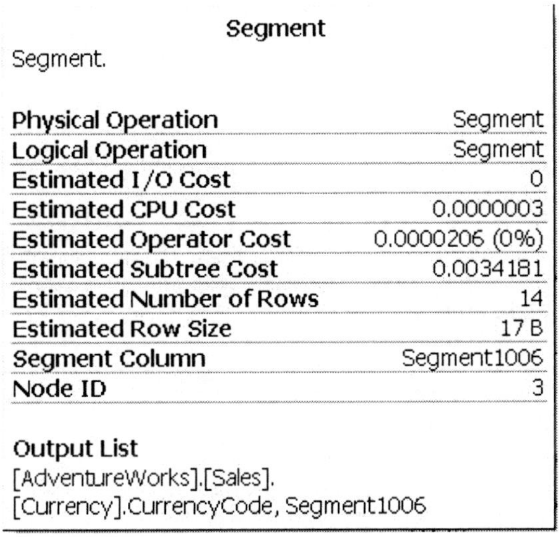

Segment	
Segment.	
Physical Operation	Segment
Logical Operation	Segment
Estimated I/O Cost	0
Estimated CPU Cost	0.0000003
Estimated Operator Cost	0.0000206 (0%)
Estimated Subtree Cost	0.0034181
Estimated Number of Rows	14
Estimated Row Size	17 B
Segment Column	Segment1006
Node ID	3
Output List	
[AdventureWorks].[Sales].	
[Currency].CurrencyCode, Segment1006	

Figure 15

Cursors require work tables and to make these tables efficient, SQL Server creates them as a clustered index with a unique key. This time, in the Static cursor, it generates the key after the segments are defined. The segments are passed on to the Compute Scalar operator, which adds a string valued "1" for the next operation, **Sequence Project**. This logical operator represents a physical task that results in a Compute Scalar operation. It's adding a new column as part of computations across the set of data. In this case, it's creating row numbers through an internal function called **i4_row_number**. These row numbers are used as the identifiers within the clustered index.

Sequence Project

Adds columns to perform computations over an ordered set.

Physical Operation	Sequence Project
Logical Operation	Compute Scalar
Estimated I/O Cost	0
Estimated CPU Cost	0.0000014
Estimated Operator Cost	0 (0%)
Estimated Subtree Cost	0.0034178
Estimated Number of Rows	14
Estimated Row Size	17 B
Node ID	1

Output List
[AdventureWorks].[Sales].
[Currency].CurrencyCode, Expr1005

Figure 16

The data, along with the new identifiers, is then passed to the Clustered Index Insert operator and then on to the Population Query cursor operator.

Population Query

The Population Query cursor operator "populates the work table for a cursor when the cursor is opened" or in other words, from a logical stand-point, this is when the data that has been marshaled by all the other operations is loaded into the work table (the clustered index).

The Fetch Query operation retrieves the rows from the cursor via an index seek on our tembdb index. Notice that, in this case, the Fetch Query operation is defined in a separate sequence, independent from the Population Query. This is because this cursor is static, meaning that it doesn't update itself as the underlying data updates, again, unlike the dynamic cursor which reads its data each time it's accessed.

Snapshot

Finally, we see the **Snapshot** cursor operator, representing a cursor that does not see changes made to the data by others.

Clearly, with a single insert operation and then a simple clustered index seek to retrieve the data, this cursor will operate much faster than the dynamic cursor we were provided by default. The Index Seek and the Fetch operations show how the data will be retrieved from the cursor.

Physical Operators

If we execute the query and display the Actual Execution plan, we get two distinct plans. The first plan is the query that loads the data into the cursor work table, as represented by the clustered index. The second plan is repeated and we see a series of plans identical to the one shown for Query 2 below, which demonstrate how the cursor is looped through by the **WHILE** statement.

Figure 10

These execution plans accurately reflect what the estimated plan intended. Note that the cursor was loaded when the **OPEN CURSOR** statement was called. We can even look at the Clustered Index Seek operator to see it using the row identifier created during the population of the cursor.

Clustered Index Seek

Scanning a particular range of rows from a clustered index.

Physical Operation	Clustered Index Seek
Logical Operation	Clustered Index Seek
Actual Number of Rows	1
Estimated I/O Cost	0.003125
Estimated CPU Cost	0.0001581
Estimated Operator Cost	0.0032831 (100%)
Estimated Subtree Cost	0.0032831
Estimated Number of Rows	1
Estimated Row Size	17 B
Actual Rebinds	0
Actual Rewinds	0
Ordered	True
Node ID	0

Object
[tempdb].[dbo].[CWT_PrimaryKey]
Output List
[CWT].COLUMN0, [CWT].ROWID
Seek Predicates
Prefix: [CWT].ROWID = Scalar Operator
(FETCH_RANGE((0)))

Figure 11

KEYSET Cursor

The dynamic cursor, our first example, retrieves data every time a **FETCH** statement is issued against the cursor, moving through the data within the cursor in any direction, so that it can "dynamically" retrieve changes to the data as well as account for inserts and deletes. The static cursor, as described above, simply retrieves the data set needed by the cursor a single time.

The Keyset cursor retrieves a defined set of keys as the data defined within the cursor, but it allows for the fact that data may be updated during the life of the cursor. This behavior leads to yet another execution plan, different from the previous two examples.

Let's change the cursor definition again:

```
DECLARE CurrencyList CURSOR KEYSET FOR
```

Logical Operators

The estimated execution plan should look as shown in Figure 19:

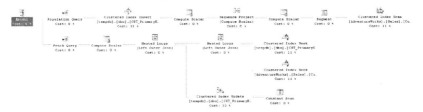

Figure 12

Now that we've worked with cursors a bit, it's easy to recognize the two paths defined in the estimated plan; one for populating the cursor and one for fetching the data from the cursor.

The top line of the plan, containing the Population Query operation, is almost exactly the same as that defined for the Static cursor. The second Scalar operation is added as a status check for the row. It ends with the Keyset cursor operator, indicating that the cursor can see updates, but not inserts.

The major difference is evident in how the Fetch Query works, in order to support the updating of data after the cursor was built. Figure 20 shows that portion of the plan in more detail:

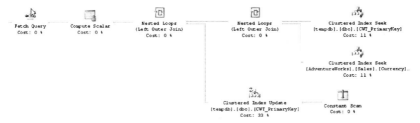

Figure 20

Going to the right and top of the Fetch Query definition, we find that it first retrieves the key from the index created in the Population Query. Then, to retrieve the data, it joins it, through a Nested Loop operation to the **Sales.Currency** table. This is how the KeySet cursor manages to get updated data into the set returned while the cursor is active.

The **Constant Scan** operator scans an internal table of constants. The data from the constant scan feeds into the **Clustered Index Update** operator, in order to be able to change the data stored, if necessary. This data is joined to the first set of data through a Nested Loop operation and finishes with a Compute Scalar representing the row number.

Physical Operators

When the cursor is executed for real, we get the plan shown in Figure 21:

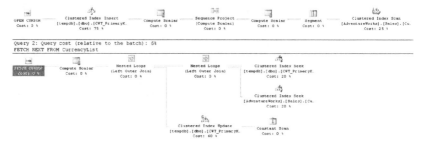

Figure 21

Step one contains the **OPEN CURSOR** operator, and populates the key set exactly as the estimated plan envisioned.

In Query 2, the **FETCH NEXT** statements against the cursor activate the **FETCH CURSOR** operation fifteen times as the cursor walks through the data. While this can be less costly than the dynamic cursors, it's clearly more costly than a static cursor. The performance issues come from the fact that the cursor queries the data twice, once to load the key set and a second time to retrieve the row data. Depending on the number of rows being retrieved into the work table, this can be a costly operation.

READ_ONLY Cursor

Each of the preceding cursors, except for static, allowed the data within the cursor to be updated. If we define the cursor as **READ_ONLY** and run "Display Estimated Execution Plan":

```
DECLARE CurrencyList CURSOR READ_ONLY FOR
```

We sacrifice the ability to capture changes in the data, but we arrive at what is known as a Fast Forward cursor:

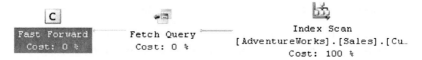

Figure 22

Clearly, this represents the simplest cursor definition plan that we've examined. Unlike for other types of cursor, there is no branch of operations within the estimated plan. It simply reads what it needs directly from the data. In our case, an Index Scan operation against **CurrencyName** index shows how this is accomplished. The amount of I/O, compared to any of the other execution plans, is reduced since there is not a requirement to populate any work tables. Instead there is a single step: get the data. The actual execution plan is identical except that it doesn't have to display the Fast Forward logical operator.

Cursors and Performance

As has been previously noted, execution plans are used in order to understand what is occurring within the query engine and the order in which it's happening. This understanding is most frequently used to improve the performance of queries and cursors are a notorious source of performance bottlenecks.

The following example will show how each of the cursors perform, how you can tweak their performance, and finally how to get rid of the cursor and use a set-based operation that performs better.

In order to satisfy a business requirement, we need a report that lists the number of sales by a particular store, assigning an order to them and then, depending on the amount sold, displays what kind of sale this is considered.

Here's a query, using a dynamic cursor, which might do the trick:

```
DECLARE @WorkTable TABLE
        (
        [DateOrderNumber] INT IDENTITY(1, 1)
        , [Name] VARCHAR(50)
        , [OrderDate] DATETIME
        , [TotalDue] MONEY
        , [SaleType] VARCHAR(50)
        )

DECLARE @DateOrderNumber INT
        , @TotalDue Money

INSERT   INTO @WorkTable
            (
            [Name]
            , [OrderDate]
            , [TotalDue]
            )
        SELECT   s.[Name]
                , soh.[OrderDate]
```

```
                    , soh.[TotalDue]
        FROM      [Sales].[SalesOrderHeader] AS soh
                  JOIN [Sales].[Store] AS s
                      ON soh.[CustomerID] = s.[CustomerID]
        WHERE     soh.[CustomerID] = 17
        ORDER BY soh.[OrderDate]

DECLARE ChangeData CURSOR
    FOR SELECT   [DateOrderNumber]
              ,[TotalDue]
        FROM     @WorkTable

OPEN ChangeData

FETCH NEXT FROM ChangeData INTO @DateOrderNumber, @TotalDue

WHILE @@FETCH_STATUS = 0
    BEGIN
    -- Normally there would be operations here using data
from cursor
        IF @TotalDue < 1000
            UPDATE   @WorkTable
            SET      SaleType = 'Poor'
            WHERE    [DateOrderNumber] = @DateOrderNumber
        ELSE
            IF @TotalDue > 1000
                AND @TotalDue < 10000
                UPDATE   @WorkTable
                SET      SaleType = 'OK'
                WHERE    [DateOrderNumber] = @DateOrderNumber
            ELSE
                IF @TotalDue > 10000
                    AND @TotalDue < 30000
                    UPDATE   @WorkTable
                    SET      SaleType = 'Good'
                    WHERE    [DateOrderNumber] =
@DateOrderNumber
                ELSE
                    UPDATE   @WorkTable
                    SET      SaleType = 'Great'
                    WHERE    [DateOrderNumber] =
@DateOrderNumber
            FETCH NEXT FROM ChangeData INTO @DateOrderNumber,
@TotalDue
    END

CLOSE ChangeData
DEALLOCATE ChangeData

SELECT  *
FROM    @WorkTable
```

Whether or not you've written a query like this, you've certainly seen them. The data returned from the query looks something like this:

Number	Name	OrderDate	TotalDue	SaleType
1	Trusted Catalog Store	2001-07-01	18830.1112	Good

2	Trusted Catalog Store	2001-10-01	13559.0006	Good
3	Trusted Catalog Store	2002-01-01	51251.2959	Great
4	Trusted Catalog Store	2002-04-01	78356.9835	Great
5	Trusted Catalog Store	2002-07-01	9712.8886	OK
6	Trusted Catalog Store	2002-10-01	2184.4578	OK
7	Trusted Catalog Store	2003-01-01	1684.8351	OK
8	Trusted Catalog Store	2003-04-01	1973.4799	OK
9	Trusted Catalog Store	2003-07-01	8897.326	OK
10	Trusted Catalog Store	2003-10-01	10745.818	Good
11	Trusted Catalog Store	2004-01-01	2026.9753	OK
12	Trusted Catalog Store	2004-04-01	702.9363	Poor

The Estimated Execution Plan (not shown here) displays the plan for populating the temporary table, and updating the temporary table, as well as the plan for the execution of the cursor. The cost to execute this script, as a dynamic cursor, includes not only the query against the database tables, **Sales.OrderHeader** and **Sales.Store**, but the insert into the temporary table, all the updates of the temporary table, and the final select from the temporary table. The result is about 27 different scans and about 113 reads.

Let's take a look at a sub-section of the Actual Execution Plan, which shows the fetch from the cursor and one of the updates:

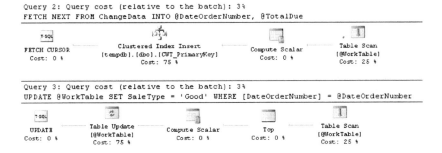

Figure 23

We can see that each of the cycles through the cursor accounts for about 6% of the total cost of the entire script, with the fetch from the cursor accounting for half that cost, repeated for each of the 12 rows.

Focusing on the top of the plan, where we see the cursor performing, we can see that 25% of the cost comes from pulling data from the temporary table. This data is then passed to a Compute Scalar, which assigns a row id value. This data is then inserted into the clustered index that is the cursor and finally the **FETCH CURSOR** operator represents the actual retrieval of the data from the cursor.

To see which cursor might perform better, we'll change this dynamic cursor to a static one by modifying the script slightly:

```
DECLARE ChangeData CURSOR STATIC
```

Now, with the rest of the code the same, let's re-examine the same subsection of the Actual Execution Plan:

```
Query 3: Query cost (relative to the batch): 1%
FETCH NEXT FROM ChangeData INTO @DateOrderNumber, @TotalDue
```

```
T-SQL                                  (.)
FETCH CURSOR            Clustered Index Seek
Cost: 0 %         [tempdb].[dbo].[CWT_PrimaryKey]
                           Cost: 100 %
```

```
Query 4: Query cost (relative to the batch): 5%
UPDATE @WorkTable SET SaleType = 'Good' WHERE [DateOrderNumber] = @DateOrderNumber
```

```
T-SQL          Table Update                                      Table Scan
UPDATE         [@WorkTable]    Compute Scalar      Top           [@WorkTable]
Cost: 0 %      Cost: 75 %      Cost: 0 %       Cost: 0 %         Cost: 25 %
```

Figure 24

Notice that the cursor is now only accounts for 1% of the total cost of the operation, because the Static cursor only has to access what's available, not worry about retrieving it from the table again. However this comes at a cost. The original query ran in approximately 46ms. This new query is running approximately 75ms. The added time comes from loading the static data.

Let's see how the Keyset cursor fairs. Change the script so that the keyset declaration reads:

```
DECLARE ChangeData CURSOR KEYSET
```

This results in the following sub-section of the Actual Execution Plan

```
Query 5: Query cost (relative to the batch): 1%
FETCH NEXT FROM ChangeData INTO @DateOrderNumber, @TotalDue
```

```
T-SQL                                  (.)
FETCH CURSOR            Clustered Index Seek
Cost: 0 %         [tempdb].[dbo].[CWT_PrimaryKey]
                           Cost: 100 %
```

```
Query 6: Query cost (relative to the batch): 5%
UPDATE @WorkTable SET SaleType = 'Good' WHERE [DateOrderNumber] = @DateOrderNumber
```

```
T-SQL          Table Update                                      Table Scan
UPDATE         [@WorkTable]    Compute Scalar      Top           [@WorkTable]
Cost: 0 %      Cost: 75 %      Cost: 0 %       Cost: 0 %         Cost: 25 %
```

Figure 25

Again, the cost relative to the overall cost of the script is only 1%, but unlike the STATIC cursor, the snapshot cursor performs slightly better

(30ms) because this time only the key values are moved into the work table for the cursor.

Let's change the cursor again to see the read only option:

```
DECLARE ChangeData CURSOR READ_ONLY
```

Now, the same sub-section of the plan looks as shown in Figure 26:

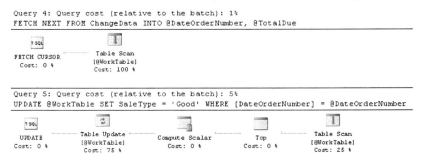

Figure 26

Here again, the **FETCH** from the cursor only accounts for 1% of the overall cost, but the load of the read only cursor takes a bit longer, so this one is back up to about 40ms.

If these tests hold relatively true, then the keyset cursor is the fastest at the moment. Let's see if we can't make it a bit faster. Change the cursor declaration so that it reads like this:

```
DECLARE ChangeData CURSOR FAST_FORWARD
```

This **FORWARD_ONLY** option causes the cursor to only go forward, and to be a **READ_ONLY** cursor. It results in the same physical plan as show above in Figure 26

In many cases, setting the cursor to **FORWARD_ONLY** and **READ_ONLY**, through the **FAST_FORWARD** setting, will result in the fastest performance. However, in this case, it didn't change anything appreciably. Let's see if we have any more luck by making the key set cursor **FORWARD_ONLY**:

```
DECLARE ChangeData CURSOR FORWARD_ONLY KEYSET
```

The resulting execution plan is the same, and the performance isn't really changed. So, short of tuning other parts of the procedure, the simple KEYSET is probably the quickest way to access this data.

However, what if we eliminate the cursor entirely? We can rewrite the script so that it looks like this:

```
SELECT ROW_NUMBER() OVER(ORDER BY soh.[OrderDate])
    , s.[Name]
    , soh.[OrderDate]
    , soh.[TotalDue]
    , CASE
        WHEN soh.[TotalDue] < 1000
        THEN 'Poor'
        HEN soh.[TotalDue] BETWEEN 1000 AND 10000
        THEN 'OK'
        WHEN soh.[TotalDue] BETWEEN 10000 AND 30000
        THEN 'Good'
        ELSE 'Great'
        END AS [SaleType]
    FROM    [Sales].[SalesOrderHeader] AS soh
        JOIN [Sales].[Store] AS s
            ON soh.[CustomerID] = s.[CustomerID]
    WHERE   soh.[CustomerID] = 17
    ORDER BY soh.[OrderDate]
```

This query returns exactly the same data. But the performance is radically different. It performs a single scan on **SalesOrderHeader** table and about 40 reads between the two tables. The execution time is recorded as 0ms, which isn't true, but gives you an indication of how much faster it is than the cursor. Instead of a stack of small execution plans, we have a single step execution plan:

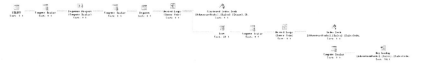

Figure 27

The plan is actually a bit too large to see clearly here but the key take-away is that the main cost for this query is the operator at the lower right. This is a key lookup operation that takes up 54% of the cost. That's a tuning opportunity, as we saw in the previous chapter. Eliminating the lookup will make this query even faster.

This example was fairly simple. The amount of data was relatively small and most of the cursors operated well enough to be within the performance margins of most large scale systems. However, even with all that, it was possible to see differences between the types of cursors and realize a major performance increase with the elimination of the cursor. It shouldn't be too difficult to see how, when working with 12,000 rows instead of 12, the same operations above would be radically costly and just how much changing from cursors to set based operations will save your production systems.

Summary

More often than not, cursors should be avoided in order to take advantage of the set-based nature of T-SQL and SQL Server. Set-based operations just work better. However, when you are faced with the necessity of a cursor, understanding what you're likely to see in the execution plans, estimated and actual, will assist you in using the cursor appropriately.

Don't forget that the estimated plan shows both how the cursor will be created, in the top part of the plan, and how the data in the cursor will be accessed, in the bottom part of the plan. The primary differences between a plan generated from a cursor and one from a set-based operation are in the estimated execution plans. Other than that, as you have seen, reading these plans is really no different than reading the plans from a set-based operation: start at the right and top and work your way to the left.. There are just a lot more plans generated by the nature of how cursors work.

CHAPTER 7: XML IN EXECUTION PLANS

With the advent of SQL Server 2005, XML is playing an ever-greater role in a large numbers of applications, and use of XML, within stored procedures, does impact the execution plans generated.

You can break down XML operations within SQL Server into four broad categories:

- Storing XML - The XML datatype is used to store XML, as well to provide a mechanism for XQuery queries and XML indexes.
- Querying XML documents using XQuery
- Inserting XML into tables - OPENXML accepts XML as a parameter and opens it within a query for storage, or manipulation, as structured data
- Converting relational data to XML - the FOR XML clause can be used to output XML from a query

We will cover the various types of XML output, using the FOR XML commands. Each form of the FOR XML command requires different T-SQL and will result in different execution plans, as well as differences in performance.

You can read XML within SQL Server using either OPENXML or XQuery. OPENXML provides a rowset view of an XML document. We will explore its use via some execution plans for a basic OPENXML query, and will outline some potential performance implications.

XQuery is a huge topic and we will barely scratch its surface in this chapter, merely examining a few simple examples via execution plans. To cover it in any depth at all would require an entire book of its own.

XML can cause performance issues in one of two ways. Firstly, the XML Parser, which is required to manipulate XML, uses memory and CPU cycles that you would normally have available only for T-SQL. In addition, the manner in which you use the XML, input or output, will affect the plans generated by SQL Server and can therefore lead to performance issues.

Secondly, manipulating XML data uses good old fashioned T-SQL statements, and poorly written XML queries can impact performance just as any other query can, and need to be tuned in the same manner as any other in the system.

FOR XML

If you want to output the result of a query in XML format, then you can use the **FOR XML** clause. You can use the FOR XML clause in one of the following four modes:

- **AUTO** – returns results as nested XML elements in a simple hierarchy (think: table = XML element)
- **RAW** – transforms each row in the results into an XML element, with a generic **<row />** identifier as the element tag.
- **EXPLICIT** – allows you to explicitly define the shape of the resulting XML tree, in the query itself
- **PATH** – A simpler alternative to **EXPLICIT** for controlling elements, attributes and the overall shape of the XML tree.

Each of these methods requires a different type of T-SQL in order to arrive at the same type of output. These queries have different performance and maintenance issues associated with them. We will explore all three options and point out where each has strengths and weaknesses.

In our first example, the requirement is to produce a simple list of employees and their addresses. There is no real requirement for any type of direct manipulation of the XML output and the query is simple and straight forward, so we'll use **XML AUTO** mode. Here's the query:

```
SELECT  c.[FirstName],
        c.[LastName],
        c.[EmailAddress],
        c.[Phone],
        e.[EmployeeID],
        e.[Gender],
        a.[AddressLine1],
        a.[AddressLine2],
        a.[City],
        a.[StateProvinceID],
        a.[PostalCode]
FROM    [Person].[Contact] c
        INNER JOIN [HumanResources].[Employee] e
        ON c.[ContactID] = e.[ContactID]
        INNER JOIN [HumanResources].[EmployeeAddress] ea
        ON e.[EmployeeID] = ea.[EmployeeID]
        INNER JOIN [Person].[Address] a
        ON ea.[AddressID] = a.[AddressID]
FOR     XML AUTO
```

This generates the actual execution plan shown in Figure 1:

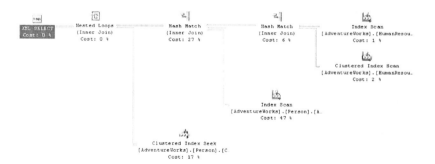

Figure 1

The difference between this execution plan and that for any "normal" query may be hard to spot. It's at the very end. Instead of a T-SQL SELECT operation, we see an **XML SELECT** operation. That is the only real change. Otherwise it's simply a query.

Let's consider a second, somewhat simpler, query and compare the output using the various modes. Starting with AUTO mode again:

```
SELECT   s.Name AS StoreName,
         c.ContactID,
         c.ContactTypeID
FROM     Sales.Store s
         JOIN [Sales].[StoreContact] c ON s.[CustomerID] =
c.[CustomerID]
ORDER BY s.[Name]
FOR      XML AUTO
```

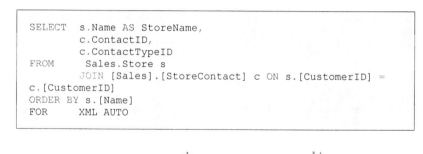

Figure 2

The estimated cost of the plan is 0.12. The XML output looks as follows:

```
<s StoreName="A Bicycle Association">
  <c ContactID="956" ContactTypeID="11" />
</s>
<s StoreName="A Bike Store">
  <c ContactID="322" ContactTypeID="11" />
```

```
</s>
```

The same results are seen, in this case, if we use **XML RAW** mode.

XML EXPLICIT mode allows you to exert some control over the format of the XML generated by the query – for example, if the application or business requirements may need a very specific XML definition, rather than the generic one supplied by **XML AUTO**.

Without getting into a tutorial on **XML EXPLICIT**, you write the query in a way that dictates the structure of the XML output, through a series of **UNION** operations. Here is a simple example:

```
SELECT  1 AS Tag,
        NULL AS Parent,
        s.Name AS [Store!1!StoreName],
        NULL AS [Contact!2!ContactID],
        NULL AS [Contact!2!ContactTypeID]
FROM    Sales.Store s
        JOIN [Sales].[StoreContact] c ON s.[CustomerID] =
            c.[CustomerID]
UNION ALL
SELECT  2 AS Tag,
        1 AS Parent,
        s.Name AS StoreName,
        c.ContactID,
        c.ContactTypeID
FROM    Sales.Store s
        JOIN [Sales].[StoreContact] c ON s.[CustomerID] =
c.[CustomerID]
ORDER BY [Store!1!StoreName],
        [Contact!2!ContactID]
FOR     XML EXPLICIT
```

The actual execution plan for this query is somewhat more complex and is shown in Figure 3:

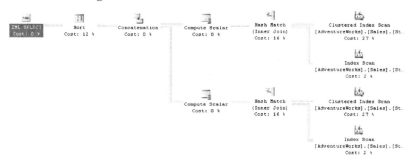

Figure 3

The estimated cost of the plan is much higher at 0.29. The XML output, in this case, looks as follows:

```
<Store StoreName="A Bicycle Association">
  <Contact ContactID="956" ContactTypeID="11" />
</Store>
<Store StoreName="A Bike Store">
  <Contact ContactID="322" ContactTypeID="11" />
</Store>
```

If you remove the **FOR XML EXPLICIT** clause and recapture the plan then you'll see that, apart from seeing the Select instead of XML Select operator, the plans are the same in every way, up to and including the cost of each of the operations. The difference isn't in the execution plan, but rather in the results. With FOR XML EXPLICIT you get XML, without it, you get an oddly-formatted result set.

Even with this relatively simple example, you can see how, because of the multiple queries unioned together, while you get more control over the XML output, it comes at the cost of increased maintenance, due to all the UNION operators and the explicit naming standards, and decreased performance due to the increased number of queries required to put the data together.

An extension of the **XML AUTO** mode allows you to specify the **TYPE** directive in order to better control the output the results of the query as the XML datatype. The following query is essentially the same as the previous one, but is expressed using this simpler syntax that is now available in SQL Server 2005:

```
SELECT  s.[Name] AS StoreName,
        ( SELECT    c.ContactID,
                    c.ContactTypeID
          FROM      [Sales].[StoreContact] c
          WHERE     c.[CustomerID] = s.[CustomerID]
        FOR
          XML AUTO,
              TYPE,
              ELEMENTS
        )
FROM    [Sales].[Store] s
ORDER BY s.[Name]
FOR     XML AUTO,
            TYPE
```

The **ELEMENTS** directive specifies that the columns within the sub-select appear as sub-elements within the outer select statement, as part of the structure of the XML:

```
<s StoreName="A Bicycle Association">
  <c>
     <ContactID>956</ContactID>
     <ContactTypeID>11</ContactTypeID>
  </c>
</s>
```

The resulting execution plan does look a little different, as shown in Figure 4:

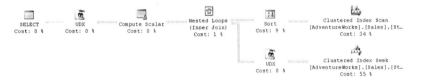

Figure 4

The estimated cost of the plan is 0.23. Two **UDX** operators have been introduced. The UDX operator is an extended operator used by XPATH and XQUERY operations. XPATH and XQUERY are two different ways to querying XML data directly. In our case, by examining the properties window, we can see that the UDX operator on the lower right of the plan is creating the XML data:

⊟ Misc	
⊞ Actual Number of Rows	701
⊞ Actual Rebinds	0
⊞ Actual Rewinds	0
⊞ Defined Values	Expr 1004
Description	UDX
Estimated CPU Cost	0.000001
Estimated I/O Cost	0
Estimated Number of Rows	1
Estimated Operator Cost	0.000701 (0%)
Estimated Rebinds	700
Estimated Rewinds	0
Estimated Row Size	1055 B
Estimated Subtree Cost	0.127211
Logical Operation	UDX
⊞ Memory Fractions	Memory Fractions Input: 0, Memory Fractions Out
Name	FOR XML
Node ID	5
⊟ Output List	Expr 1004 [...]
Column	Expr 1004
Parallel	False
Physical Operation	UDX
⊟ Used UDX Columns	[AdventureWorks].[Sales].[StoreContact].Contact
⊟ [1]	[AdventureWorks].[Sales].[StoreContact].Contact
Alias	[c]
Column	ContactID
Database	[AdventureWorks]
Schema	[Sales]
Table	[StoreContact]
⊟ [2]	[AdventureWorks].[Sales].[StoreContact].Contact
Alias	[c]
Column	ContactTypeID
Database	[AdventureWorks]
Schema	[Sales]
Table	[StoreContact]

Figure 5

The output is **Expr1004**, which consists of the two columns from the **StoreContact** table: **ContactID** and **ContactTypeID**. This data is joined with the sorted data from the clustered index scan on the **Stores** table. The next UDX operator takes this data which as been joined through a nested loop with the outer query against the Store data and then given a Scalar, probably some of the XML definitions or a checksum (calculation value), for the final output as full fledged XML.

Finally, the **XML PATH** mode simply outputs the XML data type and makes it much easier to output mixed elements and attributes. Using this mode, the query we've already walked through twice now looks like this:

```
SELECT   s.[Name] AS "@StoreName",
         c.[ContactID] AS "StoreContact/@ContactId",
         c.[ContactTypeID] AS "StoreContact/@ContactTypeID"
FROM     [Sales].[Store] s
         JOIN [Sales].[StoreContact] c ON s.[CustomerID] =
              c.[CustomerID]
ORDER BY s.[Name]
FOR      XML PATH
```

This results in the same execution plan as shown in Figure , as well as the same estimated cost (0.12). The XML output looks as follows:

```
<row StoreName="A Bicycle Association">
  <StoreContact ContactId="956" ContactTypeID="11" />
</row>
<row StoreName="A Bike Store">
  <StoreContact ContactId="322" ContactTypeID="11" />
</row>
```

Of the various methods of arriving at the same simple XML output, this clearly results in the simplest execution plan as well as the most straightforward TSQL. This makes it probably the easiest code to maintain while still exercising control over the format of the XML output. The output is transformed to XML only at the end of the process, using the familiar T-SQL XML Select operator.

From a performance standpoint, to get XML out of a query in the fastest way possible, you should use fewer XQuery or XPath operations. With that in mind, the least cost operations above, based on Reads and Scans, are the final XML PATH and the original XML AUTO which both behaved basically identically:

```
Table 'StoreContact'. Scan count 1, logical reads 7, …
Table 'Store'. Scan count 1, logical reads 103, …
```

However, since more often than not, the XML created in the AUTO doesn't meet with the application design, you'll probably end up using XML PATH most often.

XML EXPLICIT ended up fairly poorly with more scans and reads than the previous two options:

```
Table 'Worktable'. Scan count 0, logical reads 0, …
Table 'StoreContact'. Scan count 2, logical reads 8, …
Table 'Store'. Scan count 2, logical reads 206, …
```

XML AUTO with TYPE was truly horrendous due to the inclusion of the UDX operations, causing a large number of reads and scans:

```
Table 'StoreContact'. Scan count 701, logical reads 1410, …
Table 'Store'. Scan count 1, logical reads 103, …
```

OPENXML

To read XML within SQL Server, you can use OPENXML or XQuery. OPENXML takes in-memory XML data and converts it into a format that, for viewing purposes, can be treated as if it were a normal table. This allows you to use it within regular T-SQL operations. It's most often used when you need to take data from the XML format and change it into structured storage within a normalized database. In order to test this, we need an XML document.

```
<ROOT>
<Currency CurrencyCode="UTE" CurrencyName="Universal
  Transactional Exchange">
  <CurrencyRate FromCurrencyCode="USD" ToCurrencyCode="UTE"
    CurrencyRateDate="1/1/2007" AverageRate=".553"
    EndOfDateRate= ".558" />
  <CurrencyRate FromCurrencyCode="USD" ToCurrencyCode="UTE"
    CurrencyRateDate="6/1/2007" AverageRate=".928"
    EndOfDateRate= "1.057" />
</Currency>
</ROOT>
```

In this case, we're creating a new currency, the Universal Transactional Exchange, otherwise known as the UTE. We need exchange rates for the UTE to USD. We're going to take all this data and insert it, in a batch, into our database, straight from XML. Here's the script:

```
BEGIN TRAN
DECLARE @iDoc AS INTEGER
DECLARE @Xml AS NVARCHAR(MAX)

SET @Xml = '<ROOT>
<Currency CurrencyCode="UTE" CurrencyName="Universal
  Transactional Exchange">
  <CurrencyRate FromCurrencyCode="USD" ToCurrencyCode="UTE"
    CurrencyRateDate="1/1/2007" AverageRate=".553"
    EndOfDayRate= ".558" />
  <CurrencyRate FromCurrencyCode="USD" ToCurrencyCode="UTE"
    CurrencyRateDate="6/1/2007" AverageRate=".928"
    EndOfDayRate= "1.057" />
</Currency>
</ROOT>'

EXEC sp_xml_preparedocument @iDoc OUTPUT, @Xml

INSERT  INTO [Sales].[Currency]
        (
```

```
               [CurrencyCode],
               [Name],
               [ModifiedDate]
          )
          SELECT   CurrencyCode,
                   CurrencyName,
                   GETDATE()
          FROM     OPENXML (@iDoc, 'ROOT/Currency',1) WITH (
CurrencyCode NCHAR(3), CurrencyName NVARCHAR(50) )

INSERT   INTO [Sales].[CurrencyRate]
          (
               [CurrencyRateDate],
               [FromCurrencyCode],
               [ToCurrencyCode],
               [AverageRate],
               [EndOfDayRate],
               [ModifiedDate]
          )
          SELECT   CurrencyRateDate,
                   FromCurrencyCode,
                   ToCurrencyCode,
                   AverageRate,
                   EndOfDayRate,
                   GETDATE()
          FROM     OPENXML(@iDoc ,
'ROOT/Currency/CurrencyRate',2) WITH ( CurrencyRateDate
DATETIME '@CurrencyRateDate', FromCurrencyCode NCHAR(3)
'@FromCurrencyCode', ToCurrencyCode NCHAR(3)
'@ToCurrencyCode', AverageRate MONEY '@AverageRate',
EndOfDayRate MONEY '@EndOfDayRate' )

EXEC sp_xml_removedocument @iDoc
ROLLBACK TRAN
```

From this query, we get two actual execution plans, one for each
INSERT. The first **INSERT** is against the **Currency** table, as shown
in Figure 6:

Figure 6

A quick scan of the plan reveals no new XML icons. All the
OPENXML statement processing is handled within the **Remote Scan**
icon. This operator represents the opening of a DLL within SQL
Server, which will take the XML and convert it into a format within

memory that looks like a table of data to the query engine. Since the Remote Scan is not actually part of the query engine itself, the call outside the query engine is represented by the single icon.

Examining the estimated plan reveals none of the extensive XML statements that are present in this query: even the XML stored procedures **sp_xml_preparedocument** and **sp_xml_remove document** are referenced by simple logical T-SQL icons, as you can see in Figure 7.

```
Query 3: Query cost (relative to the batch): 0%
EXEC sp_xml_preparedocument @iDoc OUTPUT, @Xml

    T-SQL

EXECUTE PROC
   Cost: 0 %
```

Figure 7

The only place where we can really see the evidence of the XML is in the Output List for the **Remote Scan**. Here, in Figure 8, we can see the OPENXML statement referred to as a table, and the properties selected from the XML data listed as columns.

Figure 8

From there, it's a fairly straight-forward query with the data being sorted first for insertion into the clustered index and then a second time for addition to the other index on the table.

The second execution plan describes the **INSERT** against the **CurrencyRate** table:

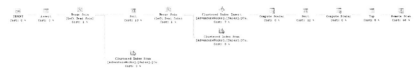

Figure 9

This query is the more complicated of the pair, because of the extra steps required for the maintenance of referential integrity between the **Currency** and **CurrencyRate** tables. Yet still, we see no XML icons because the Remote Scan operation again takes the task of gathering the new rows for the table. In this case, two comparisons against the parent table are made through the Merge Join operations. The data is sorted, first by **FromCurrencyCode** and then by **ToCurrencyCode** in order for the data to be used in a Merge Join, the operation picked by the Optimizer in this instance.

It's really that easy to bring XML data into the database for use within your queries, or for inclusion within your database. As discussed previously, OPENXML is a useful tool for importing the semi-structured data within the XML documents into the well-maintained, relational database structure. It can also allow you to pass in data for other uses. For example, you can pass in a list of variables to be used as a join in a **SELECT** statement. The main point to take away is that once the OPENXML has been formatted, you get to use it as if it were just another table within your queries..

One caveat worth mentioning: parsing XML uses a lot of memory. You should plan on opening the XML, getting the data out, and then closing and deallocating the XML parser as soon as possible. This will reduce the amount of time that the memory is allocated within your system.

XQuery

Along with the introduction of the XML data type in SQL Server 2005, came the introduction of XQuery as a method for querying XML data. Effectively, the inclusion of XQuery gives you a whole new query language to learn in addition to T-SQL. The XML data type is the mechanism used to provide the XQuery functionality through the SQL Server system. When you want to query from the XML data type, there are five basic methods, each of which is reflected in execution plans in different ways:

- **.query()**: used to query the xml data type and return the xml data type
- **.value()**: used to query the xml data type and return a non-xml scalar value
- **.nodes()**: a method for pivoting xml data into rows
- **.exist()**: queries the xml data type and returns a Bool to indicate whether or not the result set is empty , just like the **EXISTS** keyword in TSQL
- **.modify()**: a method for inserting, updating and deleting XML snippets within the XML data set.

The various options for running a query against XML, including the use of FLWOR (for, let, where, order by and return) statements within the queries, all affect the execution plans. I'm going to cover just two examples to acquaint you with the concepts and introduce you to the sort of execution plans you can expect to see. It's outside the scope of this book to cover this topic in the depth that would be required to cover all aspects of this new language.

Using the exist method

The **.exist** method is one that is likely to be used quite frequently when working with XML data. In the following example, we'll be querying the resumes of all employees to find out which of the people hired were once sales managers:

```
SELECT    c.[LastName],
          c.[FirstName],
          e.[HireDate],
          e.[Title]
FROM      [Person].[Contact] c
          INNER JOIN [HumanResources].[Employee] e
          ON c.[ContactID] = e.[ContactID]
          INNER JOIN [HumanResources].[JobCandidate] jc
          ON e.[EmployeeID] = jc.[EmployeeID]
          AND jc.[Resume].exist(' declare namespace
          res="http://schemas.microsoft.com/sqlserver/2004/07/
              adventure-works/Resume";
          /res:Resume/res:Employment/res:Emp.JobTitle[contains
              (.,"Sales Manager")]') = 1
```

The query, in this case, finds a single employee who was formerly a sales manager, and results in the execution plan in Figure 10:

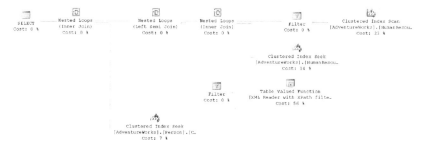

Figure 10

Starting at the usual location, top and right, we see a normal execution plan. A **Clustered Index Scan** operation against the **JobCandidate** table is followed by a **Filter** operation that ensures that the Resume field is not null. A **Nested Loop** join is used to combine this data from the filtered **JobCandidate** table with data returned from the **Employee** table, filtering us down to two rows.

Then, another **Nested Loop** operator is used combine data from a new source, a **Table Valued Function**. This Table Valued Function is subtitled "XML Reader with XPath filter". This operation represents as relational data the output from the XQuery. The role it plays is not dissimilar to that of the Remote Scan operation from the OPENXML query. However, the TVF, unlike the Remote Scan in the example above, is actually a part of the query engine and represented by a distinct icon.

The property sheet for the Table Valued Function shows that four rows were found:

Table Valued Function
Table valued function.

Physical Operation	Table Valued Function
Logical Operation	Table Valued Function
Actual Number of Rows	4
Estimated I/O Cost	0
Estimated CPU Cost	1.004
Estimated Operator Cost	0.0262892 (56%)
Estimated Subtree Cost	0.0262892
Estimated Number of Rows	5.23687
Estimated Row Size	5065 B
Actual Rebinds	2
Actual Rewinds	0
Node ID	8

Object
[XML Reader with XPath filter]
Output List
[XML Reader with XPath filter].value, [XML Reader with XPath filter].lvalue

Figure 131

These rows are then passed to a **Filter** operator that determines if the XPath query we defined equals one. This results in a single row for output to the **Nested Loop** operator. From there it's a typical execution plan, retrieving data from the **Contact** table and combining it with the rest of the data already put together.

Using the query method

The **.query** method returns XML. In our example, we'll query the Demographics data to find stores that are greater than 20000 feet in size. In addition to the query, we have to define the XML returned and, to this end, the query uses XQuery's FLWOR expressions (For, Let, Where, Order by, and Return). These constructs greatly extend the versatility of XQuery, to make it comparable to T-SQL:

- **For** – used to iterate XML nodes. The **For** expression binds some number of iterator variables, in this case, one, to input sequences, our **ss:StoreSurvey**. It works a lot like a For/Each loop

- **Where** – you can limit the results using the **Where** expressions. It works just like a **WHERE** clause in SQL

- **Order** – sorts the results, just like **ORDER BY** in SQL (not covered here)

- **Return** – simply defines the results coming back, kind of like the **SELECT** clause in T-SQL except it includes all kinds of XML commands for formatting.

There is also a **let** expression, which is not implemented in SQL Server 2005.

In this example, we need to generate a list of stores that are represented by a particular sales person. Specifically we want to look at any of the demographics for stores represented by this salesperson that have more than 20000 square feet. The demographics information is semi-structured data, so it is stored within XML in the database. To filter the XML directly, we'll be using the **.query** method. Let's look at our example query and execution plan:

```
SELECT   s.Demographics.query('
    declare namespace
ss="http://schemas.microsoft.com/sqlserver/2004/07/
    adventureworks/StoreSurvey";
    for $s in /ss:StoreSurvey
    where ss:StoreSurvey/ss:SquareFeet > 20000
    return $s
') AS Demographics
FROM     [Sales].[Store] s
WHERE    s.[SalesPersonID] = 279
```

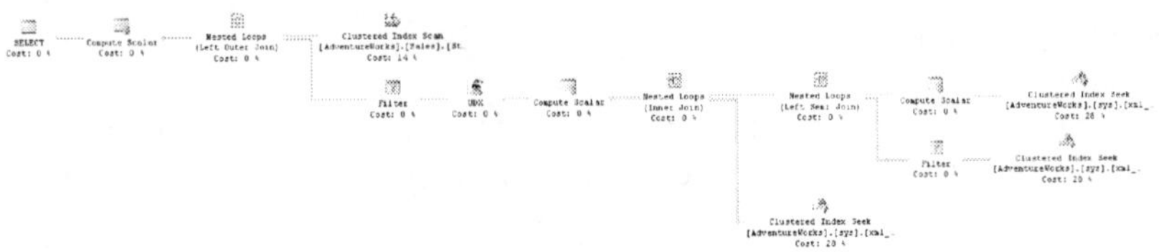

Figure 12

The query actually consisted of two simple queries

- A regular T-SQL query against the **Store** table to return the rows where the **SalesPersonId = 279,**
- A query that uses the .query method return the data where the Store's square footage was over 20000

Stated that way, it sounds simple, but a lot more work was necessary around those two queries to arrive at a result set..

As always, start at the top and right of Figure 12. The first operator is a **Clustered Index Scan** against the **Sales** table, filtered by the **SalesPersonId**. The data returned is fed into the top half of a **Nested Loop**, left outer join. Going over to the right to find the second stream of data for the join, we find a familiar operation: a **Clustered Index Seek**. This time though, it's going against an XML clustered index.

Clustered Index Seek

Scanning a particular range of rows from a clustered index.

Physical Operation	Clustered Index Seek
Logical Operation	Clustered Index Seek
Actual Number of Rows	80
Estimated I/O Cost	0.003125
Estimated CPU Cost	0.0001713
Estimated Operator Cost	0.156065 (28%)
Estimated Subtree Cost	0.156065
Estimated Number of Rows	1
Estimated Row Size	22 B
Actual Rebinds	0
Actual Rewinds	0
Ordered	True
Node ID	9

Predicate
[AdventureWorks].[sys].
[xml_index_nodes_2130106629_32000].[hid] as
[StoreSurvey:1].[hid]='À€'
Object
[AdventureWorks].[sys].
[xml_index_nodes_2130106629_32000].
[PXML_Store_Demographics] [StoreSurvey:1]
Output List
[AdventureWorks].[sys].
[xml_index_nodes_2130106629_32000].id,
[AdventureWorks].[sys].
[xml_index_nodes_2130106629_32000].hid,
[AdventureWorks].[sys].
[xml_index_nodes_2130106629_32000].pk1
Seek Predicates
Prefix: [AdventureWorks].[sys].
[xml_index_nodes_2130106629_32000].pk1 = Scalar
Operator([AdventureWorks].[Sales].[Store].
[CustomerID] as [s].[CustomerID])

Figure 13

You can see in Figure 13 that the index seek is occurring on **PXML_Store_Demographics**, returning the 80 rows from the index that match on the **CustomerId** field from the store. Below this, another **Clustered Index Seek** gathers data matching the **CustomerId**, but adds the **SquareFeet** as part of the output. This data is filtered and then the outputs are combined through a Left Join.

From there, it feeds on out joining against all the rest of the XML data before going through a **UDX** operator that outputs the formatted XML data. This is all then combined with the original rows returned from the **Store** table. Of note is the fact that the XQuery information is being treated almost as if it were T-SQL. The data above is being retrieved from an XML index which stores all the data with multiple rows for each node, sacrificing disk space for speed of recovery.

Summary

These examples don't begin to cover the depth of what's available within XQuery. Functions for aggregating XML data are available. You can pass variables from T-SQL into the XQuery commands. It really is a whole new language and syntax that you'll have to learn in order to take complete advantage of what it has to offer. For an even more thorough introduction, read this white paper offered from Microsoft :

http://msdn2.microsoft.com/en-us/library/ms345122.aspx

It can take the place of FOR XML, but you might see some performance degredation.

You can also use XQuery in place of OPENXML. The functionality provided by XQuery goes way beyond what's possible within OPENXML. Combining that with TSQL will make for a powerful combination when you have to manipulate XML data within SQL Server. As with everything else, please test the solution with all possible tools to ensure that you're using the optimal one for your situation.

CHAPTER 8: ADVANCED TOPICS

In the previous chapters, we have discussed how execution plans are generated, how to interpret them and have examined plan for some moderately complex queries, including most of the common SQL Server objects, such as stored procedures, views, indexes, cursors and so on. In our discussion of hints, we even walked through some ways in which we could exercise some control over how the execution plan was generated.

In this final chapter, we will take a tour of some of the more advanced topics related to the interpretation and manipulation of execution plans, covering the following:

- Large scale execution plans and how to interpret them
- Parallelism – why you might want to use parallelism, how to control it in your query execution and how to interpret parallel plans
- Forced parameterization – used to replace hard-coded literals with parameters and maximize the possibility of plan reuse. Used mainly in systems subject to a large amount of ad-hoc, or client-generated, SQL.
- Using Plan Guides – to exercise control over a query without changing the actual code; an invaluable tool when dealing with third party applications.
- Using Plan Forcing – to capture and reuse an execution plan, the final word in controlling many of the decisions made by the optimizer.

Reading Large Scale Execution Plans

The most important thing to remember when you're dealing with execution plans that cover large numbers of tables, and large numbers of individual plans, is that the rules haven't changed. The optimizer uses the same criteria to determine the optimal type of join, type of index, and so on, whether you're dealing with two tables or two hundred.

However, the nature of the optimizer is such that, when faced with a truly large and complex plan, it's unlikely to spend too much time trying to find the perfect execution plan. This means, as the plans become more complex, the need to understand what decisions were made by the optimizer, why, and how to change them, becomes that much more important.

Let's take a look at what I'd consider a reasonably large-scale execution plan (although I've seen much larger). The following stored procedure returns the appropriate data set, based on whether or not any special offers were used by a particular individual. In addition, if a particular special offer is being requested, then procedure executes a different query and returns a second, different result set.

```
DROP PROCEDURE [Sales].[uspGetDiscountRates] ;
GO
CREATE PROCEDURE [Sales].[uspGetDiscountRates]
   (
    @ContactId INT
   ,@SpecialOfferId INT
   )
AS
   BEGIN TRY
   -- determine if sale using special offer exists
      IF EXISTS ( SELECT * FROM [Sales].[Individual] i
                     INNER JOIN [Sales].[Customer] c
                       ON i.CustomerID = c.CustomerID
                     INNER JOIN
                        [Sales].[SalesOrderHeader] soh
                       ON soh.CustomerID = c.CustomerID
                     INNER JOIN
                        [Sales].[SalesOrderDetail] sod
                       ON soh.[SalesOrderID] =
                          sod.[SalesOrderID]
                     INNER JOIN
                        [Sales].[SpecialOffer] spo
                       ON sod.[SpecialOfferID] =
                          spo.[SpecialOfferID]
                     WHERE i.[ContactID] = @ContactId
                       AND spo.[SpecialOfferID] =
                           @SpecialOfferId )
         BEGIN
            SELECT c.[LastName] + ', ' + c.[FirstName]
              ,c.[EmailAddress]
              ,i.[Demographics]
              ,spo.[Description]
              ,spo.[DiscountPct]
              ,sod.[LineTotal]
              ,p.[Name]
              ,p.[ListPrice]
              ,sod.[UnitPriceDiscount]
            FROM [Person].[Contact] c
                INNER JOIN [Sales].[Individual] i
                  ON c.[ContactID] = i.[ContactID]
                INNER JOIN [Sales].[Customer] cu
                  ON i.[CustomerID] = cu.[CustomerID]
                INNER JOIN [Sales].[SalesOrderHeader] soh
                  ON cu.[CustomerID] = soh.[CustomerID]
                INNER JOIN [Sales].[SalesOrderDetail] sod
```

```
                        ON soh.[SalesOrderID] = sod.[SalesOrderID]
                  INNER JOIN [Sales].[SpecialOffer] spo
                     ON sod.[SpecialOfferID] =
                        spo.[SpecialOfferID]
                  INNER JOIN [Production].[Product] p
                     ON sod.[ProductID] = p.[ProductID]
                  WHERE c.ContactID = @ContactId
                        AND sod.[SpecialOfferID] =
                              @SpecialOfferId;
               END
-- use different query to return other data set
     ELSE
        BEGIN
          SELECT   c.[LastName] + ', ' + c.[FirstName]
                   ,c.[EmailAddress]
                   ,i.[Demographics]
                   ,soh.SalesOrderNumber
                   ,sod.[LineTotal]
                   ,p.[Name]
                   ,p.[ListPrice]
                   ,sod.[UnitPrice]
                   ,st.[Name] AS StoreName
                   ,ec.[LastName] + ', ' + ec.[FirstName] AS
                        SalesPersonName
              FROM [Person].[Contact] c
                  INNER JOIN [Sales].[Individual] i
                     ON c.[ContactID] = i.[ContactID]
                  INNER JOIN [Sales].[SalesOrderHeader] soh
                     ON i.[CustomerID] = soh.[CustomerID]
                  INNER JOIN [Sales].[SalesOrderDetail] sod
                     ON soh.[SalesOrderID] =
                        sod.[SalesOrderID]
                  INNER JOIN [Production].[Product] p
                     ON sod.[ProductID] = p.[ProductID]
                  LEFT JOIN [Sales].[SalesPerson] sp
                     ON soh.SalesPersonID = sp.SalesPersonID
                  LEFT JOIN [Sales].[Store] st
                     ON sp.SalesPersonID = st.SalesPersonID
                  LEFT JOIN [HumanResources].[Employee] e
                     ON sp.SalesPersonID = e.[EmployeeID]
                  LEFT JOIN Person.[Contacct] ec
                     ON e.[ContactID] = ec.[ContactID]
                  WHERE i.[ContactID] = @ContactId;
               END

  --second result SET
     IF @SpecialOfferId = 16
        BEGIN
          SELECT p.[Name]
                   ,p.[ProductLine]
              FROM  [Sales].[SpecialOfferProduct] sop
                  INNER JOIN [Production].[Product] p
                     ON sop.[ProductID] = p.[ProductID]
                  WHERE sop.[SpecialOfferID] = 16;
        END

  END TRY
  BEGIN CATCH
```

```
SELECT  ERROR_NUMBER() AS ErrorNumber
      ,ERROR_MESSAGE() AS ErrorMessage ;
RETURN ERROR_NUMBER() ;
END CATCH
RETURN 0 ;
;
```

This type of procedure does not represent an optimal way of accessing the required data. The first time the query is run, it creates a plan based on the initial parameters supplied. Because of the IF statement, the second and subsequent runs of the procedure can result in different queries being run using a very sub-optimal plan.

Unfortunately, most DBAs are going to run into things like this at some point in their career. We'll execute the procedure with the following parameters:

```
EXEC [Sales].[uspGetDiscountRates]
    @ContactId = 12298, -- int
    @SpecialOfferId = 16 -- int
```

This results in a set of data looking something like this:

	(No column name)	EmailAddress	Demographics	SalesOrderNumber	LineTotal	Name
1	Barnes, Fernando	fernando47@adventure-works.com	<IndividualSurvey xmlns="http://schemas.microso...	SO52035	8.990000	AWC Logo Cap
2	Barnes, Fernando	fernando47@adventure-works.com	<IndividualSurvey xmlns="http://schemas.microso...	SO52035	32.600000	HL Road Tire
3	Barnes, Fernando	fernando47@adventure-works.com	<IndividualSurvey xmlns="http://schemas.microso...	SO52083	29.990000	ML Mountain Tire
4	Barnes, Fernando	fernando47@adventure-works.com	<IndividualSurvey xmlns="http://schemas.microso...	SO52083	2.290000	Patch Kit/8 Patches
5	Barnes, Fernando	fernando47@adventure-works.com	<IndividualSurvey xmlns="http://schemas.microso...	SO53835	3.990000	Road Tire Tube
6	Barnes, Fernando	fernando47@adventure-works.com	<IndividualSurvey xmlns="http://schemas.microso...	SO53835	32.600000	HL Road Tire
7	Barnes, Fernando	fernando47@adventure-works.com	<IndividualSurvey xmlns="http://schemas.microso...	SO53835	54.990000	Hydration Pack - 70 oz
8	Barnes, Fernando	fernando47@adventure-works.com	<IndividualSurvey xmlns="http://schemas.microso...	SO54388	24.990000	ML Road Tire
9	Barnes, Fernando	fernando47@adventure-works.com	<IndividualSurvey xmlns="http://schemas.microso...	SO54388	49.990000	Long-Sleeve Logo Jersey, XL

	Name	ProductLine
1	Mountain-200 Black, 38	M
2	Mountain-200 Black, 46	M
3	Mountain-500 Silver, 40	M
4	Mountain-500 Silver, 42	M
5	Mountain-500 Silver, 44	M
6	Mountain-500 Silver, 48	M
7	Mountain-500 Silver, 52	M

Figure 14

This image of the data set does not include all the columns, but you can see that two result sets were returned, the first being the results that had no discounts and the second being the query that runs if the special offer is passed to the query. The estimated execution plan is shown in Figure 2:

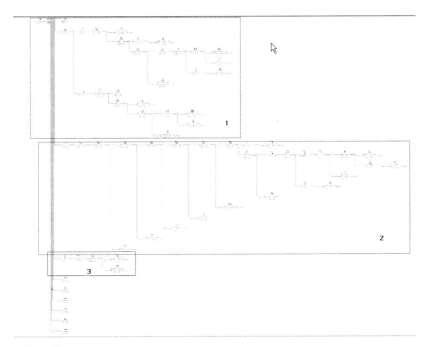

Figure 2

Obviously, this plan is unreadable without drilling down. However, even from this macro view, you can still see the logical steps of the query. The first grouping of icons describes the first query that checks for the existence of the special offer. The second, larger group of icons describes the query that runs when there are no special offers. Finally, the third group of icons describes the last query, which runs when the script receives the **SpecialOfferID** = 16.

While this execution plan may look intimidating, it is not doing anything that we haven't seen elsewhere. It's just doing a lot more of it. The key to investigating plans of this type is to not be daunted by their size and remember the basic methods for walking the plan. Start at the top and on the right and work your way through.

You have at least one tool that can help you when working with a large graphical plan. In the lower right of the results pane in the query window, when you're looking at an execution plan, you'll see a little plus sign, as shown in Figure 3:

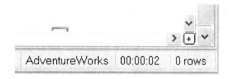

Figure 3

Click on the plus sign to open a little window, showing a representation of the entire execution plan. Keep your mouse button depressed, and drag the cursor across the window. You'll see that this moves a small "viewing rectangle" around the plan, as shown in Figure 4:

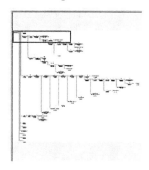

Figure 4

As you drag the viewable area, you'll notice that the main display in the results pane tracks your mouse movements. In this way, you can navigate around a large execution plan and keep track of where you are within the larger context of the plan, as well as view the individual operators that you're investigating.

As to the procedure itself, the only point worth noting here is that the majority of the cost of the query (62%), as currently written, is a **Clustered Index Scan** operator against the **Sales.Individual** table. None of the existing indexes on that table include the **ContactID** column, at least not in a way that can be used by the optimizer for these queries. Adding an index to that column radically enhances the performance of the query.

When dealing with large scale plans, you may opt to capture the XML plan and then use the search capabilities inherent in XML to track down issues such as Clustered Index Scans. Be warned, though, that as difficult as navigating a large scale execution plan in the graphical format becomes, that problem is multiplied within XML with all it's extra data on display. If you're just getting started with execution plans this large, it might be better to stay away from the XML, but be aware that it is available as an added tool.

In summary, the operations for a large scale execution plan are not different from any other you have seen in this book; there are just more of them. Don't be intimidated by them. Just start at the top right, in the normal fashion and work your way through in stages, using the scrolling window to navigate around, if necessary.

Parallelism in Execution Plans

SQL Server can take advantage of the fact that the server on which you are operating has multiple processors. It's able to take some operations and spread the processing across the processors available to it. There are a couple of basic system settings that determine if, or when, parallelism can be used by your server:

- "**Max Degree of Parallelism**", which sets the number of processors that SQL Server will use when executing a parallel query. By default this is set to "0", which uses all available processors.
- "**Cost Threshold for Parallelism**", which specifies the threshold, or minimum cost, at which SQL Server creates and runs parallel plans. This cost is an estimated number of seconds in which the query will run. The default value is "5".

Max Degree of Parallelism

SQL Server will determine the optimal number of processors to run a given parallel query (assuming that multiple processors are available). By default, it will use all available processors. If you wish to suppress parallel execution, you set this option to a value of "1". If you wish to specify the number of processors to use for a query execution, then you can set a value of greater than one, and up to 64.[13]

As described on BOL (http://msdn2.microsoft.com/en-us/library/ms181007.aspx), you can configure this option via the **sp_configure** system stored procedure, as follows:

---

[13] In addition to these system settings, you can also affect the number of processors used by a query by supplying the MAXDOP query hint, as described in Chapter 5.

```
sp_configure 'show advanced options', 1;
GO
    RECONFIGURE WITH OVERRIDE;
GO
    sp_configure 'max degree of parallelism', 3;
GO
    RECONFIGURE WITH OVERRIDE;
GO
```

Cost Threshold for Parallelism

As the optimizer assigns costs to operations within the execution plan, which is an estimation of the number of seconds each operation will take. If that cost is greater than the "Cost Threshold for Parallelism" then that operation may get defined as a parallel operation.

The actual decision process used by the optimizer is outlined as follows:

- **Does the server have multiple processors?** Parallel processing requires the server to have more than one processor.
- **Are sufficient threads available?** Threads are an operating system construct that allow multiple concurrent operations, and SQL Server must check with the OS to determine if threads are available for use prior to launching a parallel process.
- **What type of query or index operation is being performed?** Queries that cost more, such as those that sort large amounts of data or do joins between large tables, and so on, lead to a higher estimated cost for the operation. It's this cost that is compared against the cost threshold.
- **Are there a sufficient number of rows to process?** The number of rows being processed directly affects the cost of each operation, which can lead to the process meeting or not meeting the cost threshold.
- **Are the statistics current?** Depending on the operation, if the statistics are not current the optimizer may either choose not to use parallelism, or it will decide to use a lower degree of parallelism.

When the optimizer determines that a query will benefit from parallel execution, it adds marshalling and control operators, called **exchange operators**. These operators act to split the work done into multiple streams of data, pass it through the various parallel operators, and bring it all back together again.

When an execution plan is created that uses parallelism, this plan is stored in cache *twice*: once for a plan that doesn't use parallelism and once for a plan that does. When a plan is reused, it is examined for the number of threads it used the last time. The query engine, at execution time, then determines whether that same number will be used, based on the current system load and the number of threads available.

Are Parallel Plans Good or Bad?

The one thing to remember about parallelism is that it comes at a cost. It takes processing time and power to divide the operations into various threads and martial them back together. For long-running, processor-intensive, large-volume queries, parallelism makes a lot of sense. You'll see this type of thing mainly in reporting, warehouse or business intelligence systems. In an OLTP type of system, where the majority of the transactions are small and fast, parallelism can cause unwanted slow downs. A query can actually run slower with a parallel execution plan than without one.

There is no hard and fast rule for determining when parallelism will be useful, or when it will be more costly. The best approach is to observe the execution times of queries that use parallelism and, where necessary, either change the system settings to increase the cost threshold, or use the **MAXDOP** query hint in individual cases.

It all comes down to understanding the execution plans so that you can identify parallelism and then testing to see if you are receiving a benefit from the parallel processes. Query execution times are usually the surest indicator as to whether or not you are getting a benefit from parallel execution. If the time goes down with **MAXDOP** set to 1 during a test, that's an indication that the parallel plan is hurting you. If the times go down after you set the cost threshold to 3, then you're seeing a real benefit from parallel executions.

Examining a Parallel Execution Plan

If, like me, you're performing these tests on a machine with a single processor, then you won't be able to see any parallel plans. Kalen Delaney supplied a method for simulating multiple processors in SQL Server Magazine, **InstantDoc #95497** (available only to subscribers). In the SQL Server Configuration Manager, right-click the appropriate SQL Server service and edit the startup properties. Add a property "-Pn", which represents the number of processors that you want to simulate. You must then restart the service. This simulates parallel execution plans, but it does not actually give you parallel execution on a single processor machine.

For more detail, read the article. However, I'll repeat the warning from the article: ***never do this on a production system***.

We're starting with an aggregation query, or the sort that you might see in a data mart. If the data set that this query operated against was very large, it might benefit from parallelism. Here's the query:

```
SELECT   [so].[ProductID]
         ,COUNT(*) AS Order_Count
  FROM   [Sales].[SalesOrderDetail] so
  WHERE  [so].[ModifiedDate] >= '2003/02/01'
         AND [so].[ModifiedDate] < DATEADD(mm, 3,
'2003/02/01')
  GROUP BY [so].[ProductID]
  ORDER BY [so].[ProductID]
```

If we take a look at the estimated execution plan, we'll see the fairly straight forward plan shown in Figure 5:

Figure 5

There is nothing in this plan that we haven't seen before, so we'll move on to see what would happen to this plan if it were executed with the use of multiple processors. In order to force the optimizer to use a parallel plan, change the Parallelism Threshold to 1 from whatever value it is now (5 by default). Then, we can run this query and obtain a parallel execution plan:

```
sp_configure 'cost threshold for parallelism', 1 ;
GO
RECONFIGURE WITH OVERRIDE ;
GO
SET STATISTICS XML ON;
GO
SELECT   [so].[ProductID]
         ,COUNT(*) AS Order_Count
  FROM   [Sales].[SalesOrderDetail] so
  WHERE  [so].[ModifiedDate] >= '2003/02/01'
         AND [so].[ModifiedDate] < DATEADD(mm, 3,
'2003/02/01')
  GROUP BY [so].[ProductID]
  ORDER BY [so].[ProductID]
GO
SET STATISTICS XML OFF;
GO
```

Select "Include Actual Execution Plan" so that you generate both the graphical and XML versions of the plan. The graphical execution plan is shown in Figure 6:

Figure 6

The first thing that will probably jump out at you, in addition to the new operators that support parallelism, is the small yellow icon with two arrows, which is attached to the otherwise familiar operators. This icon designates that these operators as being used within a parallel processing stream. If we examine the XML plan, we begin to see how parallelism is implemented:

```
<QueryPlan DegreeOfParallelism="2" MemoryGrant="162"
  CachedPlanSize="22" CompileTime="5" CompileCPU="5"
  CompileMemory="320">
```

The value of 2, assigned to the **DegreeOfParallelism** property, indicates that the execution of this query will be split between each of the two available processors. Looking at the graphical execution plan, we'll start from the right as we usually do. As we identify the operator, we'll find its equivalent within the XML execution plan. First we find a **Clustered Index Scan** operator.

The following **RelOp** element describes that same **Clustered Index Scan** operator:

```
<RelOp NodeId="5" PhysicalOp="Clustered Index Scan"
  LogicalOp="Clustered Index Scan" EstimateRows="4987.95"
  EstimateIO="0.915718" EstimateCPU="0.0668028"
  AvgRowSize="19" EstimatedTotalSubtreeCost="0.98252"
  Parallel="1" EstimateRebinds="0" EstimateRewinds="0">
<RunTimeInformation>
<RunTimeCountersPerThread Thread="2" ActualRows="0"
  ActualEndOfScans="1" ActualExecutions="1" />
<RunTimeCountersPerThread Thread="1" ActualRows="5166"
  ActualEndOfScans="1" ActualExecutions="1" />
<RunTimeCountersPerThread Thread="0" ActualRows="0"
  ActualEndOfScans="0" ActualExecutions="0" />
</RunTimeInformation>
</RelOp>
```

Notice that the **Parallel** property is set to 1, indicating a parallel operation (it is set to zero in a non-parallel operation). Within this element, the **RunTimeInformation** sub-element defines a list of sub-elements called **RuntTimeCountersPerThread**. The three sub-elements here indicate that three threads were launched.

The next **RelOp** node describes the **Parallelism** operator:

```
<RelOp NodeId="4" PhysicalOp="Parallelism"
  LogicalOp="Repartition Streams" EstimateRows="4987.95"
  EstimateIO="0" EstimateCPU="0.0344762" AvgRowSize="11"
  EstimatedTotalSubtreeCost="1.07038" Parallel="1"
  EstimateRebinds="0" EstimateRewinds="0">
<RunTimeInformation>
<RunTimeCountersPerThread Thread="1" ActualRows="2561"
  ActualEndOfScans="1" ActualExecutions="1" />
<RunTimeCountersPerThread Thread="2" ActualRows="2605"
  ActualEndOfScans="1" ActualExecutions="1" />
<RunTimeCountersPerThread Thread="0" ActualRows="0"
  ActualEndOfScans="0" ActualExecutions="0" />
</RunTimeInformation>
</RelOp>
```

This **Repartition Streams** parallel operation simply takes the multiple streams of data and outputs multiple streams of data, spreading the data across threads.

The data then moves to a **Hash Match** which processes the rows based on the **ProductID** field, performing the grouping of the data necessary for the aggregate output:

```
<RelOp NodeId="3" PhysicalOp="Hash Match"
  LogicalOp="Aggregate" EstimateRows="261.129"
  EstimateIO="0" EstimateCPU="0.0315549" AvgRowSize="15"
  EstimatedTotalSubtreeCost="1.10193" Parallel="1"
  EstimateRebinds="0" EstimateRewinds="0">
<RunTimeInformation>
<RunTimeCountersPerThread Thread="1" ActualRows="51"
  ActualEndOfScans="1" ActualExecutions="1" />
<RunTimeCountersPerThread Thread="2" ActualRows="48"
  ActualEndOfScans="1" ActualExecutions="1" />
<RunTimeCountersPerThread Thread="0" ActualRows="0"
  ActualEndOfScans="0" ActualExecutions="0" />
</RunTimeInformation>
```

Again, as can be seen in the **RunTimeInformation** element, we're performing this operation in parallel.

The **Scalar** Operator and the **Sort** Operator follow in line, each one performing its actions against the same threads originally allocated. Finally, we arrive at another **Parallelism** operator:

```
<RelOp NodeId="0" PhysicalOp="Parallelism"
  LogicalOp="Gather Streams" EstimateRows="261.129"
  EstimateIO="0" EstimateCPU="0.0301494" AvgRowSize="15"
  EstimatedTotalSubtreeCost="1.1394" Parallel="1"
  EstimateRebinds="0" EstimateRewinds="0">
<RunTimeInformation>
<RunTimeCountersPerThread Thread="0" ActualRows="99"
  ActualEndOfScans="1" ActualExecutions="1" />
</RunTimeInformation>
```

This **Gather Streams** operation finds all the various threads from the different processors and puts it back together into a single stream of data. In addition to **Gather Streams** and **Repartition Streams**, described above, the Parallelism operator can also **Distribute Streams**, which takes a single stream of data and splits it into multiple streams for parallel processing in a logical plan.

As you can see in the **RunTimeInformation** element, after gathering the other streams together for output to the Select operator, we're now only dealing with a single thread.

Once you're done experimenting with parallelism, be sure to reset the Parallelism Threshold to where it was on your system (the default is 5).

```
sp_configure 'cost threshold for parallelism', 5 ;
GO
RECONFIGURE WITH OVERRIDE ;
GO
```

How Forced Parameterization affects Execution Plans

Forced parameterization replaces the default behavior of simple parameterization, an example of which we saw in Chapter 2. . Simple parameterization occurs automatically. When no parameters are defined within a query, and instead it uses only hard coded values such as "AddressId = 52", then the query engine will take such values and turn them into parameters.

The example we saw in Chapter 2 was a simple **DELETE** statement:

```
DELETE FROM [Person].[Address]
WHERE [AddressID] = 52;
```

The search predicate in the **Clustered Index Delete** operation from this plan used a parameter instead of the hard coded value 52, as you can see in the Seek Predicate of the property sheet:

Clustered Index Delete	
Delete rows from a clustered index.	

Physical Operation	Clustered Index Delete
Logical Operation	Delete
Estimated I/O Cost	0.04
Estimated CPU Cost	0.000004
Estimated Operator Cost	0.0432871 (72%)
Estimated Subtree Cost	0.0432871
Estimated Number of Rows	1
Estimated Row Size	11 B
Node ID	7

Object
[AdventureWorks].[Person].[Address].
[PK_Address_AddressID], [AdventureWorks].[Person].
[Address].[AK_Address_rowguid], [AdventureWorks].
[Person].[Address].
[IX_Address_AddressLine1_AddressLine2_City_StateProvi
nceID_PostalCode], [AdventureWorks].[Person].
[Address].[IX_Address_StateProvinceID]
Output List
[AdventureWorks].[Person].[Address].AddressID
Seek Predicate
Prefix: [AdventureWorks].[Person].[Address].AddressID
= Scalar Operator(CONVERT_IMPLICIT(int,[@1],0))

Figure 7

This action is performed by the optimizer in an effort to create plans that are more likely to be reused. The optimizer is only able to perform this function on relatively simple queries. The parameters created are as close to the correct data type as the optimizer can get but, since it's just an estimation, it could be wrong.

The optimizer arbitrarily provides the names for these parameters as part of the process. It may or may not generate the same parameter names, in the same order, from one generation of the execution plan of the query in question to the next. As the queries get more complex it may be unable to determine whether or not a hard-coded value should be parameterized.

This is where Forced Parameterization comes into play. Instead of the occasional parameter replacing a literal value, based on the simple rules,

SQL Server attempts to replace all literal values with a parameter, with the following important exceptions:

- Literals in the select list of any **SELECT** statement are not replaced
- Parameterization does not occur within individual T-SQL statements inside stored procedures, triggers and UDFs, which get execution plans of their own.
- XQuery literals are not replaced with parameters

A very long list of other explicit exceptions is detailed in the Books Online.

The goal of using forced parameterization is to reduce recompiles as much as possible. Even when taking this more direct control over how the optimizer behaves, you have no control over the parameter name, nor can you count on the same name being used every time the execution plan is generated. The order in which parameters are created is also arbitrary. Crucially, you also can't control the data types picked for parameterization. This means that if the optimizer picks a particular data type that requires a CAST for comparisons to a given column, then you may not see applicable indexes being used. Therefore, using forced parameterization can result in sub-optimal execution plans being selected.

So why would you want to use it? A system developed using stored procedures with good parameters of appropriate data types is very unlikely to benefit from forced parameterization. However a system that has been developed with most of the T-SQL being ad-hoc, or client generated, may contain nothing but hard-coded values. This type of system could benefit greatly from forced parameterization. As with any other attempts to force control out of the hands of the optimizer and the query engine, testing is necessary.

Normally, forced parameterization is set at the database level. You have the option of choosing to set it on for a single query using the query hint **PARAMETERIZATION FORCED**, but this hint is only available as a Plan Guide, which will be covered in the next section.

In this example, we have several literals used as part of the query, which is a search to find email addresses that start with the literal, 'david':

```
SELECT   42 AS TheAnswer
        ,c.[EmailAddress]
        ,e.[BirthDate]
        ,a.[City]
```

```
FROM      [Person].[Contact] c
          JOIN [HumanResources].[Employee] e
              ON c.[ContactID] = e.[ContactID]
          JOIN [HumanResources].[EmployeeAddress] ea
              ON e.[EmployeeID] = ea.[EmployeeID]
          JOIN [Person].[Address] a
              ON ea.[AddressID] = a.[AddressID]
          JOIN [Person].[StateProvince] sp
              ON a.[StateProvinceID] = sp.[StateProvinceID]
WHERE     c.[EmailAddress] LIKE 'david%'
          AND sp.[StateProvinceCode] = 'WA' ;
```

Run the query, and then let's take a look at the cached plans (see Chapter 1 for more details):

```
SELECT   [cp].[refcounts]
         , [cp].[usecounts]
         , [cp].[objtype]
         , [st].[dbid]
         , [st].[objectid]
         , [st].[text]
         , [qp].[query_plan]
FROM     sys.dm_exec_cached_plans cp
         CROSS APPLY sys.dm_exec_sql_text(cp.plan_handle) st
         CROSS APPLY sys.dm_exec_query_plan(cp.plan_handle)
qp ;
```

The query stored is identical with the query we wrote. In other words, no parameterization occurred. The graphical execution plan looks as shown in Figure 8:

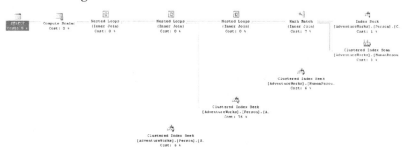

Figure 8

Let's now enable forced parameterization and clean out the buffer cache so that we're sure to see a new execution plan:

```
ALTER DATABASE AdventureWorks
SET PARAMETERIZATION FORCED
GO
```

```
DBCC freeproccache
GO
```

If you run the query again, you'll see that the execution plan is the same as that shown in Figure 8. However, the query stored in cache is not the same. It now looks like this (formatted for readability):

```
(@0 varchar(8000))
select   42 as TheAnswer
        ,c.[EmailAddress]
        ,e.[BirthDate]
        ,a.[City]
from     [Person].[Contact] c
         join [HumanResources].[Employee] e
             on c.[ContactID] = e.[ContactID]
         join [HumanResources].[EmployeeAddress] ea
             on e.[EmployeeID] = ea.[EmployeeID]
         join [Person].[Address] a
             on ea.[AddressID] = a.[AddressID]
         join [Person].[StateProvince] sp
             on a.[StateProvinceID] = sp.[StateProvinceID]
where    c.[EmailAddress] like 'david%'
         and sp.[StateProvinceCode] = @0
```

As you can see, at the top of the query, a parameter is declared, **@0 varchar(8000)**. This parameter, instead of the two character string we supplied in the original query definition, is then used to compare to the **StateProvinceCode** field. This could seriously affect performance, either positively or negatively, more likely negatively since there will be an implicit **CAST** operation to get the data from being a VARCHAR(8000) to a CHAR(3).

However, this does increase the likelihood that, if this query is called again with a different two or three character state code, the plan will be reused.

Before proceeding, be sure to reset the parameterization of the Adventureworks database:

```
ALTER DATABASE AdventureWorks
SET PARAMETERIZATION SIMPLE
GO
```

Using Plan Guides to Modify Execution Plans

Through most of the work we've been doing so far, if we wanted to change the behavior of a query we could edit the T-SQL code, add or modify an index, add some hints to the query, or all of the above.

What do you do, however, when you're dealing with a third party application where you cannot edit the T-SQL code, or where the structure and indexes are not under your control? This is where **Plan Guides** come in handy. Plan guides are simply a way of applying valid query hints to a query without actually editing the T-SQL code in any way. Plan guides can be created for stored procedures and other database objects, or for SQL statements that are not part of a database object.

The same caveat that applies to query hints obviously has to apply here: exercise due caution when implementing plan guides because changing how the optimizer deals with a query can seriously impact it's performance in a negative way.

You create a plan guide by executing the procedure, **sp_create_plan_guide** and there are three available types of plan guide:

- **Object** plan guides – applied to a stored procedure, function or DML trigger
- **SQL** plan guides – applied to strings in T-SQL statements and batches, which are outside the context of a database object
- **Template** plan guides – used specifically to control *how* a query is parameterized

Object Plan Guides

Let's assume for a moment that we've noticed that the AdventureWorks procedure, **dbo.uspGetManagerEmployees**, is generating poor plans part of the time. Testing has lead you to the conclusion that, ideally, you need to add a **RECOMPILE** hint to the stored procedure in order to get the best possible execution plan most of the time. However, this isn't a procedure you can edit. So, you decide to create a plan guide that will apply the recompile hint without editing the stored procedure.

Let's take a look at the plan guide and then I'll describe it in detail:

```
EXEC sp_create_plan_guide @name = N'MyFirstPlanGuide',
    @stmt = N'WITH [EMP_cte]([EmployeeID], [ManagerID],
        [FirstName], [LastName], [RecursionLevel])
-- CTE name and columns
```

```
        AS (
            SELECT e.[EmployeeID], e.[ManagerID], c.[FirstName],
                   c.[LastName], 0
-- Get the initial list of Employees for Manager n
            FROM [HumanResources].[Employee] e
                INNER JOIN [Person].[Contact] c
                ON e.[ContactID] = c.[ContactID]
            WHERE [ManagerID] = @ManagerID
            UNION ALL
            SELECT e.[EmployeeID], e.[ManagerID], c.[FirstName],
                   c.[LastName], [RecursionLevel] + 1
-- Join recursive member to anchor
            FROM [HumanResources].[Employee] e
                INNER JOIN [EMP_cte]
                ON e.[ManagerID] = [EMP_cte].[EmployeeID]
                INNER JOIN [Person].[Contact] c
                ON e.[ContactID] = c.[ContactID]
            )
-- Join back to Employee to return the manager name
        SELECT [EMP_cte].[RecursionLevel],
               [EMP_cte].[ManagerID], c.[FirstName] AS
               ''ManagerFirstName'', c.[LastName] AS
               ''ManagerLastName'',
               [EMP_cte].[EmployeeID], [EMP_cte].[FirstName],
               [EMP_cte].[LastName] -- Outer select from the CTE
        FROM [EMP_cte]
            INNER JOIN [HumanResources].[Employee] e
            ON [EMP_cte].[ManagerID] = e.[EmployeeID]
            INNER JOIN [Person].[Contact] c
            ON e.[ContactID] = c.[ContactID]
        ORDER BY [RecursionLevel], [ManagerID], [EmployeeID]
        OPTION (MAXRECURSION 25) ', @type = N'OBJECT',
        @module_or_batch = N'dbo.uspGetManagerEmployees',
@params = NULL,
        @hints = N'OPTION(RECOMPILE,MAXRECURSION 25)'
```

First, we use the **@name** parameter to give our plan guide a name, in this case **MyFirstPlanGuide**. Note that plan guide names operate within the context of the database, not the server.

The **@stmt** parameter has to be an exact match to the query that the query optimizer will be called on to match. White space and carriage returns don't matter, but in order to create the above, I had to include the CTE. Without it I was getting errors. When the optimizer finds code that matches, it will look up and apply the correct plan guide.

The **@type** parameter is going to be a database object, so this would be referred to as an object plan guide.

In the **@module_or_batch** parameter, we specify the name of the target object, if we're creating an object plan guide, as in this case. We supply null otherwise.

We use **@params** only if we're using a template plan guide and forced parameterization. Since we're not, it's null in this case. If we were creating a template this would be a comma separated list of parameter names and data types.

Finally, the **@hints** parameter specifies any hints that need to be applied. We apply the **RECOMPILE** hint, but notice that this query already had a hint, **MAX RECURSION**. That hint had also to be part of my **@stmt** in order to match what was inside the stored procedure. The plan guide replaces the existing **OPTION**; so if, like in this case, we need the existing **OPTION** to be carried forward, we need to add it to the plan guide.

From this point forward, without making a single change to the actual definition of the stored procedure, each execution of this procedure will be followed by a recompile.

SQL Plan Guides

Let's take a look at another example. Let's assume that we've got an application that submits primarily ad-hoc SQL to the database. Once again, we're concerned about performance and we've found that if we could only apply an **OPTIMIZE FOR** hint to the query, we'd get the execution plan that we'd like to see.

The following simple query, where we lookup addresses based on a city, should be familiar from Chapter 5:

```
SELECT * FROM [Person].[Address]
WHERE [City] = 'LONDON'
```

From Chapter 5, we already know that we can improve the performance of the above query but applying the **OPTIMIZE FOR (@City = 'Newark'))** query hint so let's enforce that behavior via a SQL plan guide:

```
EXEC sp_create_plan_guide @name = N'MySecondPlanGuide',
    @stmt = N'SELECT * FROM [Person].[Address] WHERE [City]
        = @0',
    @type = N'SQL',
    @module_or_batch = NULL,
    @params = N'@0 VARCHAR(8000)',
    @hints = N'OPTION(OPTIMIZE FOR (@0 = ''Newark''))'
```

In order to be sure of the formatting of the query with parameters as the optimizer will see it, you'll need to run the query through **sp_get_query_template**. This system procedure generates a parameterized query output so we can verify that what we've done is the same as how the query will look when it has been parameterized by the system:

```
DECLARE @my_templatetext nvarchar(max)
DECLARE @my_parameters nvarchar(max)
EXEC sp_get_query_template @templatetext = N'SELECT * FROM
[Person].[Address]
WHERE [City] = ''LONDON''',
@templatetext = @my_templatetext OUTPUT,
@parameters = @my_parameters OUTPUT

select @my_templatetext
SELECT @my_parameters
```

This returns two strings:

```
select * from [Person] . [Address] where [City] = @0
```

and

```
@0 varchar(8000)
```

You can see where we used these in the query above.

Now when we run the query, with the plan guide created and enforced by the query engine, we get the execution plan we want, as shown in Figure 9:

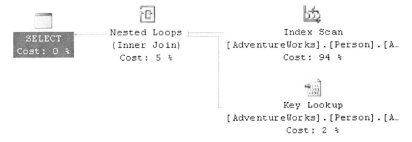

Figure 9

Template Plan Guides

As a final example, consider the query we used previously to demonstrate forced parameterization. If we determine that a procedure we cannot edit must have the parameterization set to forced, we can simply create a **template plan guide**, rather than changing the settings on the entire database.

You will need to use **sp_get_query_template** again in order to be sure of how the query is structured when parameterized.

You can then create the template guide, as follows:

```
EXEC sp_create_plan_guide @name = N'MyThirdPlanGuide',
    @stmt = N'SELECT  42 AS TheAnswer
        ,c.[EmailAddress]
        ,e.[BirthDate]
        ,a.[City]
  FROM   [Person].[Contact] c
         JOIN [HumanResources].[Employee] e
             ON c.[ContactID] = e.[ContactID]
         JOIN [HumanResources].[EmployeeAddress] ea
             ON e.[EmployeeID] = ea.[EmployeeID]
         JOIN [Person].[Address] a
             ON ea.[AddressID] = a.[AddressID]
         JOIN [Person].[StateProvince] sp
             ON a.[StateProvinceID] = sp.[StateProvinceID]
  WHERE  c.[EmailAddress] LIKE ''david%''
         AND sp.[StateProvinceCode] = ''WA''',
    @type = N'TEMPLATE',
    @module_or_batch = NULL,
    @params = N'@0 VARCHAR(8000)',
    @hints = N'OPTION(PARAMETERIZATION FORCED)'
```

Plan Guide Administration

To see a list of plan guides within the database, simply select from the dynamic management view, **sys.plan_guides**:

```
SELECT * FROM sys.plan_guides
```

Aside from the procedure to create plan guides, a second one exists, **sp_control_plan_guide**, which allows you to drop, disable or enable a specific plan guide, or drop, disable or enable all plan guides in the database.

Simply run execute the **sp_control_plan_guide** procedure, changing the **@operation** parameter appropriately.

```
EXEC sp_control_plan_guide @operation = N'DROP'
  ,@name = N'MyFourthPlanGuide'
```

Summary

With these three simple examples we've created all three types of plan guides. Don't forget, these are meant to be tools of last resort. It's almost always better to directly edit the stored procedures if you are able to. These tools are primarily for work with third party products where you can never directly modify the objects within the database but you still need a tuning and control mechanism.

Using Plan Forcing to Modify Execution Plans

The **USE PLAN** query hint, introduced in SQL Server 2005, allows you come as close as you can to gaining total control over the query execution plan. This hint allows you to take an execution plan, captured as XML, and store it "on the side", for example inside a plan guide, and then to use that plan on the query from that point forward.

You cannot force a plan on:

- INSERT, UPDATE or DELETE queries.
- Queries that use cursors other than static and fast_forward
- Distributed queries and full text queries

Forcing a plan, just like all the other possible query hints, can result in poor performance. Proper testing and due diligence must be observed prior to applying **USE PLAN**.

While you can simply attach an XML plan directly to the query in question, XML execution plans are very large. If your plan exceeds 8k in size and is attached to the query, then you query can no longer be cached because it exceeds the 8k string literal cache limit. For this reason, you should use **USE PLAN**, within a plan guide, so that the query in question will be cached appropriately, enhancing performance. Further, you avoid having to deploy and redeploy the query to your production system if you want to add or remove a plan.

Following is an example of a simple query for reporting some information from the **SalesOrderHeader** table that has been turned into a simple stored procedure:

```
CREATE PROCEDURE Sales.uspGetCreditInfo ( @SalesPersonID INT
)
AS
    SELECT   soh.[AccountNumber]
           , soh.[CreditCardApprovalCode]
           , soh.[CreditCardID]
```

```
                  , soh. [OnlineOrderFlag]
     FROM       [Sales] . [SalesOrderHeader] soh
     WHERE      soh. [SalesPersonID] = @SalesPersonID
```

When the procedure is run using the value for **@SalesPersonID** = 277, a clustered index scan results, and the plan is quite costly.

Figure 10

If the value is changed to 288, an index seek with a bookmark lookup occurs.

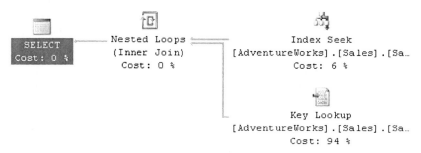

Figure 11

This is much faster than the clustered index scan. If the execution plan for the procedure takes the first value for its plan, then the later values still get the clustered index scan. While we could simply add a plan guide that uses the **OPTIMIZE FOR** hint, we're going to try **USE PLAN** instead.

First, we need to create an XML plan that behaves in the way we want. We can do this by taking the **SELECT** criteria out of the stored procedure and modifying it to behave in the correct way. This results in the correct plan. In order to capture this plan, we'll wrap it with **STATISTICS XML**, which will generate an actual execution plan in XML:

```
SET STATISTICS XML ON
GO
SELECT   soh. [AccountNumber]
         , soh. [CreditCardApprovalCode]
         , soh. [CreditCardID]
```

```
             ,soh.[OnlineOrderFlag]
    FROM     [Sales].[SalesOrderHeader] soh
    WHERE    soh.[SalesPersonID] = 288;
    GO
    SET STATISTICS XML OFF
    GO
```

This simple little query generates a 107 line XML plan, which I won't replicate here. With the XML plan in hand, we'll create a plan guide to apply it to the stored procedure (due to the size of the XML, I've left it off the following statement):

```
EXEC sp_create_plan_guide
    @name = N'UsePlanPlanGuide',
    @stmt = N'SELECT   soh.[AccountNumber]
        ,soh.[CreditCardApprovalCode]
        ,soh.[CreditCardID]
        ,soh.[OnlineOrderFlag]
    FROM     [Sales].[SalesOrderHeader] soh
    WHERE    soh.[SalesPersonID] = @SalesPersonID --288 --277',
    @type = N'OBJECT',
    @module_or_batch = N'Sales.uspGetCreditInfo',
    @params = NULL,
    @hints = N'OPTION(USE PLAN N''<ShowPlanXML...
```

Now, when the query is executed using the values that generate a bad plan:

```
    EXEC [Sales].uspGetCreditInfo @SalesPersonID = 277
```

We still get the execution plan we want, as shown in Figure 12:

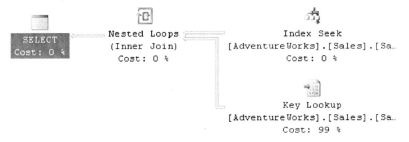

Figure 12

As a final reminder: using a plan guide, especially one that involves **USE PLAN**, should be a final attempt at solving an otherwise unsolvable problem. As the data and statistics change or new indexes are implemented, plan guides can become outdated and the exact thing that saved you so much processing time yesterday will be costing you more and more tomorrow.

Summary

With many of the options discussed in this chapter, especially **USE PLAN,** you're taking as much direct control over the optimizer and the query engine as you can. Because of that, you're taking as much of a risk with your queries as you can as well. It really is possible to mess up your system badly using these last few tools. That said, need may arise when you have that third party tool that is recompiling like crazy or a procedure that you can't edit because it would require financial testing and then having a tool like forced parameterization or plan guides can save your system. Just remember to test thoroughly before you attempt to apply any of these options to your production systems.

INDEX

SQL Tools
from Red Gate Software

SQL Compare Pro

$595

Compare and synchronize SQL Server database schemas

↗ Automate database comparisons, and synchronize your databases
↗ Simple, easy to use, 100% accurate
↗ Save hours of tedious work, and eliminate manual scripting errors
↗ Work with live databases, snapshots, script files or backups

> **"SQL Compare and SQL Data Compare are the best purchases we've made in the .NET/ SQL environment. They've saved us hours of development time, and the fast, easy-to-use database comparison gives us maximum confidence that our migration scripts are correct. We rely on these products for every deployment."**
>
> **Paul Tebbutt** Technical Lead, Universal Music Group

SQL Data Compare Pro

$595

Compare and synchronize SQL Server database contents

↗ Compare your database contents
↗ Automatically synchronize your data
↗ Row-level data restore
↗ Compare to scripts, backups, or live databases

> **"We use SQL Data Compare daily and it has become an indispensable part of delivering our service to our customers. It has also streamlined our daily update process and cut back literally a good solid hour per day."**
>
> **George Pantela** GPAnalysis.com

Visit **www.red-gate.com** for a 14-day, free trial

SQL Backup Pro $795

Compress, encrypt, and strengthen SQL Server backups

↗ Compress database backups by up to 95% for faster backups and restores

↗ Protect your data with up to 256-bit AES encryption

↗ Strengthen your backups with network resilience to enable the fault-tolerant transfer of backups across flaky networks

↗ Save time and space with the SQL Object Level Recovery Pro feature, so you can recover individual database objects instead of full database backups

> "SQL Backup has always been a great product – giving significant savings in HDD space and time over native backup and many other third-party products. With version 6 introducing a fourth level of compression and network resilience, it will be a REAL boost to any DBA."
>
> **Jonathan Allen** Senior Database Administrator

SQL Monitor

Proactive SQL Server performance monitoring and alerting

↗ Intuitive overviews at global, machine, SQL Server and database levels for up-to-the minute performance data

↗ SQL Monitor's web UI means you can check your server health and performance on the go with many mobile devices, including tablets

↗ Intelligent SQL Server alerts via email and an alert inbox in the UI, so you know about problems first

↗ Comprehensive historical data, so you can go back in time to identify the source of a problem fast

↗ Generate reports via the UI and with SQL Server Reporting Services

↗ Investigate long-running queries, SQL deadlocks, blocked processes, and more, to resolve problems sooner

↗ Fast, simple installation and administration

Due for release Q4 2010

Visit **www.red-gate.com** for a 14-day, free trial

SQL Prompt Pro $295

The fastest way to work with SQL

↗ Code-completion for SQL Server, including suggestions for complete
  join conditions

↗ Automated SQL reformatting with extensive flexibility to match your
  preferred style

↗ Rapid access to your database schema information through schema panes
  and tooltips

↗ Snippets let you insert common SQL fragments with just a few keystrokes

> **"With over 2,000 objects in one database alone,
> SQL Prompt is a lifesaver! Sure, with a few mouse
> clicks I can get to the column or stored procedure
> name I am looking for, but with SQL Prompt it is
> always right in front of me. SQL Prompt is easy
> to install, fast, and easy to use. I hate to think of
> working without it!"**
> **Michael Weiss** VP Information Technology, LTCPCMS, Inc.

SQL Data Generator $295

Test data generator for SQL Server databases

↗ Data generation in one click

↗ Realistic data based on column and table name

↗ Data can be customized if desired

↗ Eliminates hours of tedious work

> **"Red Gate's SQL Data Generator
> has overnight become the
> principal tool we use for loading
> test data to run our performance
> and load tests."**
> **Grant Fritchey** Principal DBA, FM Global

Visit **www.red-gate.com** for a 14-day, free trial

SQL Toolbelt

$1,995

The essential SQL Server tools for
database professionals

You can buy our acclaimed SQL Server tools individually or bundled. Our
most popular deal is the SQL Toolbelt: all thirteen of our SQL Server tools
in a single installer, with **a combined value of $5,635 but an actual price
of $1,995**, a saving of 65%.

Fully compatible with SQL Server 2000, 2005, and 2008.

SQL Toolbelt contains:

- ↗ **SQL Compare Pro**
- ↗ **SQL Data Compare Pro**
- ↗ **SQL Backup Pro**
- ↗ **SQL Response**
- ↗ **SQL Prompt Pro**
- ↗ **SQL Data Generator**
- ↗ **SQL Doc**

- ↗ **SQL Dependency Tracker**
- ↗ **SQL Packager**
- ↗ **SQL Multi Script Unlimited**
- ↗ **SQL Refactor**
- ↗ **SQL Comparison SDK**
- ↗ **SQL Object Level Recovery Native**

Visit **www.red-gate.com** for a 14-day, free trial

How to Become an Exceptional DBA
Brad McGehee

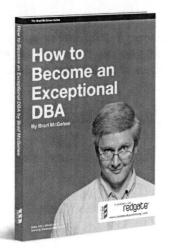

A career guide that will show you, step-by-step, exactly what you can do to differentiate yourself from the crowd so that you can be an Exceptional DBA. While Brad focuses on how to become an Exceptional SQL Server DBA, the advice in this book applies to any DBA, no matter what database software they use. If you are considering becoming a DBA, or are a DBA and want to be more than an average DBA, this is the book to get you started.

ISBN: 978-1-906434-05-2
Published: July 2008

Brad's Sure Guide to SQL Server 2008
Brad McGehee

Learning SQL Server 2008 is not as steep a learning curve as learning SQL Server 2005 was, but neither is it a simple task that you can expect to accomplish overnight. This book describes the top ten most important new features for Production DBAs in SQL Server 2008, and covers many of the key features Production DBAs will find interesting. Brad walks you through each feature, gives examples, and makes sure you're ready to tackle SQL Server 2008.

ISBN: 978-1-906434-06-9
Published: September 2008

Mastering SQL Server Profiler
Brad McGehee

For such a potentially powerful tool, Profiler is surprisingly underused. It is often hard to analyze the data you capture, and this is distressing because Profiler has so much potential to make a DBA's life more productive. Profiler records data about various SQL Server events, and this data can be used to troubleshoot a huge range of SQL Server issues. This book will make it easier for you to learn how to use Profiler, analyze the data it provides, and to take full advantage of its potential for troubleshooting SQL Server problems.

ISBN: 978-1-906434-16-8
Published: March 2009

The Art of XSD
Jacob Sebastian

This book will help you learn and use XML Schema collections in SQL Server. Prior knowledge of XSD is not required to start with this book, although any experience with XSD will make your learning process easier. A lot of applications exchange information in XML format, and this book will take you from the basics of XML schemas and walk you through everything you need to know, with examples and labs, in order to build powerful XML schemas in SQL Server.

ISBN: 978-1-906434-13-7
Planned for March 2009

CPSIA information can be obtained at www.ICGtesting.com
Printed in the USA
LVOW082104151112

307455LV00002B/11/P